THE SMALL NATION SOLUTION

THE SMALL NATION SOLUTION

How the World's Smallest Nations Can Solve the World's Biggest Problems

John H. Bodley

A division of
ROWMAN & LITTLEFIELD PUBLISHERS, INC.
Lanham • New York • Toronto • Plymouth, UK

Published by AltaMira Press
A division of
The Rowman & Littlefield Publishing Group, Inc.
A wholly owned subsidiary of The Rowman & Littlefield Publishing Group,
Inc.
4501 Forbes Boulevard, Suite 200, Lanham, Maryland 20706
www.rowman.com

10 Thornbury Road, Plymouth PL6 7PP, United Kingdom

British Library Cataloguing in Publication Information Available

Library of Congress Cataloging-in-Publication Data
Bodley, John H.
The small nation solution : how the world's smallest nations can solve the world's biggest problems
/ John H. Bodley.
pages cm
Includes index.
ISBN 978-0-7591-2220-8 (cloth : alk. paper) — ISBN 978-0-7591-2222-2 (ebook) 1. Social change.
2. Social systems. 3. Social problems 4. Culture and globalization. 5. Acculturation. 6. States,
Small—Cross-cultural studies. 7. States, Small—Economic conditions. I. Title.
GN358.B627 2013
303.4—dc23
2013005697

CONTENTS

PREFACE

The Small Nation Solution offers a very simple solution to the world's biggest problems of poverty and environmental decline. The solution is simply that first each nation needs to be the optimum size, which means *small*, preferably fewer than ten million people. Its citizens then need to reach a consensus on what they value most highly and how these valued objects can be most justly distributed. In addition to scale and consensus, the small nation solution requires adherence to two fundamental principles that apply both within individual small nations and in a small nation world system: subsidiarity and heterogeneity. Subsidiarity means getting decision making as close to the people as possible. Heterogeneity is about people in each small nation having maximum freedom to find the best solution(s) for their particular situation.

My concept of small nations is intentionally flexible, because I am interested in societies being the best size to solve human problems, not in categorizing for the sake of categorizing. There can be considerable utility in purposefully leaving some key concepts loosely defined. Of course there is a vast literature on the multiple meanings and the political-ideological significance of the terms nation, state, nation-state, and the related term "nationalism." The issue of what constitutes a nation or a state is well-trodden ground in political science and sociology, but without going too deeply into definitional issues, we can take as a useful baseline for the meaning of "nation" that it is a community of people who live in a territory and have a consensus on their cultural identity and basic values. For our purposes, we can add that the nation also has an economy and enough legal authority for people to make basic decisions that affect the conditions of their existence. This concept of nation overlaps somewhat with the meaning of ethnic group, except that the members of an ethnic group may not be occupying a shared territory, and it may not have a government, or an economy. [1] Furthermore, there are many multi-ethnic, or pluralistic small nations.

For my purposes, I will also treat autonomous subnational units and dependencies as small nations, as well as small nation states, when they suit my purpose, but I do assume that the small nation is a recognized political unit with significant decision-making authority, if not full autonomy. In some respects no government has complete autonomy in all matters. I also add the functional perspective, borrowing from Aristotle, who characterized a state (or nation) as a self-sufficient association of villages, which "came about as a means of securing life itself" and "continues in being to secure the *good* life."[2] I also agree with Aristotle that there is an important moral dimension to the small nation. As he states, unlike animals, "humans alone have perception of good and evil, just and unjust, etc. It is the sharing of a common view in these matters that makes a household and a state."[3]

I speak of *the* small nation solution, but small nation diversity means that there is no single small nation solution, beyond the basic parameters and principles outlined above. I consider three major value system options to indicate the diverse range that the small nation solution might take, but many more possibilities can be imagined. The first option takes a regulated capitalist market-based approach; the second takes a communitarian, cooperative approach to commercial activity; and the third values natural capital above financial capital. The small nation solution challenges our firmly held belief in the necessity of solving our problems by forever growing a larger economy, or that "free market" is the best solution for everyone. It also questions our belief that finance capital is the most important form of wealth.

A few disclaimers are in order. Although I am an anthropologist, and I was inspired to see scale as a solution after living as an anthropologist with tribal peoples in the Amazon, I am not advocating a return to an imaginary noble tribal past. This is not a "back to the stone age" book, and it does not condemn government, commerce, or modern technology. It is about how we can apply scale-related insights about our social life to solve contemporary problems. I have been pursuing this scale approach since the first edition of my *Anthropology and Contemporary*

Human Problems appeared in 1976, and my ideas have changed over time, even as my focus on scale has increased. After living in the small nation of Denmark in 1980, I directed my research even more toward understanding contemporary problems and the future of our large-scale world of governments and businesses. Since 1991 I have organized my research and writing in reference to three distinct cultural worlds: tribal, imperial, and commercial. The tribal world was overtaken by the larger-scale ancient imperial world organized by rulers and government, and the imperial world was in turn overtaken by our global-scale commercial world organized by the market economy. I now envision an emerging fourth world, based on small nations applying the small nation solution. The small nation world is now being constructed from the ground up and, thanks to the internet, is now more feasible than ever before.

Although I am an anthropologist by training and by profession, I also consider myself a historian and a natural historian. I was drawn early on by a series of zoological field trips to switch my career ambitions from natural history to anthropology which then led me to carry out fieldwork with tribal peoples in the Amazon. I found that the tribal Amazonians with whom I lived enjoyed highly successful lifestyles and well-adapted cultural systems, but they were also threatened by the advance of our commercial civilization. Much of my early career as an anthropologist was drawn to the issue of why tribal societies seemed so successful and yet were so vulnerable, and what could be done to help ensure their survival. I initially thought my anthropological specialty would be in tribal Amazonia, but I came to realize that a more challenging project was trying to understand the social and cultural conditions that would make our global system more sustainable. Working through these questions eventually led me to view small nations themselves as crucial solutions to global problems.

ACKNOWLEDGMENTS

I have major intellectual debts to my many students and colleagues, past and present who have shared ideas and materials, and assisted me in multiple ways over the years, especially at the Department of Anthropology at Washington State University, where I have taught since 1970. My early research in the Peruvian Amazon was supported in 1965 by a Title IV National Defense Education Act fellowship through the University of Oregon, and by grants from the National Science Foundation in 1968–1969, and by the National Science Foundation in 1976–1979 through Washington State University. Some my research was supported by sabbatical leaves from Washington State University in 1980, 1990, 1998–1999, and 2006, and by research grants from the Edward R. Meyer Fund at Washington State University in 1996–1997, 1998–2000, and 2006.

My mentors in the Anthropology Department at the University of Oregon, 1965–1969, especially Joesph G. Jorgensen, David Aberle, and Philip D. Young, gave me a solid grounding in anthropology. I am grateful to my primary Asháninka assistants in the Peruvian Amazon Rebeca Macuyama; Meyando Vasquez, Benito and Benancio Rengifo, at Shahuaya; Alberto and Moises Jumanga, Oracio Santiago at Nevati; Inketiniro at Jordan; Juan Shariwa on the Apurucayali; and Chonkiri at Shumahuani.

Elsewhere I have acknowledged in detail my intellectual debt to University of Chicago anthropologist, Sol Tax.[1] It was Tax who encouraged me to pursue my work on *Victims of Progress* in the early 1970s, and in the later 1970s helped solidify my thinking about the significance of scale and the small nation solution.

Norwegian anthropologist, and one of the founders of the International Work Group on Indigenous Affairs (IWGIA), Helge Kleivan arranged a lecture tour for me of Scandinavian anthropology departments in 1978 which gave me a chance to test my views on "cultural autonomy." In 1980 Helge hosted my extended work at IWGIA headquarters in Copenhagen. This was my first extended residence in a European small nation. In 1986 at the invitation of indigenous rights advocate and former British Columbia Chief Justice Thomas R. Berger, I held seminars in Fairbanks and Bethel, Alaska with Yupik and Inupiat Eskimo, and Athabaskan peoples from the Alaskan arctic. Special thanks to anthropologist Robert Gordon for arranging for me to teach at the University of Vermont during the summer of 2000. This gave me the opportunity to compare Vermont as a small nation with the Palouse region and Washington State. Also special thanks to St'át'imc Chiefs Saul Terry, Michael Leach, Patrick Williams, and Garry John for helping me appreciate the special value of salmon, and allowing me to contribute to the formal creation of their small nation in 2003-2005. I also thank María Elena Boisier Pons, Director of CONICYT's FONDECYT and FONDAP programs in Santiago, Chile, and María Eugenia Carmelio Rodrígues for making my recent visit to Santiago so productive.

Most recently in my home department at Washington State University, Robert and Marsha Quinlan invited me to visit Dominica in 2007 when they were conducting their 2007 field school. William Willard shared his insights on Native American small nations, and our Museum Director Mary Collins made sure I was able to attend reburial ceremonies, as our department repatriated archaeological materials to the Plateau tribes. My most recent Ph.D. students—Kerensa Allison, Christa Herrygers, Troy Wilson, Pasang Sherpa, Xianghong Feng, Ben Colombi, Brad Wazaney, and Ming Kuo Wu— helped me refine my small nation solution.

I have drawn freely on my previously published works, especially my most recent textbooks, all published by AltaMira Press: *Cultural Anthropology: Tribes, States, and the Global System*, Fifth Edition, 2011, and *Anthropology and Contemporary Human Problems*, Sixth Edition, 2012. I am grateful to Wendi Schnaufer, executive editor at

AltaMira, for supporting me in the present project, and guiding me through the publication process from proposal to finished product.

Barry C. Hicks listened to my ideas and provided me with a steady stream of references and suggestions. Brother-in-law Patrick Green was a helpful critic during numerous family reunions and summer visits. My brother Tom kept me up to date on the financial services industry. My wife, Kathleen, supported me at every stage of this work from 1968 to the present. She tells me when I have too much information and am not making any sense. As ever, I am more than grateful for her insights and endless patience. I dedicate this book to the memory of my parents, William and LaVerna Bodley, and to our children Brett and Antonie, and our grandchildren Lili and Ramona.

Part I

Big Problems, Small Nation Solutions

People can enjoy a prosperous "good life" when they live in small nations that value social justice, remain small, and find a sustainable balance among government, business, and nature. The citizens of successful small nations also have a consensus on how to protect their common wealth in community, nature, and culture. This balance of scale and justice is the small nation solution to global problems, and it just might be the best path to a truly sustainable world for all nations. Small nations appeal to our better human nature because they avoid the toxic pitfalls of hypercommercialism and social conflict that beset large nations when they ignore social justice, community, and nature in their pursuit of economic growth. Large nations, with large governments, large economies, markets, and businesses, may unintentionally promote anti-social values, attitudes, and behaviors that undermine human well-being and threaten all life on the planet. Small nations offer a genuine alternative that all nations can follow, and small nations can be the foundation for a revitalized global system.

Chapters in Part I explains why contemporary problems are really problems of scale and social power. Solving them requires optimally sized governments, economies, and business enterprises operating in a world composed of just and democratically organized nations. The well-being of individuals and households and the protection of their common wealth must be the primary goal of any successful nation. Everyone needs to have access to sufficient social, cultural, and natural wealth, or capital, to control the conditions of their daily life. These are entitlements enshrined in the 1948 UN Universal Declaration of Human Rights. When the elite few direct growth, the benefits may be concentrated as private gain, whereas the majority pays the costs and their human rights to the wealth of society, culture, and nature are diminished. The underlying scale and power problem is that elite-directed growth can make nations, economies, and businesses grow so large that they become unjust and unsustainable. Badly directed growth is doomed by multiple failings, but it is most problematic when growth is not directed at solving the fundamental problems of human existence now and for future generations.

Solutions to problems of scale and power can be readily found in successful small nations that, in part because they are small, have been forced to reach a consensus on fundamental goals and how to achieve them. Successful small nations emphasize community solidarity and balance between all forms of wealth and between cooperation and competition, and they work to ensure that everyone can enjoy an irreducible minimum of material well-being and personal security. These are the essential cultural processes that have defined human beings for at least 100,000 years. Small nations can solve human problems because they are the right size, because they have the right priorities, and because if they grow too large they can segment rather than concentrate social power. I speak of "nations" rather than states, or governments, because people come first in nations. Nations are defined by social solidarity. Nations have citizens and economies, but the citizens control the economy and put people first. This works best in small nations.

I

THE BIG PROBLEM

Elite-Directed Growth

Thus we see that a small-state world would not only solve the problems of social brutality and war: it would solve the equally terrible problems of oppression and tyranny. It would solve all problems arising from power. —Leopold Kohr, *The Breakdown of Nations*, 1978 [1957]

Living with the Asháninka, an Amazonian tribal people, in their magnificent Sira Mountain rainforest in the 1960s led me step by step to the small nation solution. My brief encounters with Chonkiri, an Asháninka big man leader called "Hummingbird," and Inketiniro, a jaguar-shaman, started me out and taught me the most. Chonkiri showed me the essential socio-political-economic heart of the small-scale tribal world. Inketiniro helped me understand the importance of the cultural illusions and delusions that persuade people to accept their way of life as natural, inevitable, and desirable. The Asháninka were not living in a perfect world, but it was working well for them. People were happy because they were in control of the conditions of their life and they were able to take care of their families. This was an enormous achievement. They could whoop with delight in the face of what seemed grueling hardships. The key to their success was their perception of social justice based on their consensus that everyone could have access to the social, cultural, and material resources they required to live a decent life. Their material culture was minimal, but they were wealthy in the social, cultural, and natural resources that they needed.[1]

Tribal culture is not the only pathway to human happiness, but living in a modern small-scale society with a shared culture, a small nation, makes it possible for people to reach a consensus on, and actually implement social justice, and political and economic democracy which are the necessary conditions for human well-being and sustainable development. Scale, justice, political democracy, and economic democracy are the essential ingredients of the small nation solution to human problems. Working together they are the small nation solution. Why and how the small nation solution works is the subject of this book. This first chapter lays the foundation.

INTRODUCING SMALL NATIONS

Fully two thirds of the world's politically independent states are small nations, each with fewer than ten million people, yet in total, the people in small nations constitute barely 5 percent of global population. The reality is that these few people have for decades been quietly developing practical solutions to global problems that can successfully prevent, reduce, or mitigate problems of environment, poverty, and conflict within their own territories. At the other extreme, the 5 percent of the world's people who are the top individual wealth holders and primary decision makers have left the world a disaster zone on the brink of catastrophe. Leaders of large nations, especially the global superpowers, and the global elite in general have directed the global economy and enjoyed most of its benefits, but they have failed to solve the most crucial global problems that confront all of humanity. Many small nation solutions are already in place and they are working, but they will ultimately fail if large nations and the dominant decision makers continue to mishandle the world. Small nation solutions are not yet widely recognized by world leaders, because small nations are, well, small, because the present world leaders view them as peripheral to the global system, and because small nation solutions are a major departure from the prevailing path of elite-directed economic globalization. Given the state of the world, it is time to consider dramatic alternatives. Small nations are models that larger nations can follow, because they work where large nations have failed.

The nations of the world can be ranked for our purposes into seven orders of magnitude by population size from nano- to giga-scale as follows: (1) *nano-nations* each of a few thousand people; (2) *micro-nations* with tens of thousands; (3) *mini-nations* with hundreds of thousands; (4) *small-nations* with a few million; (5) *large-nations* with tens of millions; (6) *mega-nations* with hundreds of millions; and (7) *giga-nations* with billions of people. In 2007, I counted seventeen nano-nations, thirty-three micro-nations, forty-seven mini-nations, and eighty-four small nations. Altogether, there were fewer than 500 million people in these 181 small nations.

For general reference, the first four ranks can conveniently be merged as small nations, and the large-, mega-, and giga-states can all be called large nations. In 2007 more than a third of the world's 6.6 billion people were crowded into just two giga-nations, China and India, both inheritors of ancient imperial world great cultural traditions. Nine more mega-states in descending order, the United States, Indonesia, Brazil, Pakistan, Bangladesh, the Russian Federation, Nigeria, Japan, and Mexico, added a billion and a half more people, such that just eleven giga- and mega-states contained more than 4 billion people, 60 percent of the world. Placing 4 billion people under the leadership for just eleven governments greatly narrows the possibilities for sociocultural system innovation to implement sustainable development at a time when global systems seem to be approaching scale limits of many sorts. Small nations number just over 400 million people, comparable to the entire population of the world in AD 1200, but they live in some 181 societies in diverse territories scattered across the globe, often in peripheral places that had little strategic or material value to the large nation world. Their relative obscurity makes it possible for each small nation to be its own unique experiment in sustainable development problem solving, relatively free of the political and ideological conflicts of larger nations.

Small nations are so numerous and so diverse that any attempt to generalize about their characteristics is risky. Nevertheless, for our purposes I can list the following minimum features that small nations by definition share: (1) fewer than 10 million people; (2) a territorial jurisdiction; (3) a functional sociocultural system; (4) consensus decision making; and (5) the power to manage their own internal affairs. As appropriate for specific problems they can also be distinguished by degree of political autonomy; by scale of total economy; by isolation, or travel time from global cities; by per capita income and wealth levels; by degree of integration with the global economy; and by degree of cultural homogeneity. Some small nations are fully independent states, some are highly autonomous subunits of larger nations, or they enjoy varying degrees of free association with larger states. In later chapters I extend this definition of small nations to include subnational jurisdictions that enjoy various degrees of autonomy to control their internal affairs following the subsidiarity principle of getting political decision making as close to the people as possible.

SCALE, POWER, AND DECEPTION: THE FATE OF HUMANITY

Over a decade ago Jared Diamond offered a grand overview of the rise of our commercial world and its future, but his approach and conclusions differ in several illuminating respects from the view offered by the small nation solution. Diamond combines biology, geography, history, and anthropology in his *Guns, Germs, and Steel* (1997), which is widely read as a verification that the commercial world and economic progress were inevitable developments, predetermined by the realities of biogeography. The combined effects of guns, germs, and steel certainly helped imperialistic Europeans conquer the world, but it would be a mistake to see biological circumstances and technology as sufficient explanations for the historical, perhaps temporary, rise of Europeans to global dominance.

The Small Nation Solution argues that the fate of humanity is determined by three variables rooted in human nature and culture: (1) the scale at which people organize their sociocultural systems; (2) how they control social power, and (3) their use of cultural deception. Over the past 200,000 years human decision making regarding these crucial variables has produced decisive differences among peoples. Peoples who live in small-scale sociocultural systems, who limit the power of their leaders, and who clearly understand the practical limits of the physical world are more likely to produce sustainable societies. They are also well able to take care of human beings, unlike those taking the opposite path in pursuit of unlimited growth. Those who allow their systems to grow continuously, who allow their leaders to become uncontrolled rulers, and who are deceived about the real limits of the physical world have produced the present unsustainable expansionist system. Unfortunately, under imperialism most people find themselves in the role of workers in a social system organized like an insect colony. This works as long as people can be deceived that imperialism benefits everyone, but it is against our human nature.

Imperialism is a deceptive goal, because in reality, throughout history the big winners in imperialist expansion have not been whole societies but primarily the top 0.5 percent of households who direct and most benefit from domination, conquest, and seemingly endless expansion. The losers, including many individuals in winning societies, are exterminated, enslaved, disempowered, and impoverished. This kind of growth is fundamentally inhuman, especially given how frequently great empires rise and fall. It is equally plausible and much more useful to see the goal of human development to be a continuous humanization process, in which people use open and overlapping sociocultural networks as tools to maintain and reproduce humanity. This is sustainable development, the opposite of the pursuit of endless growth. Taking care of people and society humanely and fairly is a tough challenge, but by 13,000 BP humanity had already won the humanization race, filling up the entire inhabitable world within perhaps 100,000 years of the emergence of speech. The unending race in pursuit of growth was started some 7,000 years ago by aggrandizing individuals who, in times of crisis, convinced their followers to accept them as rulers, rather than as leaders, and to pay them tribute.

Diamond accurately lists the geographic preconditions that made possible the technological, organizational, and ideological innovations that allowed a few aggrandizers to transform the tribal world into the contemporary commercial world in sequential developments spanning the last 13,000 years. Framing his answer geographically calls attention to how the shape and position of continents determined which plants and animals could have been most readily domesticated, where intensive farming could be practiced most productively, and where cities, kingdoms, and empires could best be created and sustained. These circumstances do not explain why societies grew into empires. It is like attributing the existence of a freeway to the peculiarities of local topography, or to the proximity of gravel quarries and asphalt. Geographical answers to such a *how* did this happen question are appealing, but we need a deeper and more helpful "why" and even a theoretically grounded "who is responsible" answer.

Assuaging guilt for the human costs of imperial expansion was not Diamond's objective, but situating the causes of global poverty and oppression in historically remote geography may help remove any collective guilt over past and continuing injustices against conquered peoples. However, this approach offers little practical guidance for finding solutions for contemporary human problems. Geography may be a necessary but not a sufficient explanation for particular historical wrongs including the current grossly unequal distribution of human costs and benefits in the world. For example, it would be more helpful to imagine that the destruction of tribal peoples and their cultures, and the recent subjugation and impoverishment of millions of people for the benefit of a relative few, were not preordained by nature but were caused by undemocratic human decision making. Otherwise, why would people act against their self-interest? This alternative view suggests that massive negative outcomes of open-ended growth possibly could have been avoided and might still be prevented by truly democratic human decision making.

We can ask the philosophical *why* question—why are some peoples unable to prevent aggrandizing individuals from expanding their personal empires at other people's expense? This is an urgent contemporary human problem, and its cause need not be situated inaccessibly in the remote past. People today maintain and reproduce present injustices. It is easy to think of whole societies in competition, anonymously moving ahead on different trajectories, but the very idea of societies and economies, can be illusory ideological tools. Inequalities are now human problems for the majority of humanity, but only a relatively few individuals, who may have too much decision-making power over the allocation of energy and materials, are the primary cause of these problems.

I have been pondering these human problems since 1965 when I began cultural anthropological fieldwork on industrial civilization's impacts on tribal peoples in the Peruvian Amazon. I interviewed scores of people, recording life histories and family genealogies, learning firsthand about forced labor, frontier violence, dispossession, and mass deaths from introduced diseases. My most valuable insights occurred in 1969 when my wife and I hiked into the rugged uplands of the Gran Pajonal, heartland of the fiercely independent Asháninka people. This vast region is today within the Sira Communal Reserve, a 6,000 km^2 protected area established for the Asháninka in 2004. We were seeking self-sufficient tribal people who were successfully avoiding damaging contacts with outsiders. By chance, we encountered Chonkiri (Hummingbird), an Asháninka bigman with his band of twenty-five family members. Chonkiri confronted us on a ridge near his house. He stood astride the trail, blocking our path and demanding to know why we had come and if we were bringing sickness. Chonkiri was supremely self-confident. His sons and sons-in-law surrounded him, all in bright red face paint and fully armed with bows, arrows, and shotguns. When he was satisfied that we were harmless, he helped himself to our useful trade goods, reciprocating with manioc, maize, and bananas from his gardens, but he had no use for our money. We learned that he and his group were virtually self-sufficient and didn't need commercial markets. They could supply everything they needed, including food, shelter, and clothing, except for the simple metal tools and guns that they obtained from their Asháninka trading partners.

Chonkiri's belligerent posturing betrayed no hint of inferiority or dependency. He was clearly telling me, "You outsiders can trade with us, but otherwise leave us alone."He was willing to trade on fair terms, but he refused to surrender his autonomy, or his way of life in the process. Chonkiri was intelligent and aggressive, so one might ask why was he just a family leader and not an imperial ruler?He knew about empires and rulers. His ancestors had traded with the Inca Empire next door, and the Asháninka still tell stories about the Inca. Asháninka land was briefly an outpost of the Spanish Empire, until they forcibly expelled the Franciscan missionaries in 1742. The Asháninka reputation for armed hostility kept outsiders away during much of the nineteenth century, and they drove out the Shining Path guerrillas late in the 1990s. The Asháninka blocked nearby roads in 2009 to show solidarity with other indigenous groups in the north who were protesting oil development in their territory. It was not a lack of ability, knowledge, or personal ambition that prevented Chonkiri from becoming a ruler. The Asháninka were sometimes violent raiders who could kill for personal revenge, but they were not centrally organized imperialists. There is no Asháninka tribe to conquer and rule as a single political body. The word "Asháninka" means "people"; it does not designate an exclusively bounded society.

The conventional geographical explanation for the "failure" of the Asháninka to become imperialists is that Amazon rainforest soils will not support intensive cultivation and their wild game is scarce and unsuitable for domestication. Indeed, when we met Chonkiri his band was collecting edible honey ants and his children were feasting on larvae. This suggested protein scarcity. However, everyone appeared to be healthy and content, and they had plenty of garden produce and leisure time to share with visitors. In fact, natural resources were abundant because population densities in the Pajonal were very low and land was not a market commodity. His family could freely clear new gardens, move their house sites, or trek to richer hunting grounds when necessary. Every household had everything it needed to make a comfortable living. There was no poverty. Chonkiri was the center of an overlapping personal network that consisted of his family, more distant relatives, and trading partners. His domain extended as far as he felt like walking in every direction, but probably did not include more than fifty to one hundred people, and he couldn't force anyone to do anything they didn't want to do. People could withdraw their support if he became too demanding, or made too many bad decisions. There was no centrally directed Asháninka society, although in times of crisis several big men like Chonkiri could draw their bands together to expel intruders. The Asháninka were, and today remain a small nation, within the larger Peruvian nation state.

THE ASHÁNINKA'S RICH TRIBAL WORLD

There were two striking features of the Asháninka social system that prevented them from becoming imperialists: the scale of their society, and their cultural view of what constituted wealth and the good life. The Asháninka were organized at the household and family levels. Consequently, there were no social hierarchies, and people differed only by age, gender, and personality. The "tribe" consisted of open and overlapping personal networks of people who spoke one of several Asháninka languages, intermarried, exchanged goods, combined for defense, and shared a cultural understanding of how people should live and relate to nature and the invisible world that they jointly recognized. Like other tribal peoples, the Asháninka attributed human-like consciousness to other animals, recognized kinship with beneficial species, and imagined that certain supernatural entities acted as monitors who punished misbehavior. The Asháninka were not poor. They lived in a rich environment and clearly valued the good life, leisure, and wealth. They were in effect tribal capitalists but dedicated to maintaining, not growing their wealth, which was primarily their tropical forest ecosystem. They situated their wealth in nature, in their shared cultural memories, and in their families. Everyone was entitled at birth to access to all the wealth they needed to be successful human beings. Nature provided most of their material needs with only modest human energy inputs, and for this reason the Asháninka treaded very lightly on their territory, taking a tiny proportion of the rainforest's annual biological product. The meaning of life for the Asháninka was taking care of their households, while enjoying sociability, prosperity, and security.

The Asháninka are living the tribal lifestyle produced by the million years of human evolution since the emergence of *Homo erectus* in the Lower Paleolithic. This system has served humanity well. By keeping their society at the family level and by defining wealth broadly and making it broadly accessible, the Asháninka found their own solution to the universal human problem of conflict of interest and factionalism addressed by James Madison, father of the U.S. Constitution. Madison correctly observed[2] that people naturally love both freedom and property, and are naturally divided into dangerous factions by their conflicting emotions, opinions, and interests. He believed that representative republican democracy would be the best form of government to control the destabilizing, sometimes violent effects of factionalism, and still protect individual freedom and property.

The Asháninka social system maximizes human freedom, and like Madison and the American Constitution, they also recognize that leaders are fallible and that even a majority might be oppressive. Their solution is to embrace factionalism and reject rulers and all forms of hierarchy. They can do this because everyone is both free and independent and can readily withdraw their support from would-be rulers by simply walking away. By guaranteeing universal access to wealth, the

Asháninka ensure that an irreducible minimum of well-being is available to everyone, thereby reducing but not eliminating the causes of interpersonal conflict. Because of natural differences in individual personality and accidents of fortune, Asháninka social power is not uniformly distributed, but their tribal system inverts the social pyramid characterizing the imperial and commercial worlds. The tribal majority is richly endowed with kin and material resources, whereas only a small minority may be impoverished by accidents of fortune. The Asháninka do not need a federal government and do not need to be imperialists.

Tribal fissioning occurs easily because there are no hierarchies and no complex division of labor. A single household can perform all the tasks needed for maintenance and reproduction. Only four people are needed to create a new self-sufficient social network based on the domestic cycle in which a household grows, and children marry and move apart. A brother and sister can each marry another brother and sister to form two halves of a self-perpetuating social network. Tribal peoples multiplied to fill the world by splitting and migrating but generally maintained optimum-sized tribal networks of 500 to 2000 people, which was the range needed to maintain and reproduce language, culture, and marriage exchanges, and provide long-term subsistence security. People were more likely to speak to and marry within such networks, but network boundaries remained permeable. At the dawn of the imperial age, 7000 years ago, there were perhaps 85 million people in the tribal world, divided into some 200,000 autonomous villages and bands. This low population level permitted a very high level of personal freedom and natural wealth per capita. In contrast, imperialist rulers at this time began organizing people into a few hundred chiefdoms, kingdoms, and empires, using taxes and tribute to intensify production, and in the process raised global population more than threefold to over 300 million by 1200 AD. Significantly, imperial expansion was an elite-directed cultural process, not a natural process. Elite-directed growth has become the world's single biggest problem. Small nations are the solution.

OF ANTS AND PEOPLE: WHY IMPERIALIST GROWTH?

It is difficult to explain why any tribal people ever surrendered their autonomy and allowed their leaders to become rulers, especially consid-

ering how easily rulers become oppressive, and how unevenly the benefits of imperialism were distributed. The most reasonable explanation is
that people were deceived by their culturally influenced perceptions to
mistakenly believe that they were acting in their own self-interest.
However, the differences between tribal cultures and our commercial
industrial world are so great that it is also likely that the first tribals to
accept rulers had to be unwillingly coerced by circumstances into
grudging submission to imperial authority.

According to myrmecologists Bert Hölldobler and Edward O. Wilson,[3] next to humans, ants are the planet's dominant animals. Ants live
almost everywhere, are voracious herbivores and predators, major
earthmovers and recyclers. They occupy the prime insect habitats and
shape the evolution of many other species. The combined biomass of
the world's ants probably exceeded the global biomass of humans before 1500 AD. An obvious difference between ants and all people is our
humanity: our human culture and our consciousness. Ants and ant societies are shaped entirely by natural selection and environment operating on their genes. In contrast, the crucial adaptive problem for humans
is not natural selection, not our genes, and not accidents of geography
or the natural environment, but cultural selection, how we deal culturally with other people and how we culturally perceive the physical
realities and the actual limits of our planet.

Like ants, people are planetary ecological dominants, in that they are
major actors in every environment. Also like ants, people adopted foraging, farming, and herding for subsistence. However, as evolutionary
biologist and entomologist Richard Alexander observed in his *Biology of
Moral Systems*,[4] the human family contains only a single species, which
is highly unusual for a biologically successful family. The genetic diversity of the hominid family actually declined over the past 5 million
years. This is a striking departure from the trend of ant genetic diversity. Ants have evolved into 12,000 species over 100 million years. The
human development of culture is the crucial difference. With culture as
a powerful tool, people have made intergroup competition so intense
that only one human species can occupy the planet. Other people became our most dangerous enemies. Thus, the main challenge for humans is learning how to live safely and productively with other people.
The real human problem is not how to grow a larger economy. The
problem is how to control the most aggressive aggrandizing individuals

in our society—those who would promote elite-directed growth in a way that benefits themselves at everyone else's expense.

Primatologist Nicholas Humphrey[5] and anthropologist Robin Dunbar,[6] along with Alexander suggest that the evolution of the human brain and culture was driven by the selective advantage to individuals of "social intelligence." This is the delicate balancing act of using the mind to deceive and outmaneuver others for access to resources while still maintaining the benefits of membership in social networks. According to Humphrey, primate group size is limited by the time required to both obtain subsistence and maintain social cohesion by face-to-face grooming. Humphrey's conclusions are supported by Dunbar's finding that the size of the forebrain, or neocortex, relative to the rest of the brain predicts group size in nonhuman primates. The forebrain supports social intelligence and presumably is required to maintain social control in larger groups. Social intelligence allowed primate societies to grow in numbers up to a threshold where the amount of interpersonal grooming time required for maintaining group cohesion would have made it impossible for individuals to get enough to eat. Human language evolved as a powerful tool for social control because it makes social intelligence more efficient by supporting gossip and improving deception. Language and more efficient subsistence technology allowed people to exceed the primate grooming threshold, and thereby allowed an individual to interact effectively within a personal network of about 150 people as predicted by their neocortex size.

It is possible that the size of human social groups may be limited by the ability of leaders to resolve intergroup conflicts over resources and to overcome people's natural preference for personal freedom. Most people today continue to spend their daily lives within networks that seldom exceed Dunbar's number of 150 people, thus comfortably accommodating our human nature. Within this small-scale social group people could generally trust each other and could expect a favor to be reciprocated. Misbehavior could be easily monitored, and noncooperators could be disciplined. The membership of personal networks in tribal bands and villages typically overlapped, but connections with outsiders varied. This made intergroup tribal alliances difficult to sustain, and helps explain why dispersed clans were rarely larger than a few hundred people, and why tribal networks were rarely larger than a few thousand people. Before 10,000 years ago the largest autonomous groups seldom exceeded 2,000 people, which is the threshold beyond which political centralization, or formal hierarchies of some kind, would become increasingly necessary in order to maintain social cohesion. Any such "unnaturally" larger groups would necessarily require leaders to devise means to bypass the limits otherwise set by our social intelligence. Aspiring rulers would need to overcome the human tendency to split off and thereby withdraw their support from would-be oppressors. Leaders could become rulers only by persuading people to believe that the costs of withdrawal would be greater than the costs of accepting life with continually increased complexity and competition.

Tribal people did become successful ecological dominants, but unlike ants, they did so without sacrificing their individual autonomy, because they kept their societies small. In contrast, ants colonies are like superorganisms composed of up to millions of individuals organized into specialized castes of workers, slaves, and queens. Large insect colonies bear striking similarities to politically centralized classical civilizations, and of course the term *caste* is derived from the extreme example of occupational specialization in Hindu South Asia. The ant analogy also applies well to market-based imperialism. Social philosopher Bernard Mandeville (1670–1733) drew the most famous analogy between social insects and early capitalist societies in his *Fable of the Bees: or Private Vices, Publick Benefits*,[7] first published in 1705. Mandeville noted that in both human and insect societies the number of distinct social roles and the material level of prosperity were directly related to the size of society. He recognized that bigger societies were necessarily more prosperous and more complex. He also characterized the opulence of large civilized societies as a public benefit naturally dependent on the "private vice" of individual self-seeking. In this view, society works well as long as everyone, like bees, pursues their own interests, but it would collapse in a "grumbling hive" if selfish behavior were banned as immoral. This correctly identifies self-interest as "natural," but overlooks the real "inhumanity" of insect society by leaving no room for concepts of justice, fairness, or equity of opportunity.

The commercial world has conquered nature more completely and more rapidly but less sustainably than did tribal people, the social insects, or the classical great civilizations. According to some estimates, in the imperial world per capita human consumption of food and fuels doubled over tribal levels, and then almost doubled again in the commercial world.[8] The scale of material wealth production in the classical empires was relatively modest compared with the contemporary world, because these earlier civilizations used only renewable energy drawn from animals, biofuels, wind, and water, rather than electricity or internal combustion engines. Our present conquest of nature is reflected in the colossal and rapidly accelerating flows of energy and material extracted from the world's natural resources to sustain wealth production.

When commercial interests succeeded in transforming land, labor, money, and the necessities of life into market commodities, the massive sociocultural and technological changes that followed were accompanied by runaway urbanization and population growth that greatly accelerated aggregate resource use. Urban people are much more costly to support per capita than rural people. Direct flow of raw materials may have increased from an estimated 1 ton per capita annually in the tribal world to 85 tons in contemporary America, which is predominately urban.[9] By 2000 AD annual aggregate human energy consumption had reached three orders of magnitude above baseline levels in the tribal world. Measured in kilocalories this is the difference between a few hundred trillion to more than a hundred quadrillion. Biologists estimate that humans and their domestic animals may now be appropriating from 20 to 40 percent of global terrestrial net primary productivity.[10] This takes food energy away from other species and reduces biodiversity. Energy expert Valcav Smil[11] estimates that global plant biomass is now half what it was 10,000 years ago, largely because of conversion of forests into cropland over the past 150 years. Humans and domesticated animals now represent nearly 97 percent of vertebrate biomass, whereas just a century ago the biomass of wild mammals may have equaled the biomass of humans. Our unwillingness to share energy with other species makes it tough to maintain biodiversity.

SOCIAL DECEPTIONS AND THE REALITIES OF PROGRESS

Human social intelligence is Machiavellian. Aggrandizing rulers use deception to control people by shaping their perceptions, but deception is also a dangerous tool. The most important tactical deception used by imperial rulers was belief in a divine king. Resistance against such a ruler would be futile, but real kings were seldom benevolent and wise, and imperial systems were perpetually subject to collapse. Tribal peoples also believed in the existence of beings endowed with supernatural powers that violated our understanding of ordinary physical reality. Like divine kings, omniscient tribal deities could monitor everyone's behavior in ways that supported the moral order; however, the risks and rewards of tribal supernaturalism were broadly distributed. The Asháninka recognition of kinship with animals and their belief that shamans could transform into jaguars or that animals could take human form were personally useful metaphors. But more importantly, when people shared and acted on such beliefs they helped overcome the disintegrating tendencies of social life and reinforced their cultural adaptation to the rainforest environment. To the extent that they made their system sustainable, such religious beliefs and practices were literally true. Tribal shamans had an inside track to the supernatural, but anyone could be a shaman and their powers could be challenged by anyone else. Enlisting the supernatural as a monitor in the tribal world discouraged cheating and stealing, as well as aggrandizing behavior, and supported egalitarianism and cooperation. The tribal system was a win-win game that rewarded cooperation. This worked because the players knew each other face to face and assumed they would continue to be players. The persistence of the tribal use of tactical deceptions for millennia suggests that such deceptions also sustained the humanization project for the long term and could thus be regarded as strategic perceptions.

Deception benefits those who are most able to shape the system. Deception encourages us to suspend our disbelief and to see the present system as natural and irresistible, not the product of human decision making. For example, in his *The Future of Capitalism* MIT economist Lester Thurow[12] compared economic globalization to the geological force of plate tectonics. Bill Gates[13] assures us in *The Road Ahead* that we need to make the best of progress, because "No one gets to vote on whether technology is going to change our lives."That would not be economic democracy. The situation was quite different in the tribal world where everyone shaped the culture and everyone enjoyed the benefits. The contrast is illustrated by the Neolithic Paradox, pointed out by French anthropologist Levi-Strauss.[14] It seems paradoxical that most of the world's great inventions were household inventions such as cooking, plant and animal domestication, weaving, and ceramics that were collectively invented thousands of years ago by tribal people worldwide, but they didn't go on to invent writing, wheels, guns, and steel. The explanation is that Neolithic technologies benefited every household, not just the builders of empires. Of course post-Neolithic technologies, such as writing, antibiotics, and electricity have brought many benefits, but these benefits have not always been widely shared.

Indeed, only an elite few decision makers produced the institutions and technologies of the modern commercial world and reaped a dispro-portionate share of the benefits while spreading the costs to society at large. The efforts and creative genius of a great many people were of course required, but their efforts were directed by a relative handful of influential elites who in effect called for the innovations and put them to work for their own ends. The prototype for commercial globalization was the private international banking, textile manufacturing, and trad-ing conglomerate created by the Medici family of Florence in 1434–1464.[15] This commercial network centered on one family was a personal imperium of interests that encompassed political partisans, religious officials, business partnerships, finance, mercantile exchanges, and real estate spread across Europe. Following the Medici model, a few hundred large investors were the principal financers and benefici-aries behind England's first large joint stock companies that initiated British colonial expansion beginning about 1600. By 1750, four London merchant families profitably commanded an interlocked commercial empire that now spanned the globe, linking West African slave stations, Caribbean sugar plantations, real estate in England and North American, military contracting in Europe, English banking and manu-facturing, and the British East India Company's interests in India. A relative handful of London-based English landowners and entrepren-eurs had already created the core institutions of capitalism by 1776 when Adam Smith wrote *The Wealth of Nations* describing the benefits of free markets and invisible hands. These benefits were real, but it was illusory to imagine that everyone benefited, whether in core or periph-ery of the global system. By 1812 about one-fourth of the UK popula-tion, some two million people, had become menial servants and home-less, even as fewer than a thousand top shareholders collected some 90 percent of the profits produced by the 40 million impoverished Indians controlled by the British East India Company. By 1890 more than a million desperately poor crowded London. In 1900 some two million people in New York's crowded tenements were living in half the household space per person as the Asháninka. By the 1930s, some 200,000 top shareholders in colonial enterprises were extracting profits from half a billion people in the British Empire, with the help of 33 million British citizens whose taxes funded the military defense of the colonies. This is the same pattern of concentrated power, grown larger, that existed throughout the ancient imperial world, and it is no accident that in 1714 Mandeville recognized that the new social hierarchy resembled an insect colony.

The social order of the contemporary commercial world is supported by very different tactical deceptions than in the tribal and imperial worlds, but in our case deceptions may be undermining our strategic perception of reality, as well as the future of humanity. Four crucial myths underpin the present order: (1) growth benefits everyone; (2) wealth is growing; (3) growth is sustainable; (4) freedom, democracy, and the rule of law are increasing. These myths work, because, like tribal myths, they contain much that is true; are often readily confirmed; seem impossible to disprove; and we want them to be true. The "growth benefits everyone" myth is readily challenged by the United Nations 2005 Millennium Development Report showing that 800 million people do not have enough food to meet their daily energy needs. This is an important benchmark because it is more than the entire population of the world in 1750, at the dawn of the industrial age. Income inequality measured relative to the standards of well-being in the high income nations suggests that as many as four billion people may be too poor to meet basic household needs without borrowing. This matters because even relative deprivation raises stress levels and reduces health.

THE PROBLEMS: POVERTY, CONFLICT, AND ENVIRONMENT

The global environment today is facing an array of problems ranging from global warming, weather anomalies, increased population, food and water resource shortages, and loss of biodiversity, to regional conflicts and poverty problems. —Hiromichi Seya, *Conditions for Survival*, 2010[16]

The global financial crisis that began in late 2007 drew an immediate crisis-mode response from government financial authorities, who committed trillions of dollars to economic stimulus and bailout-packages, but world leaders have been remarkably slow to even agree that the entire global system faces even more serious, albeit more slowly unfolding, problems.

The magnitude and scope of our contemporary human problems can most clearly be perceived when they are viewed from long-term historical, prehistorical, and cross-cultural perspective. Development experts often point to percentages and rates to show progress, but I find such measures inadequate and prefer to speak of absolute numbers of people. Rates can mislead. For example, psychologist Steven Pinker argues in his 2011 book, *The Better Angels of Our Nature*,[17] that violence has been in decline for millennia under the influence of civilization and especially more recently in the modern age. Pinker speaks of proportions, percentages, and rates, but if we look at absolute numbers and apply a broader concept of violence we can see a different picture. For example, the 200 million people who died in wars and political violence during the twentieth century[18] no doubt were a very small percent of the people who lived at that time, suggesting a very low rate of violent death for modern nations, but 200 million people are equivalent to the entire population of the world when civilization began a mere six thousand years ago.

Perhaps the most striking example of contemporary violence is the UN's estimate that by 2010, after decades of remarkable economic growth and development progress, some 1.7 billion people in 109 countries were living in "multidimensional poverty," measured by their limited access to clean water, cooking fuel, health services, basic household goods, and the standard of their house construction.[19] According to the UN, in 2010 there were a billion undernourished people who faced serious food insecurity, 1.5 billion people who lacked electricity in their homes, and 2.6 billion who lacked sanitary toilets.[20] Viewed as a percentage, the multi-dimensional poor were about one-fourth of the world's 7 billion people in 2011, but population growth has been so rapid that the number of poor would now exceed the world's total population of 1.6 billion people in AD 1900. This suggests that the human effect of progress during the twentieth century was maybe not so great. Extreme poverty is a form of violence. It is human suffering caused by social and cultural structures that allow those with more power to violate the most basic human rights to life of the weaker. For some to move ahead while others are pushed down is not optimal growth. Medical anthropologist Paul Farmer, who worked for many years among the Haitian poor, calls this process *structural violence*,[21] and it is without doubt one of the world's largest human problems.

Contemporary poverty would seem strange from the perspective of the 70 billion people who may have lived in the tribal world over the past 100,000 years. Tribal life, although relatively short for most, was probably not structurally violent, and most people in the tribal world were no doubt reasonably happy with their lives. At least, we can be fairly certain that they were successful at meeting their basic needs and were therefore not poor. Over most of this very long time span people lived as foragers in a world in which the total population remained under ten million people. Population apparently was relatively stable at this easily sustainable level because individual women controlled family-planning decisions, and there was no cultural or personal incentive for producing larger families.[22] With the entire wealth of nature at their disposal, and with their material demands relatively low, tribal people were in effect fabulously wealthy. There were also no rulers to oppress them, and people could enjoy great personal freedom. Even during the Neolithic when people began settled village life with food crops and domesticated animals in response to global warming at the end of the last Ice Age, global population remained under 100 million, and before the centralization of political power everyone remained wealthy in natural resources. Tribal life focused on the well-being of household and kin, and virtually everyone had access to the resources they needed to feel in control of the conditions of their daily life. This feeling of control is not the case for most people today, and given that our needs are social and psychological, as well as material, it is not surprising that only 27 percent of the nearly five billion people who participated in the 2005–2007 World Values Survey reported feeling "very happy" with their lives.[23]

Even though nearly two billion people in the world live in multidimensional poverty, when viewed from the top of the contemporary global hierarchy, a few people have been extraordinarily successful. According to careful estimates by researchers who maintain statistics on High Net Worth Individuals (HNWIs) for the financial services industry, in 2011 there were eleven million very wealthy people in the world, each with investible assets of a million dollars or more.[24] In the aggregate, HNWIs held investment wealth of $42 trillion, even with the downturn in the global stock market their holdings still gave them decisive control over the world of corporate business. In spite of the near collapse of the global financial system, in 2010 HNWI wealth was growing at an astounding 9.7 percent a year. HNWI investments produced a comfortable average unearned income of nearly $380,000 per HNWI, in addition to whatever salaries they earned. Most HNWIs were residents of just three countries: the United States, Japan, and Germany. Even if each HNWI represented a household of five people, they represented less than one percent of global population. In absolute numbers HNWIs would be equivalent to the entire population of the wealthy pre-Neolithic tribal world, where everyone lived in luxury from the bounty of nature, rather than from financial wealth. The relative and absolute wealth of today's HNWIs allows them to be the elite directors of the world through their investment decisions, and through the decisions of those who manage their wealth. They are able to shape the rules of the global system and make themselves the primary beneficiaries of economic growth.

The achievements of the elite directors of global economic growth have been truly remarkable, but they have also been problematic. Investments by financial elites, and their encouragement of investment of public funds in projects that also favor elite interests has certainly contributed to what some researchers call the "Great Acceleration": the dramatic elite-directed increase in global economic production, consumption, technology, and population since 1950.[25] The world's GDP increased more than seven-fold in constant dollars between 1960 and 2010, and it roughly tripled on a per capita basis. The Great Acceleration brought great advances in science and technology, including the Internet and medical care that have benefitted many, but these benefits are very costly and may be difficult to sustain, because they are pushing cultural and natural systems beyond safe limits.

It is not to disparage elite success, or to attribute evil intent to individual elites, by observing that elite direction by HNWIs and their agents has created an enormous human problem. The elite-directed growth process is especially problematic because it has failed to reduce the structural violence of poverty, and it has come at the expense of a vast degradation of the wealth of nature. This has occurred because we now live in a commercial world where elite directors have ignored the world's poor and have allowed natural resources to be treated as external to the market. By their influence the financial elite effectively control the instruments of political and economic power, but they are not counting the full human and environmental costs of the form of growth their decisions promote.

Scientists now recognize that by 1800, as industrialists began to expand their use of fossil fuels and nudged global population toward the one billion mark, commercial economic processes in the aggregate suddenly began to have a geologically visible impact on the earth's biological, chemical, and physical processes. This unexpected impact became large enough and expanded so enormously and so quickly that some scientists now designate the present age as a new geological epoch, called the Anthropocene. Prior to 1800 human activities were geologically barely visible. As recently as 1500, at the very dawn of the commercial world, there were fewer than 500 million people in the world, and technology was everywhere preindustrial. Ants probably moved more soil than humans at that time. The arrival of the Anthropocene changes everything. This new geological epoch in effect truncated and replaced the post-glacial Holocene Epoch, which began about ten thousand years ago at the end of the last great Ice Age.[26] Judging by recent climate cycles, we are currently in an interglacial period and should be anticipating another Ice Age, but instead the Great Acceleration is pushing up global temperatures and human culture is everywhere replacing nature. The Anthropocene means that humans now are really the dominant organisms determining the conditions of life on the planet. The difference this time, because we live off of fossil fuels, is that our primary by-product is carbon dioxide, not oxygen, as in previous geological epochs when cyanobacteria and vascular plants were dominant.

Ending the Holocene and replacing it with the Anthropocene was probably not a good idea, because the Holocene offered humanity absolutely ideal climatic conditions and rich ecosystems that supported the tribal world in luxury and made possible the development of modern civilization. The Anthropocene is already presenting enormous physical challenges for humanity. The UN Millennium Ecosystem Assessment team reported in 2005 that fifteen of twenty-five ecosystem services provided by nature were measurably in decline.[27] This means less naturally produced food, freshwater, soil, wood, and fiber, less natural regulation of climate, floods, and disease. We are living beyond our natural means, and the realities of nature are now more critical than what our financial balance sheets show. The loss of nature's ecosystem services immediately impacts the 1.3 billion people who directly depend on agriculture, forestry, fishing, and foraging for subsistence, but it also profoundly degrades everyone's existence. This is a vast human problem.

Research published by the World Wildlife Fund (WWF), the world's largest conservation organization, suggests that by 1976 humanity was already taking the equivalent of 100 percent of the world's baseline annual biological product, and by 2007 our global ecological footprint had grown to 150 percent of what nature could produce.[28] This biological overshoot was only possible because our extraction of fossil fuels greatly exceeded the annual capacity of nature to produce or absorb an equivalent amount by the annual production of biomass. Our factories now burn fossil fuels to make food products and materials that nature formerly produced for free. Wheat, corn, and rice replace natural grasslands and forests, and cattle, pigs, and chickens replace wild birds and animals. The overconsumption of fossil fuels allows us to degrade renewable natural resources and is the source of the climate-altering greenhouse gasses we are now pumping into the atmosphere. The human impact on nature is now so great that some authorities warn that we are exceeding the critical natural boundaries that stabilize the planet's life support systems.[29] The most dramatic of these transformative changes have occurred within a single human lifetime, and they were directed by a very few people.

THE BLUE PLANET REPORT

The scale and scope of contemporary human problems can be most simply described by the phrase "the system is broken," referring to the present humanly constructed world system. This is the central conclusion drawn from the statement of "The Problem" in the "Imperative to Act" report[30] issued in February 2012 by a distinguished team of fourteen Blue Planet Prize laureates writing for the Governing Council of the UN Environment Program in preparation for the June 2012 Rio+20 Earth Summit. The Blue Planet Prize was created by the Asahi Glass Foundation in 1992 to recognize individuals and organizations for outstanding scientific contributions to solving global environmental problems. Asahi Glass is a successful Tokyo-based multi-billion dollar global glass, chemicals, and electronics company that produces photovoltaic glass for solar batteries and takes pride in its commitment to sustainable development. The phrase "Blue Planet" forces us to think of the earth as something more than raw material for financial profit. It is how the earth was described in 1961 by Soviet cosmonaut Yuri Gagarin, who was the first person to orbit the earth. Blue Planet also recalls the first photos of the whole earth and the earth rise viewed from the moon by Apollo 8 astronauts in 1968, and the iconic "Blue Marble" photo of earth taken by Apollo 17 astronauts in 1972. Viewing the earth from space highlights the incredible beauty of earth in the void of space and its vulnerability in our hands. There no doubt are other worlds like earth out there, but they are light years away.

Blue Planet laureates are by definition "environmentalists" because they "believe in" the environment, but they also "believe in" societies and economies. The Blue Planet report commands special attention because it comes at such a precarious moment for the world, and because its authors are a cross-section of distinguished international scientists, political leaders, and directors who have thought deeply about contemporary human problems and are trying to solve them. They include directors of prominent environmental organizations such as the International Union for the Conservation of Nature, and Conservation International. They include Gro Harlem Brundtland, multiterm Norwegian prime minister and former head of the World Health Organization. Brundtland also chaired the 1983-1987 World Commission on Environment and Development (WCED) that developed the original concept of sustainable development that laid the foundation for the first Earth Summit. This was the Rio Summit that produced Agenda 21 in 1992, which still guides the international response to the environmental crisis. Several Blue Planet authors were recently listed in *Time Magazine's* "100 Most Influential People," such as Sanjit Bunker Roy (2010), founder of the Barefoot College in India; climate scientist James Hansen (2006); energy expert and MacArthur Fellow Amory Lovins (2009); Susan Solomon, atmospheric scientist and Nobel laureate (2007); as well as biologist Paul R. Ehrlich, a MacArthur Fellow; and Sir Nicholas Stern of Brentford, former World Bank Chief Economist, UK Treasury Secretary, and author of the influential *Stern Review on the Economics of Climate Change*, commissioned by the UK government of Gordon Brown.[31]

According to The Blue Planet report, "The Problem" is not just an environmental problem, it is also a human social and cultural problem. Climate change and related reductions in ecosystem services will threaten water supplies in many poor, drought-prone areas and will reduce human security in ways that may increase internal as well as external political conflicts. The report urges immediate international action, because given current political and economic realities we will not be able to create a just world or a world without poverty. There won't be a world in which society, environment, and the economy are sustainable. Our present systems of governing institutions are inadequate to reduce and mitigate the damage we have already done to the natural life-support systems of our planet. We are facing "a perfect storm of problems driven by overpopulation, overconsumption by the rich, the use of environmentally malign technologies, and gross inequalities."[32] The most spectacularly malign technologies would of course include nuclear weapons, along with other obscenely destructive military hardware, and the indiscriminate burning of fossil fuels and the production of toxic substances.

There is a pattern in the succession of similar high-level scientific reports produced since 1972. The Blue Planet assessment of global problems is remarkably similar to the "Warning to Humanity" issued in 1992, twenty years earlier, by 1,700 of the world's senior scientists associated with the Union of Concerned Scientists. This group, which included most then living Nobel science laureates, warned that we were on a "collision course" in which the greatest peril was "...to become trapped in spirals of environmental decline, poverty, and unrest, leading to social, economic, and environmental collapse."[33] Both of these reports echo the 1972 *Limits to Growth* study that graphed how just such a system collapse could occur by 2050 if growth trends in population and economic production observed since 1900 continued with no limits.[34] These multiple warnings pinpoint the problems, but how the world got into this downward spiral so quickly is best explained as a colossal failure of elite-directed growth since 1950.

THE VICIOUS CYCLE OF GROWTH AND POWER

Elite-directed growth is an ill-fated process in which elite directors set off a vicious cycle of increasing scale and complexity that causes wealth and power to be concentrated in a relatively few hands and leaves the majority to pay the costs. The problem is neither elite directors nor growth in and of themselves. The problem is an out-of-control process of elite direction that concentrates wealth and income without limit and that depends on perpetually accelerated flows of energy and materials. Those individuals who direct this kind of misguided growth receive disproportionate short-term rewards that understandably encourage them to disregard negative effects and promote even more growth.

The key feature of the elite-directed growth cycle is that elite directors are able to allocate costs and benefits as a *political distribution* that the elite, because of their power, are able to control with minimal regard for majority interests. The outcome for elite directors is that they are able to concentrate the benefits of growth in their own hands, and then they can use their outsized returns to produce more growth. In this growth process the elite "socialize" the costs, or distribute them to society at large, such that everyone else pays for growth. Socialized costs include what economists call externalities, which would include things like pollution and the human abuse of sweatshop labor, when these are part of production and distribution but are excluded from the market price of goods. These socialized costs are growth, or scale subsidies. The "subsidy" label calls attention to these otherwise hidden costs that are part of the actual "overhead," that facilitates growth in scale and complexity. This is an expanded understanding of what a subsidy means, because it covers more than support coming directly from governments. Subsides are also in effect paid by the public at large and by future generations. Subsidies make growth extra-profitable, making more profit to be concentrated in the hands of a few. Elite-directed growth is a "vicious cycle" when it enables the directors and benefactors to ignore the full costs to society and environment, allowing them to simply collect their disproportionate awards. When this occurs, the "system is broken."

Elite direction involves the exercise of power to shape majority perceptions and behavior and to gain majority consent for growth projects that ultimately harm everyone. This is not to exclusively blame elite decision makers for our problems, because elites can only do what the majority allow. There is of course elite criminality and conspiracy, but the elite generally write and follow the rules of society. They are not necessarily more selfish or greedier than the majority. Elites are intelligent and successful people, and even when they are well-intended humanitarians, their extraordinary power and influence necessarily magnify their mistakes. Solving our biggest problems means that everyone must correctly perceive the true costs of growth in scale and complexity, and the majority must set the limits of sustainable development. This is the scale solution that is most likely to be found in small nations.

ELITE DIRECTORS AND *THE POWER OF SCALE*

The big personal insight from my work on power and scale came when I began to look closely at the connection between growth and power in my home region, the state of Washington, and the United States as a nation. It was apparent that at all levels growth and power were linked by specific individuals in a dynamic circular relationship in which increases in one dimension led to increases in the other. Understanding how this worked meant putting individual human decision makers into the equation. This was very different from other common historical approaches that describe major cultural developments as if entire societies were the players as in Diamond's portrayal discussed above.[35]

The rulers of the Ur III Dynasty in ancient Mesopotamia were the first known elite directors, and they demonstrated how the process worked by successfully constructing a regional empire by about 2000 BC. In a world where a household needed 1,680 liters of barley every year to survive, King Ur-Nammu managed to extract enough "surplus" barley from the 25,000 people living in and surrounding his walled city state of Ur to allow him to launch the Ur III Dynasty of divine kings and live in luxury from the 9 million liters he extracted annually from the five million subjects of his greatly expanded personal empire. This was Pareto's scale and power law equation of skewed income distribution in action, which will be described in chapter 2. Make the system grow larger, but keep the distribution of power grossly unequal.

My earlier book, *The Power of Scale*,[36] based on five years of historical research, assembles statistical data, graphs, and tables showing the same elite-directed growth process at work throughout history. In addition to Ur III, there are case studies on the Roman Empire, 100 AD; Norman England, 1066; Florence, Italy, 1451; the Inca Empire in 1532; Stuart England, 1688; Georgian England, 1812; nineteenth-century Balinese kingdoms; and the Chakri Dynasty in Thailand in 1851. All these examples show societies consistently arranged by the same power law distributions in which the bigger or richer the empire, the more concentrated the power in the top rank. The largest empires, including the Mughal Empire with 110 million South Asian subjects under Akbar in 1605, and Ch'ing China with 370 million people in 1900, all showed the same pattern. At its height in the 1930s, the British Empire encompassed some 500 million people from whom the top 0.2 percent, perhaps a million people living in superelite households, were the principal financial investors and the principal beneficiaries. Millions languished in poverty or died in late Victorian famines.[37]

Growth in scale and complexity can almost only happen when political rulers can direct the process because, unless they are otherwise forced, people are most concerned with taking care of their own families and their immediate kin. Left to their own devices most people do not welcome changes that make their lives more complex and more vulnerable, or create unnecessary conflict. People want to make their own rules, control their personal resources, and work to meet their own needs. In the tribal world whenever local population growth caused interpersonal conflict to increase or material resources to decline, a section of the community would split off and some people would move away. People did not automatically choose to grow a bigger economy, because as long as everyone had access to the resources they needed, growing a bigger economy would only increase individual workloads. Tribal systems effectively guaranteed everyone an irreducible minimum of material well-being, and people saw no reason to change that. No one even thought of "the economy" as something separate from their daily lives that would be desirable for them to grow larger, until financial elites in eighteenth-century Europe began to construct the institutions of an income-skewed global capitalist market economy.

Given the choice, before chiefdoms, kingdoms, and empires became common, tribal people preferred to move away from would-be rulers, rather than sacrifice their freedom to political hierarchy. However, when people became too invested in particular locations, especially when subsistence required costly infrastructures such as irrigation or terracing, or other forms of permanent cultivation, it sometimes became difficult for people to move away from oppressive rulers. This also occurred when there was no place to move. Under such circumstances people made the best of bad choices, allowing aggrandizing rulers to remain in place, especially in times of crisis. Although there are many alternative ways in which centralized political power could be organized, it is easiest for people to allow monopolistic, exclusionary systems controlled by dynastic rulers to predominate. Such systems tend to be large, expansionist polities, focused on elite-directed growth. The alternative, smaller, more democratic systems such as the Greek Polis can attempt to balance and share power, but they are more difficult to maintain. Such systems can avoid the runaway growth problem of monopolistic systems, and are the path that many of today's most successful small nations have chosen.

2

FINDING THE RIGHT SIZE

Why Small Nations Succeed

It is natural for a republic to have only a small territory; otherwise it cannot long subsist. In an extensive republic there are men of large fortunes, and consequently of less moderation; there are trusts too considerable to be placed in any single subject; he has interests of his own; he soon begins to think that he may be happy and glorious, by oppressing his fellow-citizens; and that he may raise himself to grandeur on the ruins of his country. —Montesquieu, 1748[1]

Let's assume that there are optimum sizes for elephants, ants, societies, and nations. If elite-directed growth is the underlying problem caused by elites who promote growth in pursuit of their own self-interests, the critical question to ask then becomes, what is the right, or optimum size for societies, governments, economies, markets and business enterprises? If the size question can be answered, the next crucial questions are how to organize societies to achieve the right size, and what values are needed to maintain the right size? The small nation solution is finding the right size. This requires comparing successful small nations with nations that have exceeded the optimums in order to identify the qualitative changes and the costs and benefits that growth causes.

The fundamental principle which can be drawn from nature is that everything, from atomic nuclei to stars and galaxies, exists within a given optimum size range measurable by "magic numbers." The most durable and resilient objects, judging by their frequency, are the smallest things, and there is no reason to suspect that human societies and cultures are an exception to these universal natural laws. Giant objects are rare and ephemeral, because they are voracious consumers of energy and materials. Human societies are not exempt from these laws of nature. We can safely assume that in principle, the giga- and meganations, home to giant corporations and giant tera economies, are too expensive and too unstable to be the best models for humanity, and they are unlikely to last very long in their present bloated form. Nature suggests that our future is in small nations composed of small societies, small governments, small economies, and small businesses.

Anthropologists have learned that human groups, like the rest of nature, are shaped by magic numbers that set the parameters within which we can live most successfully. Two million years of biological evolution equipped us with the individual mental ability to know personally and interact effectively within an ego-based network of only about 150 people. Living together with people in a larger society is a difficult challenge, but human life cannot be sustained without small nation–sized societies situated in an even larger social world of small nations. This is how humanity arrived at its present position. Now we must get the right size to survive.

BRINGING ANTHROPOLOGY HOME: DISCOVERING THE POWER LAW

In considering human survival problems throughout my anthropological career, I focused at first on the contrast between "primitive culture" and "industrial civilization." I wanted to understand why "progress" had counterintuitively become a global survival problem. In the preface to the first edition of my anthropology text on contemporary human problems, which appeared in 1976,[2] I was critical of the many negative side effects of our civilization and especially industrial technology, but rejected "any political-economic ideology" as a problem-solving alternative, and was "emphatically not calling for a capitalist, socialist, Marxist, or communist solution" to global problems. I did acknowledge being frustrated at having no idea what form any real solutions might take, but was convinced that tribal peoples were in some way pointing us to a solution. The challenge was to discover the crucial aspects of tribal culture that most contributed to their success and identifying what could be adapted as solutions to the problems that we have struggled with in the commercial world.

In the 1970s, with the environmental movement well under way, it was easy to think that industrial technology and the dramatic increases in production and consumption that industrialization permitted were the primary sources of our troubles. This made "appropriate" or "para-primitive" technologies seem like very appealing solutions. It was not until 1983, in writing the second edition of my "human problems" text[3] that I began to realize that the absolute size of society might be more important than level of technology or specific details of ideology. To show this shift in my thinking, throughout the text I replaced the term "primitive culture" with the terms "tribal" and "tribal society" and even raised the possibility of a "Small Nation Alternative" based on small tribal-like autonomous states of under a million people. I cited the works of Leopold Kohr along with works by anthropologist Sol Tax,[4] and the British environmentalist Edward Goldsmith[5] as advocates of similar scale-based solutions, but did not yet understand why scale itself rather than technology was so important.

By the early 1990s I was outlining a more formal "culture scale approach" and began using "small, large, and global" as a simple three-part culture scale framework to organize my general *Cultural Anthropology* textbook.[6] *Small* cultures were tribal, *large* were politically centralized, and *global* were commercial-industrial sociocultural systems. The scale perspective quickly drew my attention to social power and the seemingly obvious connection between growth in the scale of society and concentration of power in the top ranks. After having focused on the problems of tribal peoples for nearly three decades, I now began to more closely examine the cultures of large-scale commercially organized societies, especially the United States. My *Cultural Anthropology* text included an entire chapter on the United States, and I also began looking closely at my own neighborhood in the Pacific Northwest for clues that might explain the connection between growth and power.

In 1996–1998 I carried out a large research project in my home territory that led quickly to a real breakthrough in my understanding of how and why growth in scale actually concentrated social power.[7] I was looking for scale effects in the distribution of real estate ownership in all twenty-seven municipalities in two counties of eastern Washington, home to some 260,000 urban people. I wanted to know how some of the wealth benefits of urban growth were actually distributed in the region where I lived. If growth benefitted everyone equally and was distributed "normally," like, say, IQ, then as the size of the economic pie, in this case property values, increased, then most people's property values would increase and everyone would be better off. There would be few negative effects. This is what our faith in growth and progress tells us to expect, but it was not what I found.

My analysis of the effects of urban growth was difficult and time consuming. It involved pouring over the assessed values of tens of thousands of parcels and property owners. At that time desktop computers were not yet up to the task, and I had to use a mainframe computer to extract great masses of mind-numbing data from large reels of computer tape supplied by the local county assessors. It took customized computer programs and spreadsheets to do the repetitive work of sorting and analysis. I found that as the population size, or scale, of urban places in the region increased, the assessed value held by the top individual owners, who were the property elites in each place, increased by orders of magnitude up to more than $100 million for the largest owner resident in the largest city. The average value held by the non-elite majority of owners increased only slightly, remaining relatively flat regardless of urban scale. However, in smaller urban places higher proportions of residents were actually property owners, rents were lower, and there was less poverty.

Real estate values held by corporate businesses also became more concentrated in larger urban places, just as they did with individual owners. Urban growth did not benefit everyone and all businesses in the same way, and this seemed to explain why urban elites used their political influence to promote growth by continually changing zoning laws and expanding urban boundaries to increase population and their total property values. Growth did more than create more wealth, it actually concentrated property value wealth, disproportionately rewarding the elite few, but leaving most people and businesses behind. How to explain this outcome remained a mystery until I searched the sociological literature on power elites and the distribution of wealth and income and uncovered the power law.

The distribution of property that I found in my own neighborhood was no mystery. It proved to be an example of a predictable mathematical pattern fortuitously called a "power law distribution" which Italian economist Vilfredo Pareto invented more than a century ago to describe the distribution of household income and wealth in many countries.[8] A "power law" describes a rank distribution in which, for example, the number of households found at a series of income ranks can be plotted from richest to poorest as a straight line on log-log graph paper measuring by powers of 10. This is a skewed distribution with a few very high income households at the very top and the majority with lower incomes. This effect is also called the Pareto Principle, or the 80–20 rule in which, for example, the top 20 percent of property owners hold 80 percent of total property value. A power law distribution occurs naturally with many things in nature, such as stars by magnitude, but it is very different from a "normal" distribution which plots as a bell curve on regular graph paper. The power law distribution is about increasing magnitudes, and displaying this requires a log graph, where each major line is 10 times greater than the next lower. A power law distribution plotted on normal graph paper produces a curiously squashed curved line.

Power laws are said to be "scale free," because the overall distribution pattern remains constant, even as the total system grows larger. This helps explain why very high income persons would favor economic growth, because they "naturally" receive much more of the larger income pie in actual quantities than most people would imagine. However, income distribution is a product of cultural rules, and income hierarchies may be limited by the cultural imposition of intentional floors and ceilings as in tribal societies that strive for social justice. Likewise, federal salary ranks are not a power law distribution, because they follow the General Schedule grade and step system in which everyone moves up.

Still not totally convinced with my evidence that the uncontrolled operation of the power law distribution rewarded the elite for promoting growth, and in effect, disempowered the majority, I expanded my research to include businesses and looked at the entire state of Washington. I also spent the summer of 2000 replicating my Washington research in the state of Vermont and found exactly the same power law effects for individual property ownership and business revenues. These findings turned out to be supported by other researchers at about the same time, who were looking at national figures based on tax returns showing that individual taxpayers by income as well as business by revenues also follow power law distributions.[9] I also found that they could readily be applied to ancient civilizations and early modern Europe.[10]

SCALE AND POWER CAUSES OF THE WORLD'S BIGGEST PROBLEMS

The really big social and environmental problems that threaten our present and future security, such as conflict, poverty, dysfunctional government, failing corporations, economic chaos, and global environmental deterioration, can all be attributed to the undesirable side effects of elite-directed growth. When nations, economies, markets, and business enterprises grow too large and too complex, really bad things can happen and now *are happening* all around us. The basic premise of this book is that the biggest problems that are happening in the world are caused by misguided growth directed by fallible human decision makers. This means that the world's biggest problems are not inevitable. They are really scale problems. They are occurring because we are living with systems that we have allowed to grow so large that they cannot be safely managed by even the best intended elites, whether individual investors, business executives, philanthropists, politicians, or the most skilled technicians. Our basic human nature cannot be changed, but solutions will be found in organizing our human social and cultural organizations and systems at a safely manageable size. Most things and systems in nature naturally find the right size, but power-seeking individuals have the capacity to override the otherwise natural size limits to secure short-term benefits for themselves.

Identifying elite-directed growth in scale and complexity as the cause of the world's biggest problems requires a different and much deeper anthropological perception of human cultural development and present realities than now prevails in popular discourse. This expanded approach to human problems is an anthropologically based scale and power theory that offers a direct challenge to the currently ruling delusion that perpetual economic growth within an elite-driven model of globalization is the solution to all our problems. From a scale perspective, unlimited growth is a problem not a solution. However, it seems ridiculously simplistic to claim to have solved all of the world's problems with a single theory, so I must qualify my claim to say that elite-directed growth is concerned with many of the world's really big problems, not all problems.

I can also appeal to Leopold Kohr's disclaimer on the far-reaching implications of his theory of political scale. Kohr (1909–1994) was an Austrian-born economist and political scientist who wrote about the "diseconomies of scale" and originally proposed that big nations needed to "break down" because they were too big. He was probably the first theorist to propose small nations as a solution to global problems. Kohr also realized how outrageous his claim would appear, and offered this carefully qualified disclaimer focusing his scale solution on the specific problem of the misuse of *political power* (which also appears as the opening quotation of chapter 1):

> Thus we see that a small-state world would not only solve the problems of social brutality and war: it would solve the equally terrible problems of oppression and tyranny. It would solve all problems arising from power.[11]

Kohr's uncommon ideas on the size of nations first appeared in 1941[12] and were quickly submerged by the war and then by postwar enthusiasm for reconstruction shaped by the interests of the elites of the great powers. Kohr's own work may not have been widely recognized at first, but it did inspire one of his students, Ernst Schumacher (1911–1977), to write the influential book, *Small Is Beautiful*, applying scale theory to economics.[13] My theory of scale and power theory was inspired in part by both Kohr and Schumacher, but it was also individually verified by my perspective as an anthropologist. The small nation solution is *anthropological* and therefore much broader in scope than Kohr and Schumacher's complementary and parallel approaches, because it holistically combines the political and the economic, placing the political-economy within entire sociocultural systems, and because it focuses on human well-being and long term sustainability. Anthropological scale theory also recognizes the importance of decision making by individual human agents, and it of course draws on the mathematical power law equation discovered by Vilfredo Pareto. The power law equation, discussed above, is the crucial explanatory underpinning of the power and scale-based small nation solution.

The small nation solution and the expanded theory of scale that it is based on is so unbelievably contrary to still prevailing, albeit failing, political and economic models and political ideology that it deserves some accounting to explain where these seemingly radical ideas come from. The following section offers an anthropological view of scale effects centered on a different stage, on insights from the tribal world, and especially from Australian Aborigines.

MAGIC NUMBERS: WHAT AUSTRALIAN ABORIGINES TELL US ABOUT VALUES AND SCALE

The archaeological and ethnographic record shows that for millennia people in the tribal world met their daily physical requirements very efficiently by living in small face-to-face residential groups of about fifty people using the very simplest material technology. The cultural development of unique languages, kinship, marriage, and lifestyle systems allowed people to form relatively self-sufficient and highly resilient minimal societies of 500 people by about 100,000 years ago. The tribal societies that flourished for tens of millennia in the prestate world are important reference points for the small nation solution, because scale-dependent aspects of tribal life seem to maximize human freedom, democracy, equality, and social justice. These are the very moral values that Americans enshrined in their Bill of Rights in 1789. They are amplified in the 1948 UN Universal Declaration of Human Rights, and in the 2009 European Union's Charter of Fundamental Rights. Fully implementing these moral values in a small nation world system would be an enormous step toward solving contemporary global problems. Tribal societies tell us that when these very basic values are in place, people can prosper even in the smallest societies, with the smallest economies, and the materially simplest technologies ever known.

Today's small nations are not tribal societies, and they do not represent a reversion to the tribal world, but because they are small, small nations can approximate the scale conditions that we know can foster the moral values needed for social justice and sustainability in the contemporary world. The durably universal values of tribal societies suggest that having the right value system is more important than developing complex technologies and maximizing the flow of energy and materials.

Australian Aborigines provide perhaps the longest-existing, best-documented example of why it is so important to have optimum-sized social groups and reach a consensus on an effective set of moral values. This might sound like an extreme claim, but Aborigines establish a baseline of sorts that defines the absolute minimum scale of a truly successful human society. They are a window on the basic small-scale social conditions that defined our human psychology and the culture of our human ancestors for at least the past 100,000 years up to the emergence of the first politically centralized societies just 7,000 years ago. This tribal period constitutes the most recent phase of what evolutionary psychologists have called the human environment of evolutionary adaptedness (EEA). This is the social world that evolution has designed us for, and it is the world that shaped our basic human nature that younger, more complex societies must work around as they grow larger.

Archaeological evidence shows that Aborigines were living in Australia by at least 50,000 years ago. DNA analysis now confirms that the ancestors of Aborigines left their original African homeland for Asia 60,000 to 75,000 years ago.[14] I saw dramatic proof of the continuity of Aboriginal culture and its cultural similarities with Ice Age Europe in the rock art at Ubirr in the Northern Territory. There were overlapping paintings of animals and stenciled hand prints reaching layer upon layer from the present far back into the remote past. Aborigines participated in the transition from archaic to Upper Paleolithic mobile forager culture based on very small, but optimally sized, social groups, which allowed people to successfully occupy all of the world's major continents fairly quickly. Speech and language was the key that made it possible for these foraging people to construct families and kinship-based social groups based on marriage and descent systems. The success and vitality of this basic Upper Paleolithic foraging cultural pattern is totally dependent on having optimally sized social groups. The success of this culture is also demonstrated by the persistence of numerous other fully self-sufficient foraging peoples who remained scattered all over the world on the fringes of permanent settlement well into the twentieth century. Given the vast length of time that these Stone Age cultures have existed and their great stability, it is legitimate to say that they represent a very basic human pattern. We know it worked well in deserts, savannahs, tropical rain forests, and the arctic, and all show precisely the same social units and broadly similar cultural patterns.

The fundamental Australian Aboriginal social group for day-to-day living is the band of twenty-five to fifty people united by an ethic of reciprocal sharing. The band was a mobile residential group, or camp composed of several small families whose members were drawn from different clans. This was the optimum number of people who could collectively provide secure subsistence by foraging, satisfy human requirements for sociability, and maintain marriage connections with outsiders. A larger band would quickly exhaust food resources and might split because of internal conflicts. Band members shared use of a territory and its natural resources with members of at least the six other bands that were its immediate neighbors. The clan was a small group of people who recognized descent from a common male ancestor and whose female members married into different clans and resided in bands in their husbands' clan territories. Ownership made clan members joint custodians and managers of property that in practice was widely shared with members of other clans. Founding histories recorded in the landscape, and in stories, songs, and dances were important clan properties that helped define estate boundaries. Clans were not totally self-sufficient but were linked by complementarity much like male and female. People married outside the clan, and songs and dances belonged to a given clan but had to be performed by a different clan. Everyone was an equal shareholder of a clan estate, and no one could be denied access to the natural and cultural resources needed for subsistence.

The cultural value that made band organization work was the shared concept of material abundance in which material needs could be easily satisfied with the simplest technology and minimal physical effort. This counterintuitive interpretation of how Stone Age economies worked to produce the "original affluent society" was first presented by anthropologist Marshall Sahlins in 1965 at the first international conference on tribal foragers.[15] Stone Age affluence meant that people's demands on nature remained very small but sufficient to satisfy their material needs and still allow time for what people valued most: leisure and sociability. The Aboriginal non-materialist value system is the exact opposite of the material scarcity that defines life in the commercial world and drives our economic activity.

The 300,000 Aborigines scattered throughout pre-European Australia extracted only a tiny fraction (0.02 percent) of the natural biological product available to them, estimating their per capita ecological footprint at about 0.1 global hectare equivalents.[16] In contrast, in 2001 Australians in the contemporary nation state of Australia were taking 40 percent of the biological product, with over 19 million people at a per capita footprint of 7.7 global hectares.[17] Aboriginal culture was emphatically anti-materialist, and the economy was stationary. People wore no clothing and slept on the ground by a fire with only a brush windscreen for shelter. Households stored no food, because compared to such relatively low total human demands natural resources were abundant. A man needed only a few spears, a spear-thrower, and a few stone tools. A woman needed only a digging stick, a wooden bowl, and grinding stones. With such a tiny material inventory it was easy for everyone to have all the required tools to control the conditions of their lives. Poverty could not exist under these conditions.

Aboriginal society was integrated by a spiritual moral order that contemporary Aborigines call the Dreaming and "The Law." The Dreaming was a moral authority equivalent to the Christian Bible, or a political constitution. It was both a cosmogony explaining where everything originated, and a cosmology explaining how everything worked. The Dreaming defined all social categories, regulated marriage and kinship, situated people within nature, structured the life cycle and age and gender roles, and personalized the landscape. It gave each person an identity and attached them to their cultural estate and country. Moral behavior was explicitly recognized, and people were labeled as "good" or "bad" in reference to whether they cared for others and shared.[18] Meaning was defined by the non-material. The moral consensus meant that material benefits were broadly shared, and the focus of the entire system was stored in people's minds, and its sole purpose was maintaining the well-being of persons, households, and nature.

The tribe of about 500 people was the largest Aboriginal social group, defined by a distinct language and culture. Five hundred people was the optimum number to maintain and reproduce a common language and culture, as well as an internal marriage system. Tribespeople talked to each other and intermarried, and society was small enough that everyone was related either by kinship or marriage or could readily be treated as if they were. Social roles were defined by age and gender, and by their knowledge. The geographic size and population density of clan and tribal territories depended entirely on the biological productivity of natural food stuffs, which was determined by rainfall or aquatic resources. Where natural resources were scarce territories were large and bands moved frequently. In normal years tribes were relatively self-sufficient, but they had no formal heads and did not constitute political units in opposition to other tribes. If tribes became too small to be internally viable, their members were absorbed by neighboring tribes. If they grew too large they subdivided. In all of Australia there were never more than about 600 tribes. The members of different tribes sometimes intermarried. They interacted by trade and shared a spiritual culture and a recognizably similar social system and material culture. The overall system remained constant for millennia but was continuously changing in detail. The evidence that Aboriginal culture persisted because it worked well for people is overwhelming.

The possibility that tribal societies were successful because they were non-materialistic and highly egalitarian and that these traits may have contributed to the extreme durability of tribal cultures has been very difficult for people to accept, quite apart from recognizing any connection between scale, moral values, and equality. The relative social equality of tribal societies is often shrugged off as pure fantasy or hopeless romanticism, even by anthropologists who should know better. As early as 1973 I felt compelled to make the case before a professional anthropological audience that describing tribal societies in positive terms was not necessarily romanticism.[19] I remember later presenting a guest lecture on tribal societies in a graduate seminar in sociology and discovering that all of the students were convinced that no society could ever be egalitarian. They all believed that classless society was a Marxist fiction. I explained that I was not describing total equality, because people are mentally and physically different and have different life experiences, but tribal societies were in fact "classless" in comparison with us. In tribal societies people were distinguished only by age, gender, and personality, and no one was denied access to the means of subsistence, or the "good life." Positions of honor or leadership were open to anyone who was qualified. This kind of social equality is certainly difficult to maintain and no doubt requires a small face-to-face society, but it is not a fiction. Speaking of this kind of equality is not to pretend that tribal peoples were "noble savages" or morally perfect peoples, or that their societies were utopias. They simply had achieved a more humane distribution of social power than the larger, more complex societies that followed them.

RIGHT SIZING: THE SMALL NATION ADVANTAGE

Dealing with other people is in many ways a more difficult human challenge than learning how to satisfy our energy and material needs from nature. That Aborigines solved both problems is a truly remarkable achievement. Rarely did such small tribes grow larger than about 2,500 people. Tribal societies of this scale proved to be remarkably successful and quickly filled the world's major continents by 12,000 years ago. Each tribe remained roughly the same size, simply segmenting as population grew too large and forming regional international exchange systems that increased security. In today's world, rural ethnic communities, villages, and urban neighborhoods resemble these original small tribes by scale and remain the bedrock of today's nations, large or small. Nations of whatever size will remain intact only as long as people can maintain a consensus about the essentials of decision making, dispute settlement, and the distribution of resources. Even with electronic information technologies, consensus becomes increasingly more difficult as nations grow larger than 10 million. We can expect that small nations will continually re-assert themselves as large nations become dysfunctional and people seek consensus through the dynamism of democratic social movements empowered by digital communication networks.

The central dilemma that has preoccupied political philosophers since Plato and Aristotle is that the civic virtues of self-government, freedom, and the good life cannot be easily achieved if the nation is too small or too large. The dilemma is how big? How small? French enlightenment philosopher Montesquieu (1689–1755) saw the most promise in the small democratic republic, equating size of territory with size of population, and he clearly understood the problem of size limits (see introductory quotation). A too-large city-state or republic even when initially governed by direct democracy would be torn apart by corrupt elites and despotism; if too small it would not be able to defend itself from outsiders.

For Montesquieu, small states could be republics, medium-sized states, monarchies, and empires would be despotic. Size was the determining influence, such that "…the spirit of this state will alter in proportion as it contracts or extends its limits."[20]

The apparent success of the American Revolution seemed to prove that representative democracy made obsolete the political scale limits recognized by classical writers, but at that time America was still a small nation. A central claim of the present work is that the question has been decided in favor of scale limits. Political scientists Robert Dahl and Edward Tufte presented a comprehensive review of the advantages of small-scale polities in a small monograph in 1973.[21] Citizens can be more actively and more emotionally involved in political decision making in small democracies, and they are more likely to share the same values and especially their understanding of what constitutes the good life. This consensus generates loyalty and will make it easier to agree on and work for the common good, which will make law enforcement easier. Dahl and Tufte also thought that the citizens of smaller polities would be able to communicate more easily and would be better informed than citizens of larger polities. The internet and cell phones may reduce some of this communication advantage of small nations, but that is still uncertain. Leaders of smaller polities might be expected to be more responsive to their citizens because of all the conditions listed above. However, it can also be argued that people in larger polities will have a larger perspective on what might be politically possible. This assertion seems reasonable, given the plausible conjecture that larger countries will have more organizations and interest groups and more complex policy-making processes.

All of the asserted political advantages of small nations can be challenged either as unproven or as value judgments. However, the political effectiveness of systems of different size can be evaluated both by the effectiveness of their citizens and the capacity of the system to deal with problems. I am interested in not only the formal properties of the political decision-making process but also with the actual outcomes produced and their effects on people.

Ten million people can be used as a rough boundary to set the upper size limit for small nations, because ten is an easy-to-remember round number, and it is an order of magnitude, a readily identified power of ten. More importantly, 10 million is less than 15 million, which is the maximum-sized nation that my authority on scale, Leopold Kohr, proposed as the absolute upper limit for a nation to be able to achieve the "*summum bonum*," the maximum good.[22] Kohr estimated that any nation larger than 15 million people would be likely to pursue what he called "post-optimum" socialized objectives such as substituting GNP for real prosperity or military power for real security. Post optimum-sized nations would reduce the *summum bonum*.

The *summum bonum* has diverse meanings, but it is fundamentally about moral values, or what political philosopher Michael Sandel calls "justice."[23] This is about how people determine what is the right thing to do in regard to the distribution of the things they value, especially wealth, rights, opportunity, and honor. These are contentious moral and political issues, and people will not always agree on what we should do. I assume that small nations are the best social environment to establish justice and for finding the best balance between the three different approaches to justice that Sandel identifies: welfare, freedom, and virtue. Small nation justice would encompass the utilitarian perspective referring to the maximum happiness or welfare for the maximum number. For libertarians it refers to individuals enjoying the freedom to raise their families, socialize, prosper materially, and have security and access to the accumulated benefits of their cultural heritage. The *summum bonum* can also refer to maximum virtue and universal human rights.

The existence of small nations suggests that, contrary to everything most people in larger nations imagine to be true, economies do not need to grow continuously for people to be happy. It takes a politically engaged citizenry to make large economies work for the majority, because social justice depends on how the economy is politically directed and how wealth is distributed and managed. Small nations show that it is possible to escape the delusional promise of perpetual growth by working toward a fairer distribution of wealth and by safeguarding all forms of wealth. Growth may still need to occur in components of GDP that foster human well-being with low flows of energy and materials. Economies just need to be the optimum size and shape that can most efficiently and sustainably meet people's needs. Some of the smallest small nations demonstrate that it is possible to take care of people and the environment even with very small economies of under $10 billion, and even with the largest businesses having revenues of under $10 million. *How* small nations succeed is the subject of Part II.

There is abundant statistical evidence from a variety of sources for the greater success of small nations in comparison with larger nations. The possibility that small nations might be especially able to promote human well-being came to public attention when the New Economics Foundation (NEF) published its Happy Planet Index (HPI) in 2006.[24] The HPI ranked 178 nations by combining years of happiness based on how satisfied people said they were with their lives, taking that times life expectancy, factoring in the ecological footprint, or the amount of biological production people consume per capita. By these measures the most successful nations would have long satisfying lives and they would make very low demands on nature. The HPI was an exploratory effort and in a number of cases values were extrapolated, but nevertheless the results were provocative. Twelve of the top fifteen, or 80 percent, of the happiest nations were either small nations (Vanuatu, Costa Rica, Dominica, Panama, Honduras, El Salvador, St. Vincent, St. Lucia, Bhutan, Samoa), or recently former small nations (Cuba, Guatemala) with populations of under 12.3 million, whereas overall only 58 percent of the 178 nations in the sample were small. Small nations were disproportionately represented in the upper ranks. This was suggestive, but not yet definitive proof of the advantages of smallness in nations, so I set out to conduct my own independent investigation.

Perhaps the main reason that the advantages of small nations have not been widely appreciated is that they are often under-represented, in the most commonly used rankings of nations. The World Bank gives population figures for 210 nations in its statistical databank, and 130 (61 percent) of these are small nations. The Bank's somewhat larger sample for its Worldwide Governance Indicators dataset covers 213 nations, 132 (62 percent) of which are small nations. The Bank offers wealth estimates for 152 nations, of which only 83 (55 percent) are small nations. The Fund for Peace *Failed States Index* for 2011 covers 177 nations, but only 99 (56 percent) are small nations. The UN Development Program's Human Development Index (HDI) also demonstrates the advantage of small nations. The HDI, which has been used with some modifications to measure living conditions in different countries since 1990, combines life expectancy at birth, average years of schooling, and per capita income. The UN Human Development Index ranks 187 nations, 56 percent of which are small nations.

I assembled a series of country databases, drawing especially on the World Bank's statistical databank,[25] in combination with numerous other cross-national statistical resources and indices. I sifted and sorted, creating dozens of graphs and ranked lists which no doubt bored my undergraduates but consistently showed that small nations outperformed large nations on a wide range of measures. I first looked at high life expectancy at birth as a clear measure of how well a country was doing at supporting the basic needs of its citizens. The World Bank's even larger 2008 list of 209 nations by population and life expectancy again showed that more than two-thirds of the 127 countries with life expectancies of seventy years or more were small nations. Small nations were even more disproportionately represented among the countries with super high life expectancies of eighty years or more.[26] Andorra, a very small nation of just 83,811 people, had the highest life expectancy of 82.5 years, and three other small nations, Hong Kong, San Marino, and Switzerland, were in the top five with life expectancies of 81.7 years or higher. This was similar to the pattern shown by the HPI, which was not surprising given that life expectancy was a prominent dimension of that index.

Several decades of medical and public health research, both within individual developed countries and cross-nationally, has consistently shown that income distribution is strongly associated with levels of individual physical and mental health and several key measures of social well-being. The pattern is that as income inequality increases well-being declines, and the reverse also holds, that as income equality increases, well-being improves.[27] The reality that poverty is bad for your health has been well known to public health authorities since the publication of Sir Edwin Chadwick's famous 1842 report on the "Sanitary Conditions of the Labouring Population of Great Britain."[28]

British social epidemiologists Richard G. Wilkinson and Kate Pickett gained wide attention with their book, *The Spirit Level*, first published in 2009.[29] In Great Britain a spirit level refers to the bubble that floats in the spirits liquid encased in a glass tube or disk used in carpenters' levels, and therefore spirit level is a metaphor for "equality." So, the level refers to finding the optimum distribution of wealth and income in a society for health and well-being. "Level" also recalls the "Levellers," an English political group who proposed a radically democratic consti-tution for England in 1647 as the civil war was ending. Levellers wanted a more just society, and they resisted land enclosures, corporate mo-nopolies, and elite privilege—elite-directed political policies that tended to increase inequality by removing income and wealth from the majority. These people were well ahead of their time.

Wilkinson and Pickett present abundant evidence for the benefits of greater income equality in wealthy developed nations, making the case that not only physical and mental health are improved by greater equal-ity but levels for socially valued objectives such as education, social mobility, trust and community life, and child well-being are all im-proved, whereas levels of social negatives such as drug abuse, imprison-ment, obesity, homicide, and teen births are all lowered by greater equality. They also point to environmental benefits of better income distribution, such as reduced status competition, and less individualism and consumerism which would reduce pressure on natural resources and make it easier to gain political support to reduce greenhouse gases to ease global warming. Higher levels of social equality would of course also benefit the upper ranks of society because it would mean more security, less disease, and more happiness for everyone.

Small nations, just by their population size, reflect virtually all of the trends reported in the *Spirit Level* statistical evidence for income equality. The obvious explanation is that small nations are somewhat more likely to be egalitarian than large nations, and the benefits of small nation equality are reflected on many measures of well-being. If we look at Gini scores for income distribution, the most egalitarian nations are most likely to be small, even accounting for the overall number of small nations. The Gini score is a standard statistical measure of distri-bution in which the smaller the score, measured in hundreths, the closer the distribution comes to perfect equality, which would be "0," where everyone has exactly the same amount of, say, income or wealth. When the score is "1" one person would have everything.

Not all nations provide enough information on wealth and income distribution for statisticians to calculate Gini scores, but I was able to assemble Gini scores for *income* for 153 nations by combining figures for a range of recent years from UN and CIA sources.[30] When I ranked these nations by Gini values, it was obvious that, just as with the Happy Planet rankings, small nations were overrepresented in the half with the lowest, or most egalitarian, scores, and there were disproportionately more large nations in the higher, less egalitarian ranks than would be expected by chance. Small nations were dramatically overrepresented among the fifteen most egalitarian nations. Thirteen nations (Serbia, Belarus, Sweden, Austria, Denmark, Slovakia, Finland, Norway, Cyprus, Luxembourg, Malta, Iceland, and Seychelles), an amazing 87 percent out of the fifteen, were small nations, even though small and large nations were virtually evenly represented in the total sample (seventy-seven large, seventy-six small). Seychelles, with a score of 0.19, was the most egalitarian. Overall, there was also a clear tendency for more egalitarian nations to show higher scores on the UN Human Development Index (HDI) scores as would be expected given *Spirit Level* findings. GDP per capita was correlated the same way with the Gini score as the HDI with the Gini, suggesting that income growth causes, or at least is associated with greater income equality. However, again, small nations were overrepresented among the higher income countries. Eleven of the top fifteen highest income countries were small (Qatar, Luxembourg, Norway, Singapore, Switzerland, Hong Kong, Ireland, Austria, Denmark, Sweden, Iceland), and Sweden, Austria, Denmark, Norway, Luxembourg, and Iceland appeared in the top fifteen for both high equality and high income. Perhaps most significantly, there was no relationship between total size of the economy and the Gini score. Growing a larger economy did not improve income equality.

It is worth noting that when I calculated Gini scores for all small nations to compare with the average for all large nations, the averages were virtually identical. Where significant differences emerged was in the subset of the most egalitarian nations, which proved to be disproportionately small nations. This is why throughout my analysis I have emphasized that I am concerned with "successful" small nations, and why they succeed. I repeatedly found that the most remarkable small nations were conspicuous outliers among nations. They stood out because they were different. I found them by sifting and sorting, but in effect the most successful small nations have sorted themselves out. They are outstanding because they are really different in ways that make them ideal models. If we only considered mathematical averages they would be invisible. In a similar way, the common tendency of international organizations to focus on per capita GDP as a measure of success overlooks the actual distribution of wealth and income within countries, which is more consequential for people.

CREDIT SUISSE GLOBAL WEALTH DATABOOK, 2010

Another critical bias in development discourse is that most assessments of inequality have focused on income, and ignore the wealth which is the *source* of income and which is often more unevenly distributed. Wealth, especially individually held wealth, is no doubt ignored because information on wealth is not routinely presented in national statistics and people are often reluctant to disclose such information. The Credit Suisse[31] study of the wealth holdings of individuals is a remarkable pioneer effort to produce usable estimates of personal wealth holdings. The Credit Suisse Global Wealth Databook, which appeared for the first time in 2010, assembled wealth Gini scores for 165 countries using sophisticated regression extrapolations to fill in gaps. The data is primarily based on estimates, but this is also true for most census data. Imperfect as the Wealth Data book is, it is the most complete study of individual wealth available and is worthy of careful consideration for what it can tells us about how to reduce global poverty.

Household wealth shows trends that are similar to those seen for income but with some revealing differences. The most obvious difference is that the income Gini ranges from 0.19 to 0.71, and the wealth Gini from 0.57 to 0.95. Wealth is therefore much more concentrated than income, suggesting that wealth equity is much more difficult for nations to achieve. Income and wealth distributions are produced by political decisions; they are political distributions. Considering how much political resistance there is in many countries to income welfare, it is not surprising that an equitable distribution of wealth is even more difficult to achieve. However, just as with income, small nations were overrepresented in the most wealth egalitarian half of the ranking of nations by wealth Gini scores, and they were underrepresented in the bottom half, even though average scores were virtually identical by scale. This suggests that wealth equity is politically more feasible in small nations where political power is likely to be less concentrated than in large nations.

At first glance it seemed surprising that Spain, a large nation of 45 million people, was the most wealth-equitable nation in the Databook sample of 165 countries, only slightly ahead of Finland. However, Spain helps make the case for the small nation solution because it is famously recognized as the most politically decentralized nation in Europe. Spain's 1978 constitution created seventeen autonomous communities, in effect creating a nation of small nations. Among Spain's autonomous communities is Euskadi, the Basque country with some 3 million people in three provinces. Euskadi is also home to the Mondragon Cooperative Corporation, which in 2005 was recognized as the seventh largest business group in Spain and is famous internationally as one of most successful cooperative systems in the world. Euskadi and Mondragon will be examined in more detail in chapter 4 as exemplars of the ecodemia small nation type.

Ten of the fifteen most wealth egalitarian nations in the Credit Suisse Databook were small nations. This is two-thirds of the fifteen, whereas small nations are just over half (56 percent) of the sample. Four of the most wealth-egalitarian small nations (Finland, Cyprus, Luxembourg, and Iceland) also appeared in the list of most income-egalitarian small nations. This surely gives these four countries an A-plus rating for social equality. Remarkably, some of the small nations that are best known for income equity, Denmark, Sweden, and Norway, are not in the top ranks for wealth equity. I suspect that this is because these countries use government income-redistribution social welfare programs to compensate for wealth inequity. Likewise, highly equitable wealth ownership in some small nations, such as Ireland, Dominica, and Tonga, can compensate for poor income distribution. Even though Dominica is officially income poor, it appears as number four in the Happy Planet Index, and certainly helps make the case that a good distribution of wealth ownership may be more important than cash income for human well-being.

COLLIER'S BOTTOM BILLION AND WHY NATIONS FAIL

For a different perspective, Oxford economist Paul Collier finds that fifty-eight countries at the "bottom of the economic system" are poor, have failed to grow, and are falling behind in the economic achievement race.[32] In 2008 these fifty-eight "failing" countries contained in the aggregate a billion people and had a paltry one trillion dollars in combined exchange rate GDP. These "Bottom Billion" poor countries are indeed failing according to global economic measures, and many of them are wracked by civil war and conflict. Unfortunately, Collier finds that the countries in this group of failing nations have one typical feature: "they are small," implying both small population and small economy. The main problem was that their per capita incomes are very low. These countries are "dirt poor" and economically "stagnant." They are "islands of chaos" mired in a fourteenth-century world of "civil war, plague, and ignorance." They have been going down as everyone else has been going up, economically speaking. The list of negative characterizations seem so horrible that Collier refuses to provide a single list of the fifty-eight countries, not wanting to stigmatize them, or to create self-fulfilling prophecy that would cause them to fail even more. If these Bottom Billion countries are small nations and if "smallness" is part of their problems, Collier's argument is a direct challenge to the small nation solution and deserves a closer look.

Collier's explanation for why these poorest countries remain poor is that they are "trapped in poverty." The idea of a "trap" as explanation for and solution to poverty was popularized by Jeffrey Sach's *The End of Poverty* book, where he described it as follows:

A large number of the extreme poor are caught in a poverty trap, unable on their own to escape from extreme material deprivation. They are trapped by disease, physical isolation, climate stress, environmental degradation, and by extreme poverty itself.[33]

Collier devotes separate chapters to four specific traps to explain poverty in the bottom billion: conflict; natural resources that are ironically too valuable; being land-locked and surrounded by bad neighbors; and bad governance. These are all plausible explanations for poverty, and they are backed up by case study materials. The case studies are skewed toward Africa, no doubt because Collier is an African specialist, but viewing this material from a small-nation-solution perspective suggests that Collier's interpretation has some shortcomings. Describing a development trap as a positive feedback cycle keeping people poor is an obvious contrast to the small nation solution which poses the dual vicious cycles of elite-directed growth and excessive material consumption linked by economic growth as the primary causes of both poverty and environmental degradation. Identifying poverty traps would certainly appeal to growth-oriented economists, whereas calling elite-directed growth a problem is still heresy for most economists. This is why the central message of the small nation solution is invariably a hard sell to most contemporary development policy experts.

A careful inspection of the fifty-eight countries making up the Bottom Billion shows that only twenty-nine, or about half, are small nations defined as countries with fewer than 10 million people. This means that small nations are underrepresented in Collier's Bottom Billion failing nations. My global list of 230 countries shows that 65 percent are small nations, so we would expect small nations to be overrepresented in the Bottom Billion, especially if smallness was a poverty trap, but this is not the case. If human, rather than purely economic development is considered, not all of the Bottom Billion countries look so terrible. Fifteen countries, or more than a fourth of the Bottom Billion, were actually listed as either High or Medium human development on the UN's 2011 Human Development Index (HDI). One of the two nations ranking High on the HDI was Azerbaijan, a small nation. Furthermore, ten of the thirteen countries ranked Medium HDI were small nations, whereas, only a third of the thirty-nine Low HDI countries in the Bottom Billion were small nations. These figures again make the case that economic growth is not by itself essential to human well-being.

Collier's Bottom Billion offer an intriguing contrast to the fourteen hypersuccessful tera-economies at the top of the economic ranks, discussed in chapter 8, where each country has an economy of a trillion dollars or more. As we will show, these economic giants are largely responsible for the linked vicious cycles of elite-directed growth and hyperconsumption that are trapping so much of the world in poverty, conflict, and environmental degradation.

Further support for the small nation solution comes indirectly from a steady stream of research by a trio of prominent economists Daron Acemoglu and Simon Johnson, both at MIT, and James Robinson at Harvard, who since 2001 have focused on the role of *institutions* in shaping which nations prosper and which remain poor. Acemoglu and Robinson pulled their material together for a popular audience in the 2012 book, *Why Nations Fail: The Origins of Power, Prosperity, and Poverty*.[34] The idea that the way a country's government and legal institutions are organized will be a major, if not the major, factor influencing the material prosperity of the country's citizens has a respectable history among economic theorists. Their argument is that national prosperity is not a simple function of geography, or the skills and hard work of people, but rather the history of its government and the form of its businesses may in fact be the primary factors. This relates to the small nation solution, because successful small nations may have less power concentrated in a few political rulers and economic elites and less political and economic power overall, than larger nations. More broadly distributed power would make it possible for them to also have more equitable institutions. Successful small nations will have more inclusive political economies, rather than the more extractive systems constructed by self-serving elites.

THE ROYAL SOCIETY ON GROWTH AND WELL-BEING

> The opportunity exists for the reinvigoration of discussions about the inter-linked issues of population size, equity, human wellbeing and sustainable development. —The Royal Society, "People and the Planet," 2012[35]

One of the strongest recent scientific assessments of the global problem whose conclusions indirectly supports the small nation solution is the "People and the Planet" report issued by the UK's London-based Royal Society. The point of departure for this report was that population numbers do matter. Demographic variables, especially absolute population size, are crucial for sustainable development and human well-being. This is a central point of the small nation solution, and it is worth considering here why the Royal Society was able to reach this conclusion even when other international organizations have overlooked this issue, and why the Royal Society's findings are so important.

The Royal Society report reaches the astounding conclusion that "wellbeing can improve without growth in GDP."[36] The report explicitly notes that improved life expectancy does not require economic growth, but that education, public health, improvement in women's reproductive health services, sanitation, good nutrition, and social support generally are important factors. Improvements in public health can stabilize or even lower population, because lower infant mortality means that families can be smaller, especially when women can control their reproductive decisions. Modest declines in population were noted for several Caribbean small nations including Barbados, Cuba, Grenada, Guyana, Jamaica, Puerto Rico, and Trinidad and Tobago.

In considering the consumption side of the population-consumption duo, the RS report distinguishes between material and nonmaterial consumption. Material consumption for water, food, energy, and minerals draws directly on and may degrade natural capital, but nonmaterial consumption is economic consumption of goods and services that may occur with few or no demands on material goods. Knowledge itself is a crucial nonmaterial good, which is not diminished by consumption. For the world's two billion or so poor and malnourished, consumption of either sort is driven by people's need for basic commodities and services to secure an adequate living standard, but for much of the rest of the world social and cultural factors, including advertising, drive consumption. Conspicuous consumption is socially driven status-seeking, but consumption may also be to simply meet or conform to, but not exceed, social conventions. Many people strive to raise income, which also tends to raise consumption. The RS report concludes that the "conventional model" linking increased consumption with improved human well-being is itself a "major obstacle" to well-being.

In making their case for human well-being being in important ways independent of economic growth, GDP per capita, or absolute size of an economy, the Royal Society report cites multiple sources showing that enough absolute material resources to meet basic needs and enough for people to live in dignity is only one dimension of well-being.[37] The ability to enjoy health, freedom of action, security, and good social relations are also critical dimensions of well-being. For example, Nobel Laureate economist Amartya Sen makes it very clear that growth in GDP or income is only a *means* to well-being, but the freedom dimension of well-being also requires social conditions such as the institutional basis for education and health care, as well as operational civil and political rights.[38] In Sen's view, the promotion of human freedom must be the primary objective of development, not increasing GDP. The poor are not necessarily suffering from income poverty; rather they are living in "unfreedom." This means not being in control of important conditions affecting your daily life and applies to people needlessly experiencing famines in income-poor countries, as well as to gender inequalities generally, and disadvantaged people in rich countries who may have reduced access to education, health care, and employment opportunities.

Royal Society People and the Planet Working Group member economist Tim Jackson[39] described a "wellbeing paradox" in 2006 at a time when then UK Prime Minister David Cameron and his government were beginning to make well-being part of the country's sustainable development strategy, rather than focusing entirely on growth in GDP. Even among policy makers who consider well-being to be the ultimate goal of economic development, they typically assume that economic growth is a good because it causes increased material consumption which presumably causes increased well-being. Given these premises, the question becomes, how big does the economy need to be to produce a particular level of well-being? The difficulty with this, of course, is that it is growth in material consumption that increases pressure on the natural environment, thereby making consumption-dependent development less sustainable. The idea that growth in GDP improves living standards has been a standard, and virtually unchallenged, guiding principle for politicians since the 1950s. The "Growth Is Good" idea is so firmly established that some economists, such as Harvard economist Benjamin M. Friedman,[40] have attributed a positive moral value to economic growth itself. Friedman attributes the positive values of increasing opportunity, tolerance, generosity, and democracy to economic growth, which is contrary to everything that tribal societies tell us. However, he adds a significant caveat that the benefits of growth need to be broadly distributed, which again is part of the small nation solution. All of this assumes that increases in GDP can be taken to represent increases in human well-being, but alternative measures of "progress," such as the Genuine Progress Indicator, as discussed in chapter 7, show that this is often not the case.

Jackson points out that one of the shortcomings of GDP as a measure of well-being is that, by definition, as "gross" product, it does not allow for the wearing out or depreciation of capital during the year. This means that people who only focus on GDP have no basis for judging important dimensions of the impact of their consumption and especially how present consumption might affect their possibilities for future consumption. This of course brings to mind the wisdom of Gro Brundtland's original definition of sustainable development that "meets the

needs of the present without compromising the ability of future generations to meet their own needs." Measuring welfare as Net Domestic
Product (NDP) would be an improvement over GDP, but it still leaves
unresolved the problem that all consumption does not equate to welfare. Furthermore, whether or not economic growth increases well-
being, economic decline is almost certain to reduce well-being. The
most critical problem then becomes how economic stability, and at
what level, can produce well-being. Jackson cites structural reasons why
growth has had such appeal for people, such as the link between growth
and tax revenues and the sense of national purpose that it involves.
Many people may simply fear that if the economy is not growing, it may
simply collapse. However, Jackson holds out another important possibility:

"It may be possible to devise economic systems that avoid structural
instability without relying on endless consumption growth. At the moment, however, we have very little experience in achieving this. . . . the
fear of collapse may be enough, not simply to keep us on the growth
path, but even to keep us from a more rigorous examination of the
alternatives."[41]

Part II

Small Nations Show the Way

The great diversity of small nations is a special virtue of their small size. Unlike large nations which must impose a single formula on everyone and may have great difficulty even persuading people to agree on what the problems are, people living in small nations know what the problems are and are free to experiment to discover solutions for their specific situations. There are many kinds of small nations, and they have followed many pathways to workable solutions to common problems, but the most successful small nations demonstrate how the negative effects of concentrated power can be overcome. Chapters in Part II examine a selected sample of small nations to show what solutions actually work and to examine why particular solutions work. The following three chapters consider three broad but overlapping small nation types representing examples of (1) regulated market capitalism; (2) nations favoring cooperative private enterprises; and (3) nations that put the environment first. These examples reflect diverse regional futurist scenarios that futurist Paul Raskin called respectively Agoria, Ecodemia, and Arcadia. Raskin imagined these scenarios could help achieve a *Great Transition* to a sustainable planetary society by 2084. All of these small nations also represent the European Commission's *Terra 2000* "Ecosocial market economy" scenario combining social justice with growth limits. They also fit the "more regional, more environmental" corner of the Intergovernmental Panel on Climate Change's (IPCC) four scenarios on greenhouse gas emissions. The crucial point is that small nations are not futurist scenarios; they are actually putting into practice solutions that futurists have only imagined. Small nations are real, and they have real, tested, and workable solutions to global problems. They are showing the rest of the world what is possible today.

3

SMALL NATION MARKET CAPITALISM

The Agoria Path

The Norwegian Labour Party has a vision of a just world without poverty, in peace and ecological balance, where people are free and equal and have influence on the conditions affecting their lives. The Norwegian Labour Party is a social democratic party committed to liberty, democracy and social justice. It is a reformist party that believes in partnership and cooperation on national as well as international level. By acting together rather than just as individuals, we can make society a better place in which to live. —Arbeiderpartiet, Norway[1]

The small Nordic nations of Denmark, Norway, Sweden, Iceland, and Finland, and the self-governing territories of Greenland, the Faroe Islands, and Åland, are firmly capitalist market-based economic systems, and they are also committed to sustainable development and social justice. These small nations, as well as many other small European states, are often deprecated by the political right wing as "socialist welfare states," but they are social democracies whose citizens use their political consensus to humanize their capitalist economies in ways that support their values of full employment, the well-being of children and families, gender equity, education, public health, art and culture, and environmental protection. These are surely humane values that most people in the world share. At the same time these nations encourage large corporate, shareholder-owned enterprises, and many have stock markets, mutual funds, and large banks. However, the government it-self may be a large shareholder, government agencies closely regulate businesses, and the tax system is designed to fairly distribute costs and benefits to people. Many of these states score at or near the top on a wide range of development, environmental, and human rights indices that place them far ahead of many much larger countries. The impor-tant point is that these small states are not the twentieth-century social-ist dictatorships that right-wing political conservatives fear. Agoria small nations have reached a consensus to organize themselves in ways that are clear alternatives to the dominant free market, growth at all costs, neoliberal economic ideologies that are currently failing in many larger nations. Agoria small nations are democracies that are working continu-ously to solve many human problems that larger countries seem unable, or unwilling, to deal with effectively.

This chapter examines the successful Nordic capitalist models, but also presents the Chilean case as an example of what can go wrong when economic elites push a small nation pursuing an agoria develop-ment path onto a neoliberal, pro-growth-at-all-costs pathway. It may prove difficult but not impossible for a former small nation to reestab-lish a sustainable development path when economically very powerful elite directors are firmly in control.

AGORIA, ECODEMIA, ARCADIA: THREE PATHWAYS TO A SUSTAINABLE SMALL NATION WORLD

The agoria path represents one of three broad ways, or pathways, that people living in small nations have been able to use to successfully organize their lives. Religions are also sometimes called pathways, and pathways require considerable commitment to make them work. They represent agreements on very fundamental values that define how peo-ple should live. In this case the values concern how to organize the economy, what kinds and what scale of commercial businesses to allow, and how to relate to the natural environment. Agoria small nations are emphatically capitalist systems, but they incorporate humane values and they accept limits of various sorts that allow their systems to be sustainable. The term *agoria* evokes the classical Greek Athenian model of the *agora*, the physical center of commerce and politics of a market-centered city-state in which commercial life was not alienated from government. Regional agoria societies in many respects resemble standard early-twenty-first-century capitalist nation-states but with the important differences that they do not assume endless economic growth unbalanced by imposed limits to make them sustainable. They are not totally unregulated free-market economies.

The other small nation pathways are based on ecodemia and arcadia value systems. Ecodemia small nations, described in chapter 4, are small nations that emphasize economic democracy, small businesses, and cooperatives. The term "ecodemia" stands for economic democracy. The third small nation type, arcadia, which is described in chapter 5, describes small nations that make environmental protection a top priority. In this book, I treat these diverse pathways as three different types of small nations. Each represents a somewhat different values consensus. People can reach a consensus on such fundamental values within a small nation, whereas it might be much more difficult to do so in a large nation.

These three designations, agoria, ecodemia, and arcadia, are terms for alternative ways of life borrowed from *The Great Transition Initiative*,[2] which is a global effort initiated by Paul Raskin of the Tellus Institute in 1995 to facilitate the construction of sustainable communities and a sustainable global system by transforming people's beliefs and practices to promote human well-being and protect the environment. The "Great Transition" envisions a transition from the present world to a truly sustainable "Planetary Society." This transition represents the magnitude of change that must occur, and it fits nicely with the concept of a future world composed of small nations.

NORWAY, NORDEN, AND THE SUCCESSFUL NORDIC MODEL

Norway can be taken as an example of the most sustainable and successful country in the world. Norway, a fully independent constitutional monarchy since 1905, is a small nation of 4.6 million people that stands out as highly successful in regard to a wide range of measures of quality of life, sustainability, and human development. Norway ranked number one at the top of the UN Human Development Index for 2011[3] and had steadily increased its standing since 1980. In comparison, the United States ranked fourth in the Human Development Index in 2011. In 2011 Norway's average life expectancy at birth was 81 years, its Gross National Income (GNI) per capita (2005 purchase power parity, PPP$) was $47,557. Only 7 percent of Norwegians were living below 50 percent of the median income (compared with 17 percent below in the United States). In 2007 Norway ranked second in the world, after Sweden, for Gender Empowerment (the United States ranked 18th), and women held 36 percent of the seats in parliament (compared with 17 percent in the United States Congress). Norwegian women held 56 percent of ministerial rank positions (compared with 24 percent cabinet rank women in the United States). Norway had a much more equitable income distribution than the United States, with the poorest Norwegians getting more and the richest less. The poorest 10 percent of Norwegians received nearly 4 percent of income, whereas the poorest 10 percent of Americans received less than 2 percent. The Norwegian top 10 percent received 23 percent, in comparison with nearly 30 percent going to the top 10 percent of Americans.

Norway is not exemplary on all sustainability measures. Although as a small nation, its total impact on the environment is low, it nevertheless has a relatively high per capita ecological footprint, ranking eighth highest in the Living Planet Report for 2008, after the United Arab Emirates, United States, Kuwait, Denmark, Australia, New Zealand, and Canada.[4] However, Norway's per capita annual carbon emissions of 9.1 tons were significantly lower than the United States at 19.9 in 2007.[5] Norway ranks sixth on the Environmental Performance Index which represent achievement of policy goals, compared with the United States at 107th out of 154 countries. Sustainable development is officially a high priority for the Norwegian government.[6] The official sustainable development strategy of 2008 links social development with environmental concerns, and it specifically takes into account the perspectives of the indigenous Saami people. Norway also accepts the conclusions of the 2006 UK government–commissioned Stern Review on the Economics of Climate Change[7] as a strong argument for urgent government-backed measures and international agreements to reduce carbon emissions. The Stern Review treated global warming as market failure[8] and concluded that the likely severity of future economic damage from climate change meant that taking significant action now to reduce car-

bon emissions would be cost effective in the long run. What is remarkable about the Norwegian government's early acceptance of the urgency of action on climate change is that they were able to reach a political
consensus, whereas consensus has been difficult for the United States
and China, the largest carbon-emitting nations.

Norway is part of Norden, the Nordic Council and Nordic Council
of Ministers. Norden is an intergovernmental organization of eight
small democratic countries with 25 million people in the north Atlantic
and Baltic region. The Nordic countries are three constitutional monarchies (Denmark, Norway, and Sweden), two republics (Iceland and
Finland), and three self-governing territories (Greenland, or Kalaallit
Nunaat, and the Faroe Islands) associated with Denmark, and the island of Åland, an autonomous part of Finland.

The sustainability of Norden countries can be attributed to important features of their sociocultural systems that contribute to a balance
between social, political, and commercial sectors. The small size of their
populations and economies probably makes balance more feasible. For
example, a careful comparison between Sweden and the United States
shows some significant scale-related differences.[9] The service sector of
Sweden and the United States are approximately the same size, but in
the United States a much higher proportion is devoted to business
services (nearly 34 percent versus 18 percent), whereas in Sweden,
social services are proportionately larger (37 percent versus 26 percent).
The higher labor cost of business in the United States may be due to the
costs of maintaining a much larger-scale economy and market in a very
large country. Sweden has proportionately more teachers, professionals
and technicians than the United States, whereas the United States has
more clerical workers and managers. Sweden also has a higher proportion of its employment in the state sector, which helps explain Sweden's
larger proportion of professionals. State and professional workers are
generally more autonomous as workers than those working under managers in very large corporations. Autonomous workers are more likely to
feel in control of the conditions of their daily life than are workers who
are simply employees.

The political struggle between capitalists and workers followed a
more balanced pathway in the Nordic states than in the United States,
which was due in part to other specific cultural historical differences.
The economic philosophy behind the social welfare state has very deep

roots in Scandinavia. Finns and Swedes claim enlightenment philosopher and clergyman Anders Chydenius (1729–1803) as a free market advocate whose primary book, *The National Gain*[10] (1766), predated Adam Smith's *Wealth of Nations* by a decade, but explicitly supported democratic human rights for everyone, including the poor.

Consensus may be the most crucial variable when costly long-range decision making must be carried out to avert long-term disaster. Nordic nations are more sustainable because they are small and culturally homogeneous enough that they can more easily maintain a consensus on basic values, especially on what sustainability means and how to achieve it. In a small nation such as Norway there will be fewer elites competing with each other, and wealth and power may be less concentrated than in larger nations, especially if there is consensus on the importance of human rights and social equality as in Norden. For example, a careful analysis of Noway's elites in 1967 found that there were only 894 elites in business (59 percent), politicians (20 percent), civil servants (12 percent), and labor (9 percent), out of a population of 3.7 million.[11] The business elite were the 527 directors and executives of the 122 largest corporations.

Norway is heavily involved in the global capitalist economy, but it distributes decision making over capital in a way that decisions can be made democratically and the benefits can be distributed equitably. This is not incompatible with good business and market principles. In 2008 the Norwegian government was a significant shareholder in some eighty Norwegian companies, employing over 280,000 people, which was about 11 percent of the workforce, in addition to the high proportion of employees in government itself and public service institutions. The Norwegian state and municipal governments owned about 35 percent of the US$190 billion in share value listed on the Oslo Børs stock exchange in 2005. The Department of Ownership within the Ministry of Trade and Industry manages most of the government's interests in state-owned companies.

Among important Norwegian state-owned companies in 2008 was the government's 63 percent ownership of StatoilHydro, one of the world's largest oil and gas companies, with revenues of US$116 billion, making it the thirty-sixth largest publicly traded company in the world at that time. The government's interests in StatoilHydro were managed by the Norwegian Ministry of Petroleum & Energy. The Norwegian government also owned 100 percent of Kommunalbanken Norway (KBN), which provides loans to local and municipal governments. The government also owned a 34 percent share of DnB Nor, Norway's largest financial services, banking, insurance, and asset management company. DnB Nor had about US$270 billion in assets under management, which is a very large sum, but significantly less than the US$2 trillion managed by Citigroup, at that time one of the largest U.S. financial services corporations. Cultural differences between the Norway and the United States were also apparent in executive salaries. Significantly, the CEO of DnB received only US$700,000 in annual compensation, whereas the Citigroup CEO received some US$10 million.

Norges Bank, the Norwegian Government's central bank, manages two large sovereign funds, the Government Pension Fund-Norway (*Folketrygdfondet*) and the Government Pension Fund-Global (*Statens pensjonsfond utland*). The *Folketrygdfondet* had about $28 billion invested in Norwegian companies in 2009, with the proceeds going to the national insurance pension fund. The Government Pension Fund - Global (*Statens pensjonsfond utland*), formerly called The Petroleum Fund of Norway, is managed by Norges Bank Investment Management (NBIM) under the Ministry of Finance and Norges Bank. This fund is derived from the government's share of revenues from StatoilHydro and oil and gas development generally.

There are obvious contradictions for a country priding itself on sustainability to at the same time have such a heavy financial interest in a fossil fuel. The purpose of Norway's petroleum fund is "ensuring that a reasonable portion of the country's petroleum wealth benefits future generations." It is oil converted into financial wealth, and it must be managed to produce "a sound return in the long term, which is contingent on sustainable development in the economic, environmental and social sense."[12] Investments are made in foreign, or "global," financial assets, not in Norwegian companies, and they are strictly controlled by ethical guidelines. These funds may not contribute to "unethical acts or omissions, such as violations of fundamental humanitarian principles, serious violations of human rights, gross corruption, or severe environmental damage." This means that companies that the fund invests in must follow the UN Global Compact and OECD Guidelines for Corporate Governance. The fund's ethical committee reviews investments and excludes companies in violation, especially manufacturers of banned military weapons, such as cluster bombs, antipersonnel mines, and nuclear weapons, or that participate in military trade with illegitimate military dictatorships. They also will not invest in tobacco companies and have excluded Walmart for its labor practices, Monsanto for allowing child labor by companies in India that supply its genetically modified cotton seed, and the mining giant Rio Tinto for environmental damage.[13]

In 2009 Norway's petroleum fund was worth more than $450 billion, or about $220,000 per household, making it the largest pension fund in Europe, and the fourth largest in the world. This fund is quite comparable in size to the $435 billion then being managed by TIAA-CREF, the retirement fund for 3.4 million American academics and professionals.

The Norwegian government's national budget was US$140 billion in 2008, or about US$30,000 per capita, and about half of its GNI. In comparison, the U.S. federal budget was $2.5 trillion in 2007, about $8,000 per capita and only 18 percent of GNI. There were also important differences in how these respective national governments allocated their expenditures. Norway transferred thousands, rather than hundreds, of dollars per capita to local governments, significantly more on social support, transportation, police and justice, and agriculture, and Norway distributed much more in foreign aid per capita than the United States, but less on national defense. These differences reflect cultural differences, as well as differences in scale and power.

The World Values Survey for 2005–2008[14] also reveals interesting differences between Norway and the United States. Norwegians report much higher levels of health, satisfaction with life, and personal autonomy than Americans, whereas Americans report somewhat higher levels of freedom. Norwegians also show much more confidence in their justice system and parliament than Americans, but they have much lower confidence in their military.[15] More Norwegians also described themselves as feeling that they were a part of their local communities; they trusted the people in their neighborhoods more, and they did not consider water, sewage, and air quality to be serious problems, because they were being adequately taken care of.

The Nordic Model is famous for enjoying peaceful labor relations, a fair income distribution, and high levels of social cohesion. Nordic countries have been able to grow their economies and keep the system sustainable in spite of high taxes, high levels of social equality and social security that critics warned would reduce incentives for workers to be productive. A central feature of the Nordic Model is collective risk sharing.[16] The Nordic Model is a welfare state that transfers income to households and publicly funds social services from income and consumption taxes. There is high public investment in childcare and education, healthcare, retirement benefits and care for the elderly, infrastructure, and research and development. Labor unions are strong, wages are considered to be fair, and unemployment benefits are generous. This combination has produced economic efficiency and social equality and kept public corruption low, all at the same time. People seem to trust their government and public institutions, and this makes them willing to judiciously embrace aspects of "free enterprise" and globalization that benefit their economy. Norwegians clearly temper economic growth with social objectives, but they do not reject growth as such. Some economists argue that the Nordic system is a "progrowth" system in which the winners in the free market compensate the losers, and the economy continues to grow.[17] This is why some observers consider them to be good models for "agoria"-type regional systems discussed in the following section. However, there is a long-term tendency for welfare costs to rise faster than GDP and continuous adjustments keep the welfare state operating sustainably.

CHILE'S SMALL NATION BACKGROUND

Chile is a microcosm of global issues and an excellent preview of how the small nation solution could put even a former small nation on an agoria path to genuine sustainability. With a population of more than 16 million people in 2012, Chile is somewhat above my threshold for small nation status, but its recent history makes it an ideal case study of the problems that elite direction can pose for small nations. Chile demonstrates how the small nation solution can help a country recover from damage inflicted by an unrestrained free market national policy of globalization, in this case forcibly applied by elite directors to one-sidedly maximize economic growth. Chile also shows that even a national sustainability project directed by the majority can be an uphill struggle if wealth and power has already become too highly concentrated.

In September 2012 I visited Chile as a member of an international review panel to evaluate proposals competing for funding to support a government-sponsored $8.5 million program to fund a new Center of Research Excellence on Indigenous Peoples. This was a program administered by CONICYT, the National Commission for Scientific Research and Technology, a special agency within the Ministry of Education, and was funded by FONDECYT, the government's National Fund for Scientific and Technological Development.[18] I was delighted that indigenous people were officially a "high national priority" for new research, ranking alongside five other high-priority areas that included proposed new research centers for sustainable agriculture and aquaculture; climate change; sustainable urban development, natural disasters, and solar energy. These priority areas demonstrated the country's commitment to sustainable development. It might have seemed curious that the government was giving indigenous peoples such a high priority, but I knew that serious conflicts caused by decades of misguided elite-directed growth remained just under the surface. There also were exciting possibilities here, because addressing conflicts with indigenous people could draw on important elements of the small nation solution.

Chile had a long history of progressive, gradual, and sometimes explicitly socialist development based on import substitution, nationally focused economic growth, strong labor organizations, and broad distribution of social benefits. In 1900 the country was a small nation of fewer than 3 million people with a formal economy of about $6 billion (International GK 1990 dollars), largely dependent on exports of nitrates and copper.[19] Up until 1973 national development was democratically directed by the state in the interests of the entire society. This was the case even though American corporations controlled much of Chile's very important copper industry. This progressive approach to development brought rapid industrialization and widely shared prosperity such that Chile was often viewed as a model for the rest of Latin America, even though its overall economic growth rate was somewhat slow. In 1973 Chile reached a population of 10 million people, the upper threshold for small nation status, at the same moment that Pinochet's right-wing military dictatorship took power and immediately began to transform the country into a free market paradise that produced an uninhibited economic growth spree. This kind of elite-directed growth dramatically concentrated wealth and income even as it severely damaged Chilean society and environment.

During the pre-Pinochet period except for periods of economic and political turmoil in the 1920s and early 1930s, Chile's per capita GDP measured in constant International GK 1990 dollars grew steadily, until it had nearly tripled. This meant that economic growth outstripped population growth. However, there were ominous indications that economic elites were directing the growth process. By the 1960s, even before the Pinochet dictatorship took power, and while Chile was still a small nation, a mere 1,611 corporately organized businesses already dominated the economy by controlling 90 percent of business assets.[20] This was much like the concentration of economic power that has characterized the United States and highlights the importance of elite directors. However, the absolute power of Chile's elite directors still remained small by international standards, because the total economy was still relatively small. Nevertheless economic power was concentrated in more important but less obvious ways as the following overview shows.

Chile's 9/11: Pinochet's "Brick" Shock Economics Hits the Country

Canadian journalist-author Naomi Klein uses Milton Friedman's enthusiastic promotion of free market economics in Chile during Pinochet's military rule as a prominent example in her book, *The Shock Doctrine: The Rise of Disaster Capitalism*.[21] Her argument is that contemporary globalization based on free market capitalism is so extreme, and so harmful to the interests of most people that it has spread only because people have been both forced and persuaded by fear to view radical free market policies as the solution to various crises and disasters. This interpretation of culture change is quite compatible with my own scale and power-based theory of elite-directed growth. Klein introduces her Shock Doctrine by describing renown economist Milton Friedman at the age of ninety-three writing an op ed column in the *Wall Street Journal* in 2005 in which he sees "an opportunity to radically reform the educational system" of New Orleans in the wake of disastrous Hurricane Katrina.[22] His proposal of course was the use of a voucher system as a free market alternative to a single system of publicly funded schools.

The connection between Friedman, crisis as opportunity, and education reform immediately brought to mind an incident that I had observed in Santiago, Chile, in 2012. While walking with my fellow panelists to our daily meeting at the CONICYT office one morning, we noted a crowd of high school students blocking the road barely two blocks from our hotel on Condell Street in the relatively affluent commune of Providencia, adjacent to the center of Santiago. Students held bold banners demanding equal access to education, and a young man was tending a small bonfire of broken chairs burning in the center of the street. We recognized this as a small aftershock from the massive demonstrations that had rocked Santiago only days earlier, resulting in hundreds of arrests and many injuries as well as still-visible property destruction. A young woman explained to us the purpose of their demonstration. She told us that they were commemorating one of their students who had been killed by the police ten years ago, and they were demanding release of some of their classmates who were now being held in prison following their most recent demonstrations. The primary issue was widespread public dissatisfaction with the still-in-effect free market reforms of the education system dating to the Pinochet era. These reforms reduced public funding and provided vouchers so that students could pay for part of their education at any school of their choice. This meant that the wealthier few who could pay more could receive a better education in well-funded schools, whereas the poorer majority was forced to attend poorer-quality and now-deteriorating schools. They were being forced into an education ghetto.

The central focus of Pinochet's military regime (1973–1990) was to develop the Chilean economy following the guidelines of what would now be called a "neoliberal" economic program. Pinochet used military force and political terror to apply the radical free market economic policies that were designed by a small group of Chilean economists, the "Chicago Boys," who were trained by conservative economists from the University of Chicago in the 1950s following Milton Friedman's market-centered theories. Chileans received their economic training in Chicago and at the Pontifical Catholic University of Chile beginning in 1956, in what was called the Chile Project funded by grants from the Ford Foundation and by a forerunner of the U.S. Agency for International Development (USAID). This American academic intervention was part of the historic left vs. Cold War right, and specifically reflected the fears of the American economic elite that the Cuban Revolution, begun in 1953, would spread throughout Latin America and cause large American corporations to be nationalized. In the case of Chile, which already had a history of "leftist" prosocial welfare and economically nationalist tendencies, American intervention was no doubt specifically intended to prevent the Chilean government from making any further moves to the left that might adversely affect the mining holdings in Chile of Anaconda and Kennecott Copper companies.

The policies of the Chicago Boys called for reducing the Chilean government's role in the economy; reducing government regulation on private business; transferring publically owned property and businesses to the private commercial sector; encouraging foreign investment, in other words, U.S. capital; eliminating tariffs to promote global trade; promoting production for export; and letting the "free market" determine prices. The Chicago Boys presented their program in a written report which gained the colorfully descriptive title of "El Ladrillo" (the Brick). It was presented to Pinochet as soon as he took power on September 11, 1973, in a violent coup d'état (Chile's 9/11) in which the presidential palace was bombed and assaulted, and President Allende committed suicide rather than surrender.

With a military dictator in power, "The Brick" was indeed a cudgel. Chile became an ideal test case for the most extreme free market policies that made growing the economy as large and as fast as possible the supreme goal of government. This was the very opposite of the Agoria Path. In theory government needed to step aside so that investors and business elites could produce wealth, but the Chilean people did not favor this approach, and Pinochet needed brute force to implement the program. The regime killed or tortured more than 40,000 people according to cases that could later be documented by official commissions,[23] and no political opposition was tolerated. The brutal reality of these events is powerfully presented in the Museum of Memory and Human Rights (Museo de la Memoria y las Derechos Humanos) which opened in Santiago in 2010 under the leadership of Socialist President Michelle Bachelet, who was herself tortured by the Pinochet regime. The Brick itself remained a secret directive until finally being made public in 1992, shortly after Pinochet was forced out of office by a referendum.

These forcibly imposed economic policies did produce growth as we will see. Beginning in about 1980, the same policies were widely adopted by right-wing, conservative governments in the United States and the UK, and elsewhere in Europe. They were the foundations of the era of rapid economic globalization. The small nation of Chile was the first test case. Pinochet's neoliberal experiment in Chile deregulated the labor market, attacked labor unions, discontinued minimum wage laws, cheapened Chilean labor relative to the external market, and reversed the agrarian reform, taking land from small holders and returning it to their former large landowners. Pinochet privatized government-owned businesses and public institutions including health services and education, virtually giving them away at absurdly low prices. He promoted growth of the financial sector and greatly reduced or eliminated tariffs as well as public expenditures on social services. Forests and fisheries were thrown open for virtually unlimited exploitation. The industrial system, which was geared for import substitution, and internal investment and consumption were suddenly replaced by an export economy based on natural resources and foreign investment. The Chilean economy immediately contracted and unemployment rose, but exports from fisheries and forest products increased, and GDP began to grow rapidly, based on extractive, or natural resource–based, industries including mining and agriculture. Poverty increased and wealth and income became more concentrated.

The formal economic outcome of the Friedman-Pinochet high-speed growth formula was dramatic. Indeed, between 1973 and 2011 the country's GDP grew more than five-fold in constant 2000 dollars. Population grew less rapidly, and per capita GDP increased nearly two and a half times. Growth in GDP per capita was nearly as dramatic as what occurred between 1900 and 1971, but in about half the time. Chile's growth between 1973 and 2011 was also significantly greater and more rapid than experienced by the United States over the same time. In 2005 PPP dollars, Chile's GDP reached more than $263 billion in 2011 and per capita GDP was more than $15,000, qualifying it as a "High Income" country by World Bank rankings. Chile even joined the OECD's exclusive thirty-four-member club of wealthy developed nations in 2010, and it ranked "Very High" in the 2011 UN Human Development Index. However, per capita measures of progress can be deceptive. A closer look shows that the benefits of Chile's economic progress, especially during its most rapid growth since about 1983, were quite unevenly distributed, and largely bypassed its large indigenous population. This, in spite of the fact that natural resources from indigenous territories have helped fuel Chile's growth in its export economy.

Tiger Without a Jungle: Impacts of Chile's Economic Miracle

> The actual Chilean economic growth path is not capable of sustaining itself in the future. *Every tiger*, no matter how enterprising, *needs the jungle that sustains it.* —*Ecología Política*, 1995[24]

The burst of economic growth resulting from Pinochet's free market economic "reforms" was quickly trumpeted around the world as an "economic miracle" and Chile was declared to be "the economic tiger" of South America. Conservative commentators were still repeating the "success" story in 2012.[25] However, by the 1990s it was very clear to the Mapuche Indians, living in their formerly forested homelands of Araucania in southern Chile, that a social and environmental disaster was transforming their lives. The Mapuche felt some of the first really bad impacts of the Chilean economic miracle. In 1994 ecological researchers associated with the Instituto de Ecología Política (Institute of Political Ecology) added up the negative "externalities" that were subsidizing the miracle, and warned that the economic tiger was proving to be so destructive that it was becoming a "tiger without a jungle."[26]

My view of the Chilean situation was initially indirect and shaped by my work in 1980 as a visiting researcher at IWGIA,[27] a human rights organization in Copenhagen, Denmark, where I was updating my *Victims of Progress* book on indigenous people. At that time IWGIA was supporting the efforts of exiled Mapuche Indian activists who were trying to draw international attention to the suffering of their people under the Pinochet regime.[28] This was soon after the military coup and the impacts were mostly political, but they were hitting the Mapuche especially hard. As part of my work I handed off a cash-filled envelope to a Mapuche man who IWGIA was helping to gain a hearing at the UN. The Mapuche were especially distressed because Pinochet's Decree Law No. 2568, which he had just signed in 1979, revoked protections put in place by prior governments, thereby opening Mapuche lands to legal invasion by large forestry corporations and estate owners.

Later, when I taught a graduate course on indigenous people as a visiting professor at Uppsala University in Sweden in 1985, I met more Chilean exiles who were students in my class. It was obvious that Pinochet was driving dissidents out of the country. Something was seriously wrong.

Fast-forward to Santiago, Chile, 2012. I had at first wondered why the Chilean government was treating indigenous people as a high priority, but on September 8, 2012, the day I left Chile, bold headlines on the front page of the conservative newspaper *El Mercurio* shouted out the explanation: "Hooded Ones Burn 10 Forestry Vehicles in the Largest Fire Attack in BioBío." BioBío was 300 miles south of Santiago. The "hooded ones" were frustrated Mapuche activists who were continuing a series of violent attacks against the forestry companies that were converting ancestral Mapuche lands into tree plantations. In this case their target was equipment belonging to a timber company called Forestal Arauco. In 2009 there were 1.2 million indigenous people in Chile, and they represented nearly 7 percent of the national population. There were nearly a million Mapuche. No wonder the government was taking their concerns seriously. In comparison, there were just over 5 million Native Americans in the United States in 2010, and they were only 1.6 percent of the total population.

In order to make sense out of the headlines, I looked further to understand what had happened to the Mapuche and their lands since the 1980s. I turned to a report on conditions in the predominately Mapuche rural Commune of Lumaco, in the Araucania region, produced by a team of Chilean researchers from universities in southern Chile working in association with the local Mapuche Ñankjuchew Association, the Latin American Observatory of Environmental Conflicts (OLCA), and the Plantations Watch program of the World Rainforest Movement.[29] This turned out to be an impoverished region. The 2002 Chilean Census showed that over 60 percent of the Lumaco population of 13,000 was living below the official poverty line. The 9,000 Mapuche residents held only 15 percent of the land, in small plots, mostly on nonarable soils unsuitable for intensive cultivation. Before the arrival of Europeans in 1550 and up to the military conquest of their territory by the Chilean State in 1883, the Mapuche had prospered, and their land use practices had not degraded these vulnerable ecosystems, even after centuries of use.

When the Chilean military occupied Mapuche lands in 1883 the Mapuche people were confined to very small, unproductive plots, appropriately called "reductions" (*reducciones*). This was a dispossession process that began with the Spanish conquest and was applied throughout Latin America. As soon as the Mapuche were "reduced," their prime ancestral lands were turned over to European settlers and corporations. Large tracts were quickly deforested, and soils were eroded and depleted, but the Mapuche were able to make a precarious adaptation as small farmers.

The military coup of 1973 made the situation much worse when Pinochet quickly disbanded the existing state agencies which had administered Chile's forests in the broad public interest. By Decree 701 Chile's forests and forestry activities were privatized in 1974. State lands and lands that previous governments had expropriated on behalf of small holders like the Mapuche during the Agrarian Reform process were auctioned off. Huge subsidies and tax incentives were given to private timber companies to take over vast tracts of forest and convert them to tree plantations producing for export. Many forested areas still held by the Mapuche were turned over to private companies. Mapuche who were badly in debt were forced to sell off their small holdings. By 2002 half of Lumaco Commune had been converted to tree plantations, whereas in 1973, less than 2 percent was in plantations. The new export-led approach to economic development made it even more difficult for the Mapuche to make a living by small-scale mixed farming on their marginal lands, because their products were priced out of the market by lower-priced imports. The rising costs of energy and the inputs required for industrial agriculture also disadvantaged Mapuche farmers, but the negative environmental impacts were even worse.

The giant corporately owned plantations were composed of two alien tree species, the Monterrey pine and a eucalyptus that totally displaced the biologically rich native forest. The introduced trees were voracious water consumers that quickly dried out surface waters and lowered the water table, producing drought conditions that led to fires. Water shortages became so acute that municipal governments have had to distribute water to communities for household consumption. The monocrop plantations attracted disease and insect pests, including an invasive woodwasp that killed trees. The Mapuche also attributed health problems to the pesticides sprayed on the plantations and to water contamination. From the Mapuche perspective, and indeed from the view of any impartial observer, these impacts were one-sided costs that were seriously unjust, because the benefits were going almost entirely to the remote shareholders of the timber companies.

Just who these remote beneficiaries of the conversion of Mapuche forests into monocrop plantations were became clear as soon as I worked out the corporate genealogy of Forestal Arauco, the timber company mentioned on the front page of *El Mercurio* as the target of the Mapuche attacks. It turned out that Arauco was owned by Empresas Copac, a large Chilean energy and natural resources conglomerate involved in fossil fuel distribution, electric power, forestry, fisheries, and mining. Copac's majority owner was AntarChile, a Forbes 2000 global-scale corporation, which in turn was majority owned by Roberto Angelini Rossi and family, one of six Chilean billionaires. This discovery made me rethink what I had seen in Santiago in the context of Chile's recent tumultuous history.

Sanhattan Billionaires, Skyscrapers, and the Chilean 500

As we explored central Santiago on foot in 2012 my wife and I found ourselves orienting by a spectacular tall building clad in blue glass standing next to three other very tall buildings still under construction in the northeast corner of Providencia. My obsession with scale automatically drew my attention to this gigantic structure. Looking at the building through anthropological eyes gave me a better understanding of the elite-directed scale changes that had suddenly transformed Chile, amplified social inequality, and reduced sustainability. This part of Santiago was immediately adjacent to La Golf barrio of Las Condes Comune where the wealthiest Chileans live in the shadow of a cluster of some twenty very tall buildings. These tall buildings were mostly offices and they housed the headquarters of the largest foreign and domestic corporations in the country. They were all very new skyscrapers with at least twenty or more floors, standing 75 meters (250 feet) or more tall[30] These buildings constitute the most impressive visible center of Santiago's seventy tall buildings that stand at least twelve floors or higher.[31] These particular twenty extra-tall buildings are also the financial and commercial center of Chile. All of Santiago's tall skyscrapers were constructed since 1980 and most since 1990. Chileans, blending awe and ironic humor, call this district *Sanhatten*, designating it "Manhattan in Santiago." Such monumental constructions represent the triumph of Chile's elite-directed economic growth and globalization project which was set in motion by the Pinochet dictatorship. This is also why many of the wealthiest Chileans still consider Pinochet a heroic figure.

It is hard not to be impressed by such a conspicuous concentration of economic power, but this many very tall buildings in such a small country are a sure marker of Chile's departure from the agoria pathway to sustainable growth. In contrast, Oslo, the capital of Norway, an exemplar of an agoria small nation, has only two buildings taller than 75 meters, and only five buildings have more than twenty floors. Oslo's tallest building is just thirty-seven floors, and 117 meters, well less than half the size of Santiago's tallest. Norway's economic growth has been directed in a more balanced way.

Skyscrapers in general are an important measure of increasing scale and complexity as well as of overly concentrated social power. Everything about standard skyscrapers is large scale. Their construction requires structural steel produced by large steel mills. Electricity from large-scale generators is required for lighting, heating, cooling, and to operate elevators. Skyscrapers are large carbon emitters and they have large ecological footprints that make enormous demands on nature. It is of course possible to build "green" skyscrapers with reduced ecological footprints, but this may even increase their already giant financial footprint. Skyscrapers are mountains of wealth and monuments to the egos of their owners. This is the same elite-directed wealth concentrating process that I saw on a much smaller scale in Washington State. In Chile and in the Washington Palouse, when elites increase urban density with larger and larger commercial buildings they distort urban property values, displace residents, and overpower small and medium business enterprises in the neighborhood.

Skyscrapers and the wealth they represent also distort national and regional economies, and their impacts can be seen globally. A sustainable world could do without them. There were no skyscrapers anywhere in the world before 1890 when the Home Insurance Company Building in Chicago reached what was then the amazing height of twelve stories and 42 meters (138 feet). This first skyscraper is of course dwarfed by the Burj Khalifa in Dubai with 163 floors reaching 828 meters, which is more than twice the height of the blue clad tower we saw in Santiago. It is hard to imagine that any of these giant structures contribute to social justice and sustainability. Many small nations have small cities with no skyscrapers, and their absence both reflects and contributes to their human-scale qualities and sustainability. Modestly sized, locally owned residential high rises can be part of the small nation solution. This is not what Chile's skyscrapers represent, but Santiago's skyscrapers did make it easy for visitors to orient.

The physical scale of skyscrapers alone makes them important, but their use as business headquarters draws closer attention to the concentrated wealth and economic control that they represent. By the year 2000 Santiago's skyline already boasted thirty-seven skyscrapers and the city ranked sixtieth out of 315 world cities, based on the presence of offices representing forty-four of the 100 most important global accounting, advertising, legal, finance, insurance, and management consultancy firms, the so-called advanced producer firms that serve the business interests of multinational corporations.[32] In 2008 Santiago was also on the list of world business "command and control centers" for serving as headquarters for nine companies on the Forbes list of the world's 2000 largest public companies (the Forbes Global 2000).[33] The Chilean Global 2000 companies were worth nearly $342 billion, ranking Chile ninth in the world for market capitalization in the Forbes 2000.

Chile is still a small enough country that it is possible to outline the economic power structure in some detail using publicly available information. The link between Chile's global billionaires and their majority ownership of five of the nine Chilean Global 2000 companies makes it very clear who are all the prime beneficiaries of the country's rapid economic globalization. Chile's five billionaire families together were worth more than $40 billion in 2011, based on their holdings in some of the largest mining, retail, fisheries, paper and forestry companies. These families benefited enormously from the Friedman-Pinochet program of free market privatization. Chilean President Sebastián Piñera was a global billionaire when he took office in 2010. Piñera became a major owner of the formerly state-owned LAN Chile Airlines in 1994, shortly after it was privatized in 1989.

The tallest building that we used as our reference point in Santiago stood out as a giant among giants. It was a true landmark, specifically designed to be a central icon for the city. It also proved to be a powerful cultural symbol. It was named the "Gran Torre" of the Costanera Center. It towered sixty-two floors to its maximum height of 300 meters, which it reached in February 2012, even as construction continued. At that time it was the tallest building in Latin America, the second tallest in the southern hemisphere, and seventieth tallest in the world out of more than 64,000 skyscrapers ranked. Santiago's second largest skyscraper, the Titanium Portada at fifty-five floors and 192 meters high, stood a few blocks from the Gran Torre. It was jointly owned by two Chilean conglomerates, major owners of some of Chile's largest and most conspicuous buildings and companies in the retail, transportation, agriculture, wine making, commercial real estate construction, horse racing, health, communication, and finance sectors.

A bit of research revealed that the Gran Torre was built for CENCOSUD, another Forbes Global 2000 Chilean-based retailer business conglomerate and second largest company in the country. CENCOSUD was second only after CODELCO, the giant copper mining company which is still owned by the Chilean government. CENCOSUD had revenues of $15 billion in 2011, making it 611th largest in the world in the Forbes 2000. It was majority owned by the Paulmann family, another one of the five billionaire families in Chile. CENCOSUD owns and operates hundreds of stores in malls and big box retail chains throughout Argentina, Brazil, Chile, Columbia, and Peru. Appropriately, Costanera Center, a glamorous six-level shopping mall, stands beside the Gran Torre. It contained more than 300 shops featuring world-famous fashion and consumer brands.

Global-scale elite directors certainly do work together in furthering their mutual interests in wealth growth and consolidation. CENCOSUD's billionaire owner, Horst Paulman, made use of the business services of corporate giants JP Morgan Chase and Swiss UBS in promoting his company to global investors and in helping him beat out Walmart in his quest to buy up the biggest supermarket chains in Brazil.[34] Morgan Chase is the largest company in the Global 2000, and Morgan Chase and UBS ranked six and nine, respectively, in the controlling "super entity" at the top of the global network of corporations in 2007.[35]

I began to assess the concentrated power held by the major owners and directors of Chile's largest companies by carefully sorting through the list of Chile's 500 Largest Companies in 2010 compiled by *América Economía*.[36] This ranking of companies differs from the more familiar rankings by Forbes and Fortune because the Chilean list includes all types of companies, publically traded, private, state-owned, and foreign-owned. Subsidiaries are also listed separately along with parent companies. My first sort of the Chilean 500 to eliminate double counting of subsidiaries owned by other companies produced a shorter list of 347 parent companies with total revenues of some $212 billion U.S. dollars. It was immediately obvious that a few very large companies at the top were very powerful. This is the sort of concentrated power that the power law distribution predicts. The top 5 percent of these (the seventeen largest companies) produced more than half of total revenues, but a third of these companies were foreign owned. Nearly a fourth of the total revenues of the 347 were from the nine large publically traded Chilean companies that also appeared on the Forbes Global 2000 list. The total revenues of these global-scale companies were more than $50 billion dollars. Both the conspicuous presence of foreign companies and the global status of Chilean companies were clear reminders of how closely Chile's recent economic growth was linked with the global economy. The presence of foreign corporations was especially striking in mining, which was the largest component of GDP at 15 percent, and accounted for more than 20 percent of total corporate revenues. Significantly, nearly half of mining revenues went to foreign corporations. CODELCO, the largest mining company and still owned by the Chilean state, received only a third of mining revenues, even though it is the largest copper producer in the world.

Economic Groups and the New "Owners of Chile"

It is hard to get excited about the cold statistical facts of corporate power. What really matters is how corporate power benefits (or harms) real people. When I saw the links between newly raised Chilean skyscrapers and local billionaires, and their links to the Chilean 500 largest corporations, I immediately uncovered a maze of connections that demanded extensive research to unravel. Fortunately, I soon discovered the distribution of economic power was a topic of great and long-standing interest to Chilean intellectuals on all sides of the political spectrum. Chileans understand that this kind of power affects their lives and it matters greatly to them.

The foundational study on economic power in Chile was Ricardo Lagos Escobar's[37] 1960 law degree thesis, "The Concentration of Economic Power." This is a remarkable document because Lagos served as center-left president of Chile from 2000 to 2006 for the democratic coalition, the *Concertación* that governed after Pinochet. In his prologue to the Lagos thesis, economist Alberto Baltra Cortés, former Chilean Minister of the Economy and Commerce and president of the social-democratic Radical Party, notes that the growing concentration of corporate economic power was a characteristic feature of modern economic development that was linked to technological advances, but he cautiously argued that the power of society needed to consider placing this growing economic power "at the service of the interests of the majority and pull it away from the exclusive benefit of certain sectors." This was an agoria, small nation view, but it was not what happened in Chile.

When Lagos wrote more than a hundred top Chilean corporations had national legislators or former legislators on their boards. A former president sat on six corporate boards and a former minister was on twelve. Lagos also worried that the economic groups would become so powerful that they would take over companies that the state had developed and that still retained important ownership. He called the economic power of the "groups" a true monopoly, and argued that standard anti-monopoly laws would have only palliative effects in treating this "illness." He speaks of the "law of capital concentration," arguing that the growth of corporate enterprises and greater concentration cannot be overcome with laws, because large-scale production is an "imperious necessity of modern economies." He threw up his hands in despair, declaring that the only true solution was the familiar Marxist call for "the abolition of private ownership of the means of production." Lagos of course recognized that such a profound change would be resisted by those in power, so he advocated gradual change by means of government control over finance capital.[38]

Neither the Marxist extreme nor the gradual nationalization of capital that Lagos advocated would match the small nation solution which prescribes government decentralization, corporate downsizing, and restructuring of ownership, rather than the abolition of private property. The virtue of small nations is that they avoid the problem in the first place by not allowing great accumulations of capital to develop. The

Chilean case makes it possible to identify the specific cultural features that can facilitate the emergence of elite directors and that make it possible for them to promote a period of rapid economic growth and wealth concentration. Pinochet's neoliberal reforms and their continuation under the democratic coalition that followed caused an almost complete replacement of the economic elites who controlled the national economy in 1960 with a new group of elites.[39] The new elite groups were from the same social segment as the earlier elites, and even though the proportion of poverty in the country declined overall, inequality continued to be a problem. The names of the top economic groups and their leaders changed, along with changes in details of how they worked and how they were viewed by the majority, but the basic economic order remained the same.

Chilean journalists and academic researchers found that the elite who came to power under Pinochet's free market model were more than an economic elite, they were also part of the political order, and they were a relatively closed sociocultural class. There are sociocultural and economic barriers that make it difficult for those in the lower-income ranks to enter the top 10 percent, although there is considerable mobility below that top rank. This helps explain why democratization under the *concertación* did not significantly reduce actual economic inequality even though it succeeded in reducing poverty. The business management theory and the belief promoted by the elite was that everyone could succeed, and even become wealthy as an entrepreneur if they were bold and worked hard. The Chilean reality was that the economic elite largely came from the same social rank and shared the advantage of social and cultural capital in who they knew, what connections they had, and the education they received. It was found that students with the same academic qualifications, but from lower socioeconomic origins, were earning half of what students coming from the elite ranks were earning.

Human-Scale Development and the Sustainable Chile Program

Pinochet was not removed until 1990, when he was democratically voted out of office after a fiercely contested referendum which was dramatized in the award-winning 2012 Chilean film *No* directed by Pablo Larraín. Post-Pinochet damage control and the recovery process began immediately after his removal, but reconstructing the country has proven to be very difficult. Pinochet's decree laws were embedded in the Chilean Constitution, and the concentrated economic and political power that accompanied Chile's rapid growth made it politically difficult for the opposition to reform even obviously destructive laws. A vocal and powerful minority still revered Pinochet, who died in 2006, believing that he had saved Chile from communism. In 2010, after more than two decades of left-wing leadership, the right-wing businessman, politician, and billionaire Sebastian Piñera was elected president. Piñera's victory was due in part to control of the major media by Chile's wealthiest families. By 2012 the country remained seriously divided over its future pathway.

As soon as Pinochet was out of office it became possible for Chileans to openly document the negative impacts that had occurred in Chile while the free market economic model was given free rein. People could propose and gain political support for viable political and economic alternatives for the country. In 1997 a network of Chilean ecologists, academics, and intellectuals formed the Sustainable Chile Program (*Programa Chile Sustentable*, PCS) to promote a new citizen initiative for a major social, political, and economic transformation of the country based on principles of social and environmental sustainability. In many respects this is a program for as sweeping a change as proposed in the Brick the Chicago Boys presented to Pinochet in 1973, but there were some very crucial differences. The Sustainable Chile Program was fully transparent, assumed broad citizen support, and was offered as a replacement for the failures of previous economic growth-centered development programs that had been imposed on Chile. The new program was also an intellectually grounded alternative to the established "developmentalism" of international agencies such as the UN Economic Commission for Latin America (ECLA), the Interamerican Development Bank (IBD), and the multi-lateral trade organizations. It was of course also a very firm rejection of Pinochet's neoliberal growth model.

The Sustainable Chile Program is strongly scale-based and totally compatible with the agoria small nation solution. Its intellectual roots go back to a 1989 project on "Human Scale Development" organized by the Dag Hammarskjöld Foundation (DHF) in Sweden and a Chilean NGO, the Development Alternatives Centre (CEPAUR).[40] The Human Scale project involved a diverse group of social scientists, economists, and development experts from throughout Latin America, and Sweden. Their final report offered a sharp critique of standard approaches to development, whether based on neoliberal ideology or not. All were seen to be failing because they were too narrowly economic and too focused on growth as an end in itself, and because they ignored the social and political environment in which markets operated. The neoliberal models were specifically failing because they inflicted so much social damage that they could be sustained only by political oppression, as in Chile. Elegant classical economic models failed in countries where great masses of impoverished people were too poor to be effective market participants, and where there were no effective controls on decision makers directing vast amounts of economic power. Standard economic models did not eliminate poverty, unemployment, and underemployment and did not prevent governments from accumulating unsustainable foreign debts.

Project participants did not propose a specific model for how states should be organized to promote Human Scale Development, because one of their main conclusions was that there can be no single model when citizens are actually the decision makers rather than remotely headquartered corporate directors, foreign investors, and intergovernmental development banks and institutions. What is needed is an "open option," not a static model. Human scale means local communities, ethnic groups, and regional and national citizen organizations are the protagonists, and governments must reflect and accommodate their expressed needs and objectives. They seek to promote "social democracy," or a "democracy of day-to-day living," to counteract the prevailing hyper-individualism, and atomization of society under free market conditions. The key to the human-scale approach was its focus on the ability of people to satisfy their fundamental human needs, which they listed as subsistence, protection, affection, understanding, idleness, creation, identity, and freedom. This was a pioneer effort to systematize human needs and needs satisfaction, which has only recently been adopted in various forms by major development agencies.

A useful few guidelines suggested by the Human Scale Development perspective are for a country to reduce its imports and carefully monitor its exports to increase self-reliance. Financial, technological, cultural, and political dependencies also need to be reduced, at national, regional, and local levels. This in effect means escaping domination by walking away from centralized political and economic power. Self-reliance is an intrinsic part of putting people and their fundamental needs first as the objective of development. The human-scale part absolutely requires that individuals operate within localized families, small groups, and communities. Only in this way can the synergistic effects of satisfying multiple needs simultaneously be realized. There is of course still an important role for national government in redistributing resources, and in promoting and supporting local self-reliance and autonomy. This anticipated the principles of subsidiarity and heterogeneity, which mean accepting considerable cultural diversity. There must be higher levels of political authority to mediate disputes between different areas with diverse interests, and to represent the nation to the larger international community.

PCS director Manfred Max-Neef is an economist and a principal author of the Human Scale Development Project. Max-Neef, together with his source of inspiration on the importance of scale, Leopold Kohr, won The Right Livelihood Award (the Alternative Nobel Prize) in 1983. Kohr received the award in recognition for his earlier work on scale, especially *The Breakdown of Nations* (1957). Max-Neel was recognized for his 1982 book, *From the Outside Looking in: Experiences in Barefoot Economics,*[41] and for his contribution to the concept of "Human Scale Development."

Max-Neef added two growth and scale concepts to his theoretical toolkit: the ideas of the *ecoson*, an "ecological person," which could be used to derive the concept of an *economic threshold* where growth would stop. The *ecoson* is a quantifiable measure representing the amount of resource consumption required for one person to "attain an acceptable quality of life."[42] He did not offer specific calculations, but proposed that such a measure could be based on basic requirements for food, clothing, and housing, and suggested that it might reveal that, for example, a resident of the United States might represent fifty *ecosons*, whereas a South Asian might be the equivalent of only a fractional *ecoson*. He warned that the natural world might already be bearing the weight of 50 billion *ecosons*. Consumption exceeding the *ecoson* could be considered "waste surplus," which in scale terms would reveal "the magnitude of the problem caused by the worship of giant dimensions." Originally appearing in 1982, Max-Neef's *ecoson* concept anticipated the concept of the ecological footprint,[43] which began to appear a decade later and did not gain widespread attention until after 2000.

The *ecoson* relates directly to Max-Neef's notion of an "economic threshold," which he defined as the point at which economic growth no longer brings improvements in human well-being or the quality of life. Growth beyond the threshold can be expected to have negative impacts on well-being. At that point growth in quantity would need to be replaced by *development* to improve quality, which implies a focus on distribution over production. This calls attention to issues of social justice and the human right to a fair distribution. It also addresses the question of how big an economy should be.

Members of the Sustainable Chile Program (PCS) formed alliances and formulated a political agenda. Sara Larraín, who served as the first PCS director from 1997-2001 and was PCS director in 2012, was also a director for the International Forum on Globalization. Larraín ran for President of Chile in 1999, helping to elect Ricardo Lagos, the scholar who earlier had investigated the concentrated power of Chile's economic groups. Larraín also served as vice president of the Partida Ecologista Verde de Chile (Green Ecologist Party of Chile, PEV), which was legally formed in 2008 and affiliated with the Global Greens network of Green parties and political movements. Another PCS Director, Alejandro San Martin, served as PEV president beginning in 2010.

It will not be surprising to find that many of these basic power and scale-related perspectives and the concern for human well-being developed in Latin America will figure prominently in later chapters, especially in Part III where we consider how the small nation solution can be, and in some cases is already being, applied to existing large nations, including the United States and Europe.

4

SMALL NATION ECONOMIC DEMOCRACIES

A co-operative is an autonomous association of persons united volun-
tarily to meet their common economy, social, and cultural needs and
aspirations through a jointly-owned and democratically controlled
enterprise. —International Co-operative Alliance (ICA), 2012[1]

Mondragón considers its core mission to be the production and sale
of goods, services and distribution; using democratic methods in its
organizational structure and distributing the assets generated for the
benefit of its members and the community, as a measure of solidarity. —José María Aldecoa, president of the Mondragón Corporation
General Council, 2012[2]

The focus here is on examples of organizing economic life according to
cooperative principles. This is the essence of the ecodemia small nation
pathway to sustainability. At the same time, indigenous small nations
consistently make supporting their culture and environmental protection high priorities. These small nations are effectively combining political and economic democracy. Indigenous people organized in small
nations such as the Nunavut of arctic Canada, the Basques of northeast
Spain, Australian Aborigines, and various Native American nations have
readily adopted their traditionally cooperative economic forms to commercial markets in ways that also effectively protect and share the
wealth and fairly distribute benefits to people. They have the special
advantage of cultural consensus and deeply rooted cooperative patterns

of decision making and sharing that draw on heritages reaching back millennia. Some indigenous nations control large territories that may be rich in natural resources, others jointly own and manage a wide variety of corporate business enterprises and use the proceeds to benefit all their members. Indigenous marketing and buying cooperatives support smaller businesses and consumers, as well as networks of diversified individual cooperative businesses that may sometimes be strictly limited in size. The object of these businesses is to share management decisions with worker-owners, ensure that pay scales are fair, to minimize risk, and to maximize returns to the community.

The basic principles of economic democracy were also independently invented by Robert Owen who founded the cooperative movement at the dawn of the industrial age in the small nation of Scotland. The following sections illustrate the development of cooperatives and employee owned businesses in the United Kingdom, along with examples from indigenous nations. These case studies demonstrate that cooperative forms of business work extremely well.

ECONOMIC DEMOCRACY, ROBERT OWEN, AND THE COOPERATIVE MOVEMENT

> Co-operatives are based on the values of self-help, self-responsibility, democracy, equality, equity and solidarity. In the tradition of their founders, co-operative members believe in the values of honesty, openness, social responsibility and caring for others. —International Co-operative Alliance (ICA), 2012[3]

In 2002, after completing the first draft of my *Power of Scale* book, I made a personal pilgrimage to the World Heritage Site of New Lanark on the River Clyde in southern Scotland. I wanted to see firsthand the place where the modern cooperative movement began. New Lanark beautifully preserves the original cotton mills, worker housing, school, and village store that Welsh social reformer Robert Owen (1771–1858) developed and operated here from 1800 to 1825 as a social experiment to prove that factory workers could actually benefit from a humanely operated capitalist business enterprise.[4] Workers at New Lanark received schooling for their children, housing, health benefits, and special prices at the company store. Profits from the store helped support the school. Overall the social welfare aspects of Owen's management program were dramatically different from the way other factories were operated in Great Britain at the time. Working conditions at New Lanark were good, hours and wages were reasonable, and workers had real opportunities for self-improvement, unlike the horrific conditions that prevailed for factory workers elsewhere during this early phase of industrialization. The basic idea that profits from capitalist enterprises could be more widely shared implied a blurring of the line between capitalist owners and workers and opened the way for economic democracy. Owen campaigned for public support for education and wanted new Parliamentary legislation for regulations to improve worker conditions generally. His proposals were opposed by the church as well as by free market factory owners who argued that social welfare would make workers improvident and immoral.

In 1817 Owen began a public campaign to promote an ambitious series of agricultural and manufacturing cooperative communities of 500 to 1,500 people. He clearly understood that the size of social groups mattered. His new communities were designed on the model of New Lanark. They were to be laid out in great squares with factories in the center and the sides lined with apartments, surrounded by walks and gardens. People would sign up for membership in a particular type of village association at a central registry office in London. Communal dining, education, and medical care would be provided, and marketing would be cooperative with surpluses shared for greater economic efficiency. No one would work more than eight hours daily, and children would be trained for both agricultural and manufacturing work. Members were assigned to particular age grades, each with distinct social functions, and they were to be governed by a general committee drawn from the oldest grades. There were to be subcommittees for health, instruction, agriculture, manufactures, merchandise, domestic economy, and external communication. In spite of the age differences and internal rankings by investment rank, the villages were to be highly egalitarian.

Among those who were inspired by Owen's ideas were those who founded the Rochdale Society of Equitable Pioneers in Rochdale, Lancashire, England, in 1844. This was the foundation of the modern cooperative movement based on the seven Rochdale Principles: as expressed in 2012 by the International Co-operative Alliance (ICA): (1) voluntary and open membership; (2) democratic member control; (3) member economic participation; (4) autonomy and independence; (5) education, training and information; (6) co-operation among co-operatives; (7) concern for community. The cooperative movement has proven highly successful, as indicated by the fact that The International Co-operative Alliance had 275 members, organizations of co-ops in ninety-eight countries worldwide, and claimed more than a billion individual members in 2012.[5] The United Nations recognized 2012 as the International Year of Cooperatives, and UN Secretary-General Ban Ki-moon praised cooperatives as a reminder that economic viability and social responsibility could be combined.[6]

The Co-operative Group in the UK is the largest consumer co-operative organization descended from Owen's original experiment at New Lanark and the Rochdale Society. As of 2012 the Co-operative Group had 7.5 million individual members and eighty independent co-operative organizations also belonged. The individual members represent about 12 percent of the total UK population of nearly 63 million. The group offered its members food sales, banking, and specialty businesses in pharmacy, funeral services, legal services, life insurance, business services, auto sales, consumer appliances, travel services, and clothing. Its annual revenues were over ten billion dollars, and members held equity of more than $8 billion. The group produced profits of $279 million, and held $129 billion in assets, including a real estate portfolio of thousands of properties across the UK. It employed more than 100,000 workers, and operated over 5,000 retail outlets.[7]

The UK Co-operative Group is large enough on every metric, revenues, profits, assets, and shareholder value to qualify as a Forbes Global 2000 corporation. However, because it is a cooperative, it is organized democratically and demonstrates that even very large corporations can be democratized on the basis of one member one vote. Members are represented by elected representatives drawn from forty-eight area committees, who send representatives to the seven Regional Boards, who are in turn represented on the UK level twenty-member Group Board, which includes fifteen Regional Board members. There are also subsidiary boards for the different business groups. The Co-op Group has been a pioneer in the Fair Trade movement and in efforts to mitigate climate change.

INDIGENOUS PEOPLE SMALL NATIONS: NUNAVUT

What we want is to have the tools to run our own lives and to participate as equals in the greater life of Canada as a whole. The principal
tools are, simply, reasonable Inuit land claims settlements and a Nunavut territorial government.[8]

Indigenous people are a prime example of how the small nation solution can be implemented. This section first explains who indigenous
people are and why they are such a special type of small nation. This is
followed with a case study on the First Nations Canadian Territory of
Nunavut, showing how it was created and how its economy is organized
as a small nation economic democracy. I was personally interested in
the Nunavut case because immediately before I arrived in Copenhagen
to work at the International Work Group for Indigenous Affairs (IW-
GIA) in 1980, Denmark had just passed the Home Rule Act of 1979
giving limited political autonomy to Greenland, home of the Kalaallit,
the indigenous Greenlandic Inuit people. IWGIA is a human rights
organization, and my host at IWGIA, Norwegian anthropologist and
human rights advocate Helga Kleivan, was an Inuit specialist and had
tirelessly campaigned for Inuit rights to self-determination. He clearly
saw Kalaallit Home Rule as a huge victory for indigenous rights. The
Kalaallit are closely related to the Inuit in the Canadian arctic, and the
Kalaallit victory helped inspire the creation of Nunavut, which took
place twenty years later. A decade after Nunavut was created, Greenland officially became the small nation of Kalaallit Nunaat, "the land of
the Kalaallit," an autonomous country with fewer than 60,000 people
within the Kingdom of Denmark. Both of these events are major land-
marks in the worldwide struggle for the rights of indigenous people to
maintain themselves as small nations.

The label "indigenous peoples" is a self-designation used by individuals and organizations working for the human rights of peoples to maintain their historically shared attachment to ancestral territory, identity,
and culture. It is these deeply held attachments that make indigenous
people small nations. After decades of deliberation in the UN system,
the human rights of indigenous peoples to exist were at last formally
recognized internationally by the UN Declaration on the Rights of Indigenous Peoples (UNDRIP), which was finally adopted by the UN
General Assembly in 2007. The key UNDRIP articles include Article 3

on the right to self-determination, "to freely determine their political status and freely pursue their economic, social and cultural development," and Article 26, "Indigenous peoples have the right to the lands, territories and resources which they have traditionally owned, occupied or otherwise used or acquired," as well as a right to compensation for resource confiscation without their consent (Article 28). These articles in effect make it possible for indigenous peoples to organize themselves as small nations.

The indigenous Inuit peoples of the former Northwest Territory in the Canadian arctic became the small nation of Nunavut in 1999 in part as a result of a formal agreement between the Inuit and the Canadian government. The agreement refers to the Inuit as "all those members of the aboriginal people, sometimes known as Eskimos, that has traditionally used and occupied, and currently uses and occupies, the lands and waters of the Nunavut Settlement Area." The agreement further states in Article 35 that "Inuit are best able to define who is an Inuk" (a single Inuit person) and specifies that a Designated Inuit Organization will establish an enrollment list of Inuit for the purposes of the agreement. Aside from being alive and Canadian, and self-identified as Inuit, a qualified person must be Inuit by Inuit custom, and be associated with the territory.[9]

The establishment of the Inuit-governed Canadian Territory of Nunavut was one of the most comprehensive recent agreements negotiated by indigenous peoples and took place as part of a comprehensive settlement of Inuit land claims signed in 1993. It is a most remarkable example of a newly created small nation. In this exceptional case most of the demands of the indigenous group were met. The negotiation process began in 1976 when the Inuit Tapirisat organization of Canada presented the Canadian government with a proposal for the establishment of a special territory to be known as Nunavut, which means "our land" in the Inuit language. Nunavut would consist of the nearly 2 million square kilometers of land that the Inuit had never surrendered by treaty, and where the Inuit continued to be the dominant inhabitants. The Inuit wanted full ownership of some 648,000 square kilometers and exclusive hunting and fishing rights over the remainder. They also proposed that they should, as the majority population, control the regional government as well as the regulation of any resource development of Nunavut. Such ownership and control would ensure their primary objective of self-sufficiency.

In their 1982 letter to the provincial prime ministers of Canada, the Inuit Committee on National Issues (ICNI) eloquently presented their position on the constitutional guarantees that the Inuit required as the minimum conditions for the recognition of their basic rights and to set the stage for the creation of Nunavut. Specifically, they wanted the following principles to be protected:

1. the collective recognition of the aboriginal peoples as distinct peoples in Canada due to our occupation of our lands since time immemorial, including the protection of our cultures, histories and lifestyles, and flowing from this principle;
2. the recognition of our political rights to self-governing institutions (structures) of various kinds within the Canadian Confederation; and
3. the recognition of our economic rights to our lands and waters, their resources and their benefits, as a base for self-sufficiency and the development of native communities and families, including the protection of our traditional livelihoods.[10]

In 1982, the Inuit voted overwhelmingly in a plebiscite in favor of the establishment of Nunavut as a politically separate Inuit territory. Shortly thereafter, the Nunavut Constitutional Forum (NCF) and the Canadian federal government agreed in principle to the establishment of Nunavut.[11] The forum made it clear that what they were seeking was not an ethnically or racially based political division, but rather a division based on peoples who were permanent residents of a natural region and who practiced a self-sufficient economy based on renewable resources. Additional and more detailed proposals for the design of Nunavut were presented by Inuit representatives at a constitutional conference held in 1983, in which the Inuit emphasized that Nunavut was to be a form of self-government within the Canadian federal tradition. Final agreements on specific boundaries of Nunavut were not completed until 1988, and Nunavut Territory became official in April 1999. At that time Nunavut contained 26,000 people, 85 percent of whom were Inuit, and a total of 770,000 square miles (1,993,530 km^2), an area larger than Mexico. The Inuit received a cash settlement of $840 million over fourteen years, as well as mineral rights to 14,000 square miles (35,250 km²), and direct title to 136,000 (352,104) square kilometers.

Nunavut is a small nation within a nation, with its own government, the Government of Nunavut, which has a full complement of government agencies, including a premier, seven ministerial departments, and a nineteen-person assembly to represent three regional communities. Nunavut also sends a representative to the Canadian Parliament. A special organization, Nunavut Tunngavik Inc. (NTI), manages the land and resources collectively owned by the Inuit, and promotes Inuit well-being generally, according to the terms of the Nunavut Land Claims Agreement Act. The NTI also issues an annual report on the "State of Inuit Culture and Society"[12] and maintains a registry of Inuit owned business corporations operating in Nunavut.[13]

Nunavut is a unique experiment in which indigenous peoples are attempting to create a truly sustainable society in the commercial world based on social and cultural principles that proved successful in the tribal world. A formal Nunavut Economic Development Strategy was issued in 2003 by the newly formed Sivummut Economic Development Strategy (SEDS) Group, a coalition of some twenty Inuit organizations convened by the Nunavut Economic Forum (NEF). The Strategy Group's goal was "a high and sustainable quality of life" to be achieved "without compromising the unique culture, values, and connections to the land that have supported Inuit society over countless generations."[14] The Nunavut Development Strategy emphasizes sustainability and self-reliance, environmental stewardship, traditional knowledge, and social equity based on four principles: cultural integrity, determination and realism, community control, and cooperation and coordination.[15] The Inuit envision a mixed economy, balancing a wage and salary sector with a strong "land-based economy," drawing on natural resources. Hunting, fishing, and foraging are dominant features of Inuit culture and identity but also provide at least half of Nunavut's food, and are important sources of income.[16]

Nunavut's development goals are more likely to be achieved because Nunavut is a small-scale society. There are only twenty-eight communities, and they average just 820 persons. Iqaluit, the capital, was the largest settlement, with an Inuit population of 2,956 in 1999. In 1995 there were about 100 Inuit-owned commercial businesses, most very small, operating in the territory, but by 2007 there were 243 businesses.

Nunasi Corporation, headquartered in Iqaluit, is collectively owned by all the Nunavut Inuit and produced revenues of over $200 million US in 2005, making it the largest Inuit business in Nunavut.[17] Nunasi owns a holding company, NorTerra, jointly with the Inuit of the Western Arctic. In turn, NorTerra owns Canadian North, an airline operating Boeing 737 jetliners in the arctic; the Northern Transportation Company Limited (NTCL), which operates maritime shipping in the Canadian arctic; and Weldco-Beales (WBM), a heavy-equipment manufacturing company with plants in Alberta, British Columbia, and Washington State.[18]

NATIVE AMERICAN TRIBAL NATION ECONOMIES

In June 2010 I stood in the hot sun with a small group of Colville, Nez Perce, Wanapum, and Yakama tribal elders, Army Corps of Engineers officials, and anthropologists on a high, sagebrush-covered bluff where the Palouse River joins the Snake in southeast Washington State.[19] We were gathered for a reburial ceremony, returning to the earth a few fragments of human bones and cultural materials of 10,000-year-old Native Americans uncovered by archaeologists at the nearby Marmes Rockshelter in 1968. What we were witnessing was an implementation of the Native American Graves Protection and Recovery Act (NAGPRA) of 1990 which requires federal agencies and other federally funded agencies, the Department of Anthropology at Washington State University (WSU) in this case, to return human remains and cultural materials that they might be holding to their affiliated people. My WSU archaeologist colleagues had carried out the original excavations under federal contracts to remove and curate any human or cultural materials before they were inundated by rising waters behind Lower Monumental Dam.

Much of the recovery work involved relatively recent, even historic materials and human remains, including the recovery of one of the Jefferson Peace Medals given to Indian chiefs by Lewis and Clark in 1805. The big surprise was that the deepest remains were securely radiocarbon dated at more than 10,000 years, which made them one of the earliest verified human evidences of human occupation in the hemisphere. Even more remarkable, after consultation with the tribes and archaeologists, it was possible for the Army Corps of Engineers to make the determination that "there is a relationship of shared group identity" between existing tribes and the Marmes remains. This meant that current members of the Confederated Tribes of the Colville Reservation, Washington; Confederated Tribes of the Umatilla Indian Reservation, Oregon; Confederated Tribes and Bands of the Yakama Nation, Washington; the Nez Perce Tribe, Idaho; and the Wanapum Band, a nonfederally recognized Indian group in Washington, can all legitimately claim that they are "affiliated peoples" and that their cultural roots in this region go back at least 10,000 years. They of course already knew they were the descendants of the first peoples to occupy this land since the beginning of time, according to their oral traditions, but it was a nice touch to have this legally acknowledged by the Army Corps.

All of these indigenous peoples and their relatives in Canada share a broadly similar Plateau Culture, based on fishing, hunting, foraging, and life in small villages. They are also successfully adapting their ancient small nation culture to the contemporary demands of the commercial world. They are small nations, and like many other indigenous peoples throughout the world, they have retained key elements of their small scale, domestically organized, communal lifestyle. They are showing that ecodemia-style, cooperatively based small nations can be a solution for many contemporary problems.

These indigenous Plateau peoples have remained connected to their past and culturally intact for millennia, even after their very recent invasion and occupation of their territory by Euro-Americans and their political and economic incorporation into the commercial world. In the nineteenth century the immediate ancestors of these peoples fought against the invaders until they were forced to sign treaties and settle on reservations that were only small fractions of the territories that had supported them for millennia. Their ancestral family-based subsistence was fully dependent on the great Columbia River salmon fisheries and diverse natural ecosystems of the Pacific Northwest. Their foraging activities were part of a regional system of mutual cross-utilization of resources which extended throughout the Columbia Basin and beyond, and involved peoples speaking several different languages.[20] Their way of life was absolutely sustainable, as evidenced by the wealth of natural resources and healthy intact ecosystems that the Lewis and Clark Expedition "discovered" in 1805. In chapter 6, I explore the sustainability challenge confronting the Pacific Northwest today as a consequence of the biological transformation that followed Euro-American settlement and of the commercial exploitation that followed. Here what matters is the creative cultural transformation that the tribes are putting in place.

In 2010 there were some 25,000 enrolled members of these tribes on twenty-seven federally recognized reservations in Washington State. They were, and are, in effect small nations. The Yakama, for example, specifically call themselves the "Yakama Nation." Indian tribes are also constitutionally recognized by the federal government as locally sovereign governments, distinguished as "domestic dependent nations." All of these peoples in Washington State, with the exception of the Wanapam Band, which is not federally recognized, now have their own tribal governments, most with formal constitutions set up under the Indian Reorganization Act of 1934 and the Indian Self-Determination and Education Assistance Act of 1975. This means that Native Americans are legally well positioned to run their own economic and internal cultural affairs as small nations.

In the United States nationally there were some 560 self-governing Indian nations in "Indian Country," and nearly 5 million people self-identified as Native American or part Native American in the 2010 Census.[21] Changes in federal policies such as the Indian Self-Determination Act of 1975 and the Indian Gaming Regulatory Act of 1988 have encouraged tribal nations to grow their own economies for the benefit of their people.

Regardless of their small numbers, Washington's twenty-nine (as of 2012) small tribal nations have thriving tribal government-owned economies that are remarkable models for how any community with a shared and deeply valued culture might organize their economic lives by sharing their wealth within a larger commercial economy. Tribal nations in the Pacific Northwest already have significant natural wealth within their reservation holdings, and by means of the treaty claims on hunting and fishing and foraging rights to the territories that they traditionally utilized. A system in which economic assets are tribally owned and managed and the benefits are distributed to the owners is not fundamentally different from any capitalist corporate business enterprise. What differs is the scale of operations and this makes a huge difference. In the tribal case, management is highly democratic and the benefits are distributed equitably. This is what we would expect given scale and power principles.

Tribes continue to receive many benefits from the federal government, especially in the areas of health care and education, but this is a fully justified form of redistribution given tribal treaty rights and the fact that the federal government still holds much tribal wealth in trust for the tribes. What is important for small nation solutions is that tribal governments demonstrate that publicly owned resources, infrastructures, and business enterprises can be democratically managed by small nations in ways that benefit everyone. This makes them interesting models for any nation interested in solving development problems. Having freedom to develop the tribal commonwealth is a relatively new phenomenon for tribal governments. They have only recently begun to significantly increase their economic wealth and autonomy. Washington's Indians who are employed support more other dependents than the average for the state, and they have a lower proportion of their labor force employed in the formal economy.[22] Many reservations in the country resemble less-developed nations, and they generally still have relatively high rates of poverty and a multitude of health and social problems. These economic and social realities are not surprising for peoples whose recent ancestors were invaded, militarily subdued, and deprived of most of their natural resources.

THE YAKAMA NATION'S PEOPLE'S GOVERNMENT, PEOPLE'S ECONOMY

The Yakama Nation, like many contemporary tribal nations, is a readily documented example of a successful ecodemia-style small nation solution. The Yakama can make this solution work because with just over 10,000 enrolled members, they are a very small, micro-scale nation. Their shared history of resistance and pride in their cultural heritage is also an important factor. Fourteen Yakama bands signed a treaty with Washington Territorial Governor Isaac Stevens in 1855, ceding some 29,000 square miles of their traditional territory and agreeing to move to a much reduced reservation of only some 2,200 square miles in the southeast corner of their original territory. Before the Yakama could even relocate, miners and settlers begin entering Indian Territory, and many of the tribes felt betrayed and began an organized armed resistance. Fighting continued sporadically throughout the Washington Territory from 1855 to 1858 in what was called the Yakima War, but the Yakama did finally accept their reservation and agreed to live in peace with their new neighbors.

Rather than being governed by an Indian Reorganization Act constitution, the Yakama govern themselves democratically by their traditional laws and ordinances as approved by a General Council and a fourteen-person elected Tribal Council organized into eight standing committees and five special committees. The General Council consists of all tribal members eighteen and older. This is a potential voting population of about 6,000 people, which is a small enough number that all could assemble in one place. This is direct, not representative, democracy. There are no political parties. The General Council is the effective legislative body of the whole tribe, and the Tribal Council operates like the executive. The General Council holds an annual meeting and frequent special sessions in which members vote on issues, make laws, and select the members of the Tribal Council. A minimum of 250 members constitutes a quorum. Because the Yakama Nation is a self-determining sovereign nation there are many more issues for the government to consider than would be the case in a typical municipal or county government of comparable size. There are no government ministries as such, but the standing committees allocate resources to more than fifty "programs." There are ten different tribally owned business enterprises that help fund the government. The amazing number of programs cover virtually all the services that people need, and include, for example: Departments of Natural Resources, Fisheries, Public Safety, Emergency Management, Data Processing; an Environmental Management Program; Human Resources; Purchasing; Tourism; Ambulance and Health Clinic; Wildlife Resource Management; Tribal Insurance; the *Yakama Nation Review*, a tribal newspaper; and a radio station. Two of the larger tribally owned businesses are Yakama Nation Legends Casino and Yakama Nation Forest Products. There is also a Resort RV park, an electric power company, a land office, low-cost internet access for everyone within the reservation, and a public transit system.

This is a truly remarkable range of services for any government to provide and can only work because people often hold multiple positions, and spend a great deal of their personal time attending meetings, making decisions, and generally trying to stay informed on what fellow tribe members are thinking and saying. Direct democracy is a hard task, but it must be very satisfying for people to have this much control over the conditions of their daily life.

POWER TO THE PEOPLE: YAKAMA POWER

Further exercising their autonomy as a sovereign nation, in 2006 the Yakama formed their own electric utility, Yakama Power, which they organized as a nonprofit, cooperatively owned public utility.[23] This is a remarkable success story that draws a sharp contrast between the costs and benefits of giant companies versus small nation systems. Yakama Power demonstrates that a very small nation can do quite well on its own. The primary motivation in this case was the desire of the Yakama Nation for greater economic self-determination, but owning and operating their own electric power system also brought many other benefits including reduced energy costs to households, greater energy efficiency, and opportunities to develop other forms of renewable energy, and it provided a way to address the problem of climate change.

Having this much control over the production and distribution of something as basic to one's daily life as electric power must be a source of great personal satisfaction for the Yakama people. Even as they took control of their electric utility, the Yakama Nation also took operational control over the Wapato Irrigation Project, the largest water district in the Yakima River Basin in acre-feet per year. This system of 1,100 miles of irrigation canals was built originally by the Bureau of Indian Affairs in 1868 and continues to serve tribal and nontribal farmers and ranchers on the reservation, which includes some of the richest and most productive agricultural land in the state.

Before Yakama Power began operations in 2006, the Yakama Nation's electric power came from Pacificorp's subsidiary Pacific Power, which started in 1910 as Pacific Power and Light (PP&L), a small regional power company serving limited areas in Oregon and Washington. PP&L was a for-profit company, and eventually it began to acquire other companies and then grew much much larger. What happened then was a complex and confusing series of corporate mergers that had little to do with providing better electric service to the Yakama people, but that did help grow the economic power of global elites. It is worth tracing this sordid business history because it shows how Pacificorp ended up under the control of an American billionaire, and further explains why Yakama Power is such a superior human-scale alternative to global-scale corporate mergers run amok.

Pacific Power was swallowed up by the economic globalization process, in 1987 becoming a wholly owned subsidiary of Pacificorp by the merger of PP&L with Utah P&L. PP&L suddenly became Pacific Power and Utah P&L became Rocky Mountain Power, both under Pacificorp. Then suddenly in 2001, Pacificorp was purchased by ScottishPower, headquartered in Glasgow, but itself a subsidiary of Iberdrola, a private multinational electric utility headquartered in Spain and operating in forty countries. ScottishPower was formed as part of the free market wave of deregulations and privatizations in which governments worldwide busily divested themselves of the public's assets that were quickly snatched up by expanding multi-nationals. The directors of Iberdrola must have decided that ScottishPower may have overreached and didn't need to own power companies in the American West, and in 2005 ScottishPower sold Pacificorp to MidAmerican Energy Holdings. MidAmerican in turn was a subsidiary of Berkshire Hathaway, headquartered in Omaha, Nebraska, which was ranked in the 2012 Forbes Global 2000 as the eighth largest publically traded company in the world. Berkshire's revenues were over $100 billion, and its assets approached $400 billion. Berkshire's individual shares are recognized to be the most valuable in the world. It is about one-third owned by Warren Buffett, who was ranked by Forbes in 2012 as the world's third wealthiest individual with $44 billion.[24] Buffett bought Pacificorp in 2005 for $5 billion, in what was called the second biggest deal of his career. "The energy sector has long interested us, and this is the right fit," Buffett declared.[25]

It would be hard to argue that Berkshire Hathaway, a gigantic, multi-layered corporate conglomerate with a billionaire as the prime beneficiary at the top, serves a human need that cannot be successfully met by an organization on the scale of the Yakama Nation, the corporate owner of Yakama Power. After all, members of the Tribal Council also sit on the board of Yakama Power and are clearly capable of managing the company. This is a good reminder of the utility of the subsidiarity principle that decision making (and ownership) should be exercised at the lowest possible level. If Yakama Power can do the job, Pacificorp should step aside, along with MidAmerican Energy Holdings, Berkshire Hathaway, and Warren Buffett. This is in fact what happened, because when Yakama Power was formed, the Washington Utilities and Transportation Commission made sure that Pacificorp transferred its distribution system to Yakama Power.

Earlier the Yakama Nation had formed a partnership with Benton Rural Electric Association, a nonprofit public utility cooperative, and contracted for power from Bonneville Power Administration (BPA), the federal nonprofit wholesale distributor of electric power produced by the thirty-one federal hydro projects scattered throughout the Columbia Basin. By 2008 Yakima Power began supplying electricity to the tribal government facilities throughout the reservation, and to its casino. Its slogan is "Power to the People," and Yakama Power intends to extend services to residents and other commercial businesses in the area. The Yakama Nation hopes to become energy self-sufficient in renewable electric power, and is exploring all forms of renewable energy. As a step in that direction, following a resolution of the General Council Yakama Power began a development/demonstration project in 2008 to develop a small-scale hydroelectric system on the existing Wapato Irrigation Project. This was a $2 million effort supported in part by the federal Department of Energy's Tribal Energy Program within their Office of Energy Efficiency and Renewable Energy (EERE). In addition to renewable energy production and low-cost distribution, the Yakama took advantage of the Department of Energy's "Building America Program" to retrofit homes on the reservation to make them more energy efficient. This program virtually cut household energy use in half.[26]

The nation made good use of the Federal Energy Regulatory Commission (FERC) relicensing requirements for Grant County PUCs to continue operation of its Priest Rapids Hydroelectric Project after its license expired in 2005.[27] This shows that higher levels of authority such as FERC have important roles to play in mediating interactions between lower level agents, in this case a tribal nation and a public utility, when both had a common interest in resources associated with a stretch of river. Such higher authority would be absolutely necessary in a small nation world. Surpra-national regulatory institutions have a crucial role to play in the small nation solution. What also matters is that none of the contending parties should have overwhelming power because of gigantic size.

Because of the complex history of the region, in addition to FERC, many other interested parties were involved with the Yakama Nation's negotiations with Grant County PUC, the small electric cooperative that built and owned the Priest Rapids Hydroelectric Project. Six county governments were involved because the project was within their jurisdictions. Five federal agencies were involved as landowners within the affected area: the Bureau of Reclamation, Bureau of Land Management (BLM), the U.S. Department of the Army, the U.S. Fish and Wildlife Service, and the U.S. Department of Energy. Other government agencies that took an interest in the relicensing process included: the Department of the Interior, The Bonneville Power Administration, the National Marine Fisheries Service, Washington State's Fish and Wildlife Department, and Alaska Fish and Game. Several other public utilities, Avista, a very large for-profit energy company, as well as American Rivers, an environmental organization, were also part of the discussion. This is why running a small nation is a complex, difficult, and time-consuming project for the people involved.

In 2007 The Yakama reached an agreement with a neighboring public utility, Grant County PUD, to allow sharing of benefits from the nearby Priest Rapids Hydro Project and joint efforts to restore and maintain fish and wildlife. The agreement contained an important "whereas" statement that demonstrated their long-term interests in sustainable development: "WHEREAS, the Yakama Nation places the greatest importance on preserving the fish, wildlife, and cultural resources reserved in the Treaty for the benefit of present and future generations . . . ."[28] This agreement added specific management plans for protection of Pacific lamprey and white sturgeon, two fish species of special cultural significance for the Yakama. A prior agreement contained detailed requirements for fish passage, hatcheries and habitat improvement for chinook, sockeye, and coho salmon, and steelhead.[29] There can be no doubt that the Yakama are environmentalists who believe in the Endangered Species Act. They have engaged with many federal and state agencies in their efforts to protect fish and wildlife.

TRIBAL NATION CASINOS VS. BILLIONAIRES: ADELSON AND TRUMP CASINOS

The scale and power contrasts between the tribally owned gaming enterprises just described and the global-scale operations of American billionaire's Sheldon Adelson and Donald Trump, who own and direct similar business operations, help explain why the small nation ecodemia approach supports sustainable development and social justice, and why global 2000 corporations may often fail to do so.

According to figures provided by the National Indian Gaming Commission, the industry's federal regulatory agency, in the 2011 fiscal year the forty-nine gaming operations (casinos) in the states of Alaska, Idaho, Oregon, and Washington produced average revenues of $56 million.[30] This may seem like a very modest amount, but as we have seen, each tribal nation is the sole owner of its casino and casino revenues loom very large in the tribal nation economies by supporting government operations which supply benefits to all tribal members. The scale of the largest comparable shareholder owned and publically traded casino operating corporations is difficult to fathom in comparison with tribal casinos. As an example, Las Vegas Sands, headquartered in Las Vegas, is a Forbes Global 2000 Corporation with revenues of nearly $10 billion and assets of $22 billion in 2011. The Sands revenue was almost two hundred times more than the average revenue of a tribal casino, but the Sands owned and operated more than 11,000 slot machines in nine integrated resorts in the United States, China (Macao), and Singapore. In comparison the Yakama Nation's Legends Casino has 1,400 slots. Everything about the Sands operation is overwhelming. By its own not so modest claims, it is "the pre-eminent developer and operator of world-class integrated resorts that feature luxury hotels; world-class gaming, retail, entertainment, convention, and exhibition facilities; celebrity chef restaurants, and many other amenities." The Sands' Marina Bay Sands resort in Singapore which opened in 2010 is a gigantic complex with three fifty-five-story towers containing 2,600 rooms, connected by a sky bridge adorned with an "infinity" swimming pool that seems to have no edge. This structure caught my attention because my brother Tom lives in a nearby high rise and watched the towers being constructed. The Sands richly rewards its managers, giving the top five annual base salaries of $1 to 3 million, which was augmented to total compensation of more than $50 million with their various bonuses, incentives, and benefits. The majority owners and prime beneficiaries of the company are members of the Sheldon G. Adelson family and friends, who owned 87 percent of the company in 2011.[31] Adelson himself is ranked as the twelfth richest individual in the world, worth nearly $25 billion.

THE VEGAS SANDS ECO 360° VISION
OF GLOBAL SUSTAINABILITY

> Mission: Las Vegas Sands Corp. is committed to environmental responsibility by promoting sustainable development, reducing the impact of our operations on the natural environment, and enhancing the resort experience of our guests as well as the quality of life in the communities where we operate.[32]

Sheldon Adelson is a controversial figure. He became very prominent during the 2012 U.S. presidential campaign for personally contributing tens of millions of dollars to various Republican candidates and for being an outspoken opponent of labor unions and any policies that he considered to be "socialist" redistribution. His business approach is very different from the models of economic democracy pioneered by Robert Owen. As the billionaire owner of the Vegas Sands gambling resort empire Adelson is a clear example of an elite director, but he takes on added significance because his company is offering itself as a model for solving global sustainability problems. This makes the Sands worth a closer look because its sustainability strategy can by contrast help to highlight the distinctive features of the small nations solution that are so very different from the solutions proposed by many global elites.

The Sands presents its "ECO 360° Global Sustainability" strategy as their business model, but they also present it as "environmental stewardship" reflecting their responsibility to the planet and their desire "to leave a responsible, cleaner, and safer world for future generations."[33] These are the same goals that small nations like the Yakama are promoting, based on revenues produced by the same entertainment industry. As described above, the Yakama have already worked hard to influence government policies to restore Columbia River salmon, and they have implemented energy and environment policies in their own territory to benefit the salmon and other wildlife. They are also using casino revenues to directly benefit the 10,000 tribal members who are the joint owners. The Yakama Nation has no problem with labor unions and has adopted a formal policy to protect worker rights.[34] Their small nation solution is working.

The Sands Corporation hires some 40,000 employees to run its worldwide operations but has concentrated the primary profits in a single extended family. This makes the Sands a prime example of concentrated social power in a giant Forbes Global 2000 company. Furthermore, according to news reports, the Sands allowed no collective bargaining (labor union representation) by any of its employees until June 2012, when 130 security guards working at the Sands Casino Resort in Bethlehem, Pennsylvania, won a ruling from the National Labor Relations Board (NLRB), forcing the Sands to allow them to organize.[35] This matters because sustainability also means social sustainability and social justice. The right of workers to form and to join trade unions is guaranteed by Article 23 of the United Nations Universal Declaration of Human Rights, 1948. I remember this article specifically, because I just read it at the Museo de la Memoria in Santiago, where it was displayed on a courtyard wall as one of thirty bronze plaques for each of the thirty articles of the Universal Declaration of Human Rights. By itself, the Sands' resistance to fair labor practices leads me to question the seriousness of ECO 360° Global Sustainability commitment to enhancing "the quality of life in the communities where we operate." The narrow materialist approach to sustainability raises further warning signs. Proposed solutions to global problems that actually divert attention from the very fundamental changes in the distribution of social power that must be made in order for every society to be sustainable can in themselves be part of the problem, rather than a solution.

The Sands 360° sustainability strategy is portrayed as a circle with four sections: green buildings, environmentally responsible operations, green meetings, and stakeholder engagement. If high-rise, very large resorts are needed to meet the entertainment and conferencing needs of the global elite and high net worth individuals then it is certainly commendable that they be designed and built to minimize their environmental costs. At the same time we should remember that the Yakama Nation also meets entertainment and conferencing needs of people with a resort of just six stories, and also succeeds in doing a more equitable job of distributing the benefits among their "stakeholders," as Robert Owen would hope. The high-rise Sands resorts qualify as "green" buildings. They have won architectural awards for innovative design features and green technologies such as the nano-filtration system to save water and solar-thermal heating for swimming pools. Giving resort guests the option of reusing towels and linens also "greens" Sands' resorts, as does planting 250 trees on top of the Marina Bay Sands skypark green roof in Singapore. Conferences that recycle and reduce wasted paper products is good practice. However, scale still matters. Even with all of the Sand's very admirable green practices they reported a carbon footprint for all of their operations in 2010 at 844,055 MT CO_2e (metric tons of carbon dioxide equivalent) emissions. There were thirty-five small nations that actually had lower carbon emissions in 2010, including Bermuda, a prosperous island nation of 65,000 people. As the Marina Bay Sands casino came on line in 2011, Sands' carbon emissions actually increased to 904,812 MT CO_2e.

There is a contradiction in promoting sustainability solutions on the one hand, and on the other building giant resort casinos in cities such as Singapore and Las Vegas that are themselves not self-sufficient in food, water, and fuel, and are totally dependent on global systems of fossil fuel energy and concentrated wealth and power. Trump's casinos in Atlantic City were of course hit by hurricane Sandy and emerged with only minor damage, but their vulnerability to rising seas and storm surges was a powerful reminder that the carbon emissions that allow global-scale casino companies to thrive also cause global warming.

The implications of the Yakama Nation case are profound. The obvious point is that if the Yakama can meet their needs without depending on a giant corporation to supply them with employment, or electric power, or return on investments, then maybe many more small regional communities could do the same. What any new small nation will need, and what will be a challenge to create, is a cultural consensus on how to restructure to manage all forms of capital justly and sustainably. Everyone in the world does in fact have a common heritage of a 10,000-year-old sustainable culture, with essential elements that can be revived. A deep sense of shared humanity and shared crisis will help.

AUSTRALIAN ABORIGINAL
BAWINANGA CORPORATION

In the previous chapter the scale aspects of Australian Aboriginal social organization and related Aboriginal value systems were described as they existed before Europeans arrived in 1788. This section describes how Aborigines have adopted modern corporate legal forms to suite their tribal patterns of economic democracy. The Northern Land Council created by the Northern Territory Land Rights Act of 1971 is an Aboriginal organization that operates like a small nation government mediating between traditional Aboriginal landowners and outsiders seeking to extract resources from Aboriginal lands. Individual Aboriginal communities also have their own local governments and economic structures. The Bawinanga Aboriginal Corporation (BAC), discussed in this section, is essentially a consumer cooperative, in principle resembling the vastly larger Co-operative Group in the UK but based on Aboriginal values of sharing. Bawinanga serves the needs of many Aborigines living in a vast region of the Northern Territory that was designated as the Arnhem Land Aboriginal Reserve in 1931. Much of this area is now part of the newly created West Arnhem Shire, an area of some 50,000 km² with some 5,000 resident Aborigines speaking several different languages. Many Aborigines in this region maintain attachments to their clan estates and live largely by self-provisioning on their own countries in outstations, which are a continuation of their traditional band social structure. Bawinanga Corporation is located in the Aboriginal settlement of Maningrida, which is a supply center offering basic goods and services to people living in more remote areas.

Australia's federal Corporations (Aboriginal and Torres Strait Islander) Act 2006[36] specifies in detail how indigenous corporations must be organized in Australia and requires that they register with a special government agency, the Registrar of Indigenous Corporations, and meet specific financial reporting rules. This does not mean that the national society is totally imposing external forms on Aboriginal culture because Aborigines are able to organize their affairs by using both systems, as will be shown below. As of 2009 there were more than 2,700 indigenous corporations in the country. Most were in remote areas where they provided social and public services for which they received significant public funds. Even though Aboriginal culture is sometimes described as biased toward males, nearly a third of the directors of Aboriginal corporations were women, where gender was reported. Indigenous corporations were small and nearly half had incomes of under about US$25,000 and assets of under US$100,000. The largest had incomes and assets of tens of millions of US dollars, which would qualify them as small businesses.

The Bawinanga Aboriginal Corporation is the second-largest Aboriginal corporation in Australia, with revenue of US$78 million and assets of nearly US$14 million in 2008.[37] It was incorporated in 1979 initially as an outstation resource agency to provide support for people living in outstations on their clan lands. The corporation expanded into a wide range of activities, and it soon took on additional welfare and economic development functions. The name "Ba-win-anga" combines parts of the names of three language groups in the region, Barada, Gunwinggu, and Rambarranga.[38] At first BAC was federally funded by the Department of Aboriginal Affairs, and from 1980 to 2005 its chief executive was a *balanda* (non-Aboriginal) man. In 1997 BAC began to administer the federal Community Development Employment Projects (CDEP) funds flowing into the region, and its annual revenues began to exceed US$10 million.

The Aborigines have succeeded in governing the Bawinanga corporation by combining the informal, open discussion characteristic of small, face-to-face, domestically based societies with the formality of legally chartered corporate institutions required by the federal government. In effect this is an intercultural blend of small- and large-scale cultural structures that must satisfy both Australian legal requirements and the expectations of Aborigines in the "very remote" Maningrida settlement and the linguistically and culturally diverse Aborigines living in outstations dispersed over a vast territory.

BAC is governed by an all-Aboriginal ten- to fifteen-person Executive Committee elected annually by the members representing different language groups and outstations. Executive Committee members include new leaders who understand the *balanda* world, and "customary" leaders who are especially knowledgeable about local Aboriginal culture and local affairs. A few executive members are leaders in both respects, and most were likely to serve in multiple organizations. The annual election means that executive leadership changes frequently, and this reduces the possibility of a single cultural group dominating the organization. There were few Aborgines qualified by prior training, English fluency, and business experience to manage such a complex organization, but whoever receives the most votes becomes Executive Committee chair, The executive chair is a prized salaried position and comes with access to a motor vehicle, but it is consistently rotated among the different language groups. In this way the potential for abuse of executive power is severely limited.

The distinctive feature of BAC is that it is an indigenously owned and directed community corporation that operates businesses, promotes community development and the general welfare. Like virtually all co-ops, BAC aims "to promote, in all its endeavours, the common good and mutual benefit of its members through fair, equitable and representative action and enterprise." BAC membership is open to all adult Aboriginal persons who are permanent residents of, or who have "traditional rights, affiliations and interests" in, Maningrida and the out-stations that it serves. A very special feature of BAC, and its first objective, is "to promote the maintenance of language, culture and traditional practice." There are no membership fees and no dividends paid.

In 2009 BAC reported 246 registered Aboriginal members, serving 800 Aboriginal "clients" in thirty-two outstations. BAC functions include agriculture, forestry, fishing, manufacturing, municipal services, construction, wholesale trade, shops, accommodation, cafes, restaurants, transport and storage, communication services, housing, education, health and community services, art services, personal and other services, employment and training, and land management. Its activities are organized in several business segments including the BAC Housing and Welding Shop; the Barlmarrk Supermarket; BAC Outdoors for hardware and merchandise; a Buildings Activities for construction; a financial services division for banking; Good Food Kitchen preparing take-out foods; Maningrida Arts & Culture division, selling local art works nationally and internationally; a road construction and maintenance division, a Workshop for vehicle maintenance, as well as a wide range of other activities.

BAC's hired senior managers are stable and experienced, but they are *balanda* (non-Aboriginal). It is not surprising that many non-Aboriginals would have management roles in Bawinanga businesses, because Aborigines know what they want, but most do not yet have the formal expertise required to run all the various businesses that the community needs. Native American tribal nation governing bodies such as the Yakama tribal council also hire outside business managers when necessary. BAC's senior management adds an element of stability to the entire organization. They try to stay current with the interpersonal details of community life in a way that would be difficult in a larger-scale society. They help the Executive Committee mediate between national and customary law, and they offer a level of neutrality between different Aboriginal language groups. The legal requirements of BAC as a formal corporations means that the Aboriginal Executive Committee members must avoid conflicts of interest, but at the same time they do represent the interests of their close kin, clans, language groups, and outstation residents. Finding a successful balance between formal corporate practice and kinship-based customary practice has been improved by government supported opportunities for Aboriginal leaders to gain training in business practices and for the non-Aboriginal staff to gain training in Aboriginal culture. Balance is also achieved by the frequency of elections, and because Executive Committee members encourage others to participate as observers in their formal meetings, and they hold informal discussions, as would be customary practice.

The apparent success of BAC and Maningrida generally has caused people to begin moving from outstations back to Maningrida, and some members are concerned that Maningrida itself may become too big, which would undermine some of its original goals of supporting outstations. A more critical problem has been BAC's continued reliance on funding from the Australian government. BAC receives funding from several Commonwealth programs including CDEP, an employment program, and the Community Housing and Infrastructure Program (CHIP) both of which became part of the Commonwealth's Department of Family and Community Services (FACS). There was considerable confusion and disarray in Aboriginal Policy caused by the abolition of the Aboriginal and Torres Strait Islander Commission (ATSIC), the threatened abolition of CDEP, and the declaration of a "State of Emergency" in the Northern Territory in 2007 that brought in direct federal intervention in local affairs. Most of these policy changes were modified after a new federal government was elected in late 2007.

THE MONDRAGÓN COOPERATIVE MODEL

The Basques of northern Spain have already shown that sustainable cultural systems can be designed that effectively integrate industrial technologies and commercialization within an existing nation-state. A successful, highly democratic, and economically just cultural system has been operating quietly in northern Spain since the 1950s.[39] Stubbornly independent Basques have created an integrated regional society of some 250,000 people, based on a system of numerous small-scale, worker-owned cooperatives centered on the town of Mondragón. Each Mondragón industrial cooperative is limited in size to no more than 500 members, who each have an equal vote in management decisions. There are no giant, remotely owned corporations. The scale limit is crucial, because the Basques have learned that it is almost impossible for larger production units to remain truly democratic. Likewise, the pay scale normally increases by no more than a factor of six from top to bottom, which both rewards hard work and sets a ceiling on executive pay. Everyone shares in annual profits, and a proportion goes to support local community projects and the Basque cultural heritage.

The crucial principles of the Mondragón cooperative system is that workers and community are considered to be more important than capital, and workers are both owners and managers. This is called "solidarity." Decision making is based on democratic principles.[40] The primacy of workers is reflected in the salary scale which gave entry-level workers a livable wage of US$16,480 in 2005, and in which the highest income rank topped out at $98,880, which was just six times higher than the minimum. Workers buy shares in their cooperative and receive annual dividends.

Mondragón cooperatives manufacture world-class computerized robots and a wide range of exported industrial goods and consumer durables. They also run their own consumer co-ops and cooperative banking, social insurance, education, and child care services that respond directly to the needs of local people. The Mondragón mission statement makes employment, community, equity, education, and environment the primary objectives, and Basque cultural autonomy is a key to their achievement. The Basques are a unique people, who claim to be descendants of the Ice Age peoples who produced the great paintings on the cave walls at Lascaux and Altamira 30,000 years ago. In fact, their language and genetic roots do connect them with the most ancient Europeans. The Basques have learned that general welfare and domestic tranquility can best be achieved when everyone is allowed to manage the human, cultural, and natural resources that produce wealth.

This example shows how localization processes are actually being implemented in a particular region. The Basques are attempting to maintain high degrees of local cultural autonomy based on economic self-reliance. They are using industrial technology and capitalist economics within an integrated network of worker-owned, small-scale corporate business enterprises that strive to be highly democratic and egalitarian while supporting households and local communities.

Known as MCC (Mondragón Corporación Cooperativa), the Mondragón cooperative system is one of the most famous examples of how corporate commercial businesses can be intentionally organized to put community and employees and long-term sustainability ahead of short-term profits. From 1955 to 2005 the Mondragón cooperatives had grown to some 63,500 member shareowners, producing revenues of $15 billion.[41] By 2008 the Mondragón Cooperatives had become the seventh largest business group in Spain, and it was the most prominent system of cooperatives in the world. By 2010 there were 109 cooperatives, 125 subsidiary companies, all primarily worker owned, and twenty-four other entities including training and research centers, with a total workforce of 83,000.[42] By 2011 revenues stood at $19 billion; profits $162 million; total assets US$42 billion; and there was $5 billion in shareholder value. These figures would qualify MCC as a Global 2000 ranked corporation. There are now MCC-affiliated cooperative corporations scattered throughout the world, all following the same cooperative principles.

Mondragón cooperatives are organized in three functional groups: financial (banking), industrial (manufacturing), and distribution (retail markets), under a democratically elected congress with a general council and standing committees. The distribution group operates 2,300 supermarkets, shops, and restaurants under the EROSKI brand in Spain and France. MCC manufactures a wide variety of high-tech components, equipment, tools, and household appliances. It was the tenth-largest business corporation in Spain in 2011, and operated ninety-three production plants in twenty countries worldwide.

MCC demonstrates that industrial production can be organized democratically and in a way that diffuses, rather than concentrates, decision making power as well as wages, benefits, and profits. Worker management and ownership, democratic decision making, and scale limits on number of employees in individual cooperatives and companies are central MCC "human and participatory" organizational principles. The success of the Mondragón system is clearly shown by the fact that the Basque districts of Spain have some of the highest GDPs and household incomes in the country.[43] Furthermore they have been an island of comparative economic stability during the continuing turmoil that followed the global financial crisis that began in 2008.

5

ARCADIA

Environmentally Friendly Small Nations

Mother earth has . . . the right to the maintenance of the integrity of the systems of life and the natural processes that sustain them, as well as the capacities and conditions for their regeneration. —Law of the Rights of Mother Earth, Plurinational State of Bolivia[1]

Arcadia is the mythical home of Pan, the Greek god of nature. This original meaning refers to an idyllic natural place, where nature was protected and enjoyed. An arcadian small nation would be an environmentalist paradise. Arcadian small nations know that the shared gift of natural capital is humanity's greatest form of wealth, and their citizens agree on the importance of ecosystem and biodiversity protection and the urgency of the climate change threat. The present chapter looks in detail at indigenous tribal peoples living in the Amazonian rainforest, the Caribbean island nation of Dominica, the predominately indigenous Plurinational State of Bolivia, and a sampling of Pacific island nations. Small island nations are among the most prominent arcadian nations for the obvious reason that they know that they absolutely *must* protect nature right now. Their land, freshwater, biodiversity, and marine resources are either extremely limited or very vulnerable to overexploitation, and they are always exposed to catastrophic natural events such as typhoons and tsunamis. Pacific island nations consider themselves to be the first victims of climate change, and islanders feel especially vulnerable to sea level rise and the loss of their coral reefs which they blame on the unjust actions of larger nations. Islanders have a strong consensus on environmental protection and are taking specific actions that make them exemplary models of sustainability. Not all arcadian nations are indigenous or island nations. The Himalayan Buddhist kingdom of Bhutan has the most intact forests in South Asia and has placed more than half of its territory under constitutional protection. Bhutan's forests absorb five times more carbon dioxide than the kingdom emits, making Bhutan a carbon storehouse, rather than an emitter, even as its mountain glaciers are melting due to global warming. Like Bhutan, the Commonwealth of Dominica has the best preserved forests in the region and calls itself the "nature island of the Caribbean." Arcadian small nations know that they cannot solve the global environmental crisis by themselves; they can only show the world that real solutions are actually possible.

SMALL NATIONS PROTECTING AND MANAGING THE ENVIRONMENT

Systematic cross-national research shows that small nations rank very well as managers of their environments and natural resources and on overall environmental sustainability. The Yale Center for Environmental Law and Policy and the Center for International Earth Science Information Network (CIESIN) working in collaboration with the World Economic Forum and the European Commission's Joint Research Centre in 2008 produced an Environmental Performance Index (EPI) for the governments of 149 countries.[2] The EPI considers twenty-five indicators measuring government effectiveness on two important policy objectives: (1) environmental health, managing air pollution, protecting drinking water, and generally reducing mortality caused by poor environmental conditions; and (2) ecosystem vitality considering policies directed at reducing the effects of air and water pollution and stress on the environment, maintaining productive natural resources, and confronting climate change.

The government with the best overall environmental performance was Switzerland, a small nation, with a rank of 96 out of 100, measuring percent of environmental goals met. The top eight governments were all small nations, and fourteen (70 percent) of the top twenty countries with scores of 85 and above were small nations. In general, environmental performance is strongly correlated with per capita GDP, suggesting that it is better to have a relatively high performance commercial economy. At first glance the data generally supports that conclusion; however, there are striking small nation outliers. A closer look shows that small nations can perform at the top even with small economies and low per capita incomes. Nearly all of the top twenty on overall environmental performance were high income countries with GDPs/capita above $12,000. However, Costa Rica was a small nation outlier in the top group even with its upper-middle income rank of under $10,000 and a performance of 90.

The environmental performance database covers more countries for ecosystem vitality measures, and this allows more small nations to appear in the sample where they can show even more clearly the distinct advantages of small nations for effective resource management. Overall ecosystem vitality rankings for 154 countries showed that the top seven countries meeting 87 percent or more of their ecosystem goals were all small nations: Laos, Switzerland, Congo, Costa Rica, Bhutan, Norway, and Sweden. They ranged in income from Congo with a low of $1,159 per capita to Norway with $32,775. These rankings demonstrate again that a country does not need to be financially rich or large in population to take care of its natural environment.

Small nations absolutely excel at maintaining productive natural resources and at having effective government policies to safeguard forests, and prevent overfishing, and degradation of agricultural soils and rangelands. This is an area where most countries do poorly, and only 25 percent of 214 countries were achieving 90 percent or more of their resource management goals. Most remarkably, fifty out of the fifty-five countries in the 90 percent rank for natural resource productivity were small nations. You could confidently predict that any country that is successfully managing its natural resources is a small nation. As the population scale of a country goes down, success at maintaining natural resource productivity goes up. This is not about population density, because there is no correlation between *density* and effectiveness of resource management policies. Many highly effective resource management countries are small nations with very high population densities. The issue is that people in small nations are better able to reach a consensus about their resource management goals and can make and implement effective policy decisions. Small nations were overwhelm-ingly represented at the very top, with eleven small nations achieving 100 percent of their resource management goals, and thirty-four of the top thirty-five countries ranking at 95 percent or higher were small nations. This is a remarkable achievement.

SMALL NATIONS ENDING POVERTY AND MEETING CLIMATE CHANGE GOALS

Effective climate change policies would of course be expected of an arcadian small nation. The Environmental Performance Index (EPI, see above) measures a country's progress toward this goal by estimating the percentage that it has reached the goal of carbon emissions of 2.24 metric tons per capita per year, zero grams of carbon per kWh of elec-tricity, and .85 tons of carbon per US $1000 of industrial GDP output. The assumption is that in combination achieving these goals would produce a 50 percent reduction in global greenhouse gas emissions by 2050. As of 2005 most countries were doing very poorly on climate policy. Fewer than 12 percent of countries were within 90 percent of the goal, but more than half at 90 percent or above were small nations.

The use of fossil fuels is of course a critical climate change policy issue, and small nations show how much diversity is possible in the energy sector, and they demonstrate that fossil fuel use can be reduced while keeping human well-being and income levels high. The IPCC Fourth Assessment Report shows that fossil fuel use contributed more than half of the greenhouse gases (GHG) causing global warming.[3] The enormous acceleration of fossil fuel related CO_2 emissions since 1970 can be attributed to four crucial factors: (1) carbon intensity, the amount of CO_2 emitted per unit of energy production; (2) energy inten-sity, energy used per unit of GDP; (3) GDP per capita; and (4) popula-tion.[4] Improvements in carbon and energy intensity have not offset the increases in population and GDP per capita. Small nations are crucial because their populations have remained small in absolute numbers, even as on average they have grown at similar rates as larger nations.

The 1992 UN Framework Convention on Climate Change (UNFCC) committed the nations of the world to stabilizing atmospher-ic greenhouse gases at a level that would prevent "dangerous anthropogenic interference with the climate system" (article 2). There has been agreement that global temperatures should not rise more than 1.7 to 2° C (3 to 3.6° F) above preindustrial levels, but there has been less political certainty over exactly what level of CO_2 in the atmosphere constitutes "dangerous interference." [5]

According to climate models that speak carefully of probabilities, the "very likely" probability of remaining below 2°C, and thus avoiding dangerous climate change impacts, would require cumulative CO_2 emissions of just 500 Gt from 2000 to 2049, when carbon balance with zero emissions would hopefully be achieved.[6] A cumulative total of 1,000 Gt is "likely," but not "very likely," to keep the world below the 2°C safety threshold, suggesting that if a small risk of catastrophic failure is assumed, then the necessary cultural changes may be more achievable. It is also "likely" that cumulative emissions are already so high that long term climate stabilization over centuries may require that carbon emission remain at near-zero levels indefinitely into the future,[7] which means that drastic sociocultural changes along the lines of an arcadian small nation solution will be needed to assure sustainability. Between 2000 and 2006 the commercial world had already burned through 234 Gt, and at that rate within twenty-five years will exceed the 1,000 Gt cumulative total, long before the 2050 target date for stabilization.

The problem with setting severe restrictions on carbon emissions is that most development authorities believe that improving living standards to meet human needs in the impoverished world will require poor countries to increase their energy use, which will put them in conflict with global efforts to reduce carbon emissions. The real question is how best to prevent "dangerous" anthropogenic climate change and at the same time assure that every nation can achieve sustainable development.

In order to resolve this apparent dilemma, The Greenhouse Development Rights (GDR) framework developed by the Stockholm Environment Institute and Ecoequity[8] set a target development threshold of $7,500 PPP GDP/capita per year, which is well above the World Bank's "extreme poverty" line of $1 or $2 dollars per capita per day (<$1,000/year). A $7,500 "development threshold" is also higher than the World Bank's global "poverty" line of about $16 PPP per capita ($5,800/year). A threshold of $7,500 is intended to be above basic subsistence needs and would allow a country to achieve a high Human Development

Index. This is what I have elsewhere called a "maintenance level" to meet basic needs with a comfortable security margin, but it would not cover high levels of consumption, luxury, or "affluence," such as has characterized "developed" consumer cultures in high income nations. Countries below the development threshold have done little to cause global warming and would not be expected to sacrifice to reduce carbon emissions. The GDR framework provides a basis for calculating the capacity of high income countries to reduce emissions and continue to meet the basic needs of their citizens.

It is possible to imagine the magnitude of cultural changes that will be needed and to identify the kinds of already developed cultural systems that meet the challenge and can serve as models for other countries. According to the U.S. Energy Information Administration (EIA), in 2006 global carbon emissions averaged just under 6 metric tons per capita.[9] If we assume a stationary global economy and population of 6.5 billion people in 2007, the average global emission rate would need to be 0.92 metric tons per capita to achieve the target cumulative emissions of 500 Gt by 2050. The somewhat riskier 1000 Gt target could be achieved with a global per capita emission rate that did not exceed 2.6 metric tons. The 2007 global average rate of just under 5 tons per capita was already fivefold too high for the 0.92 target. The United States at 20 tons per capita was more than twenty-fold over that target, but it was also far above the $7,500 well-being threshold.

The good news is that nearly half of the 207 countries in the EIA database are already below the 2.6 ton "likely safe" per capita emission threshold and nearly a third, were at or below the 0.92 "very likely" safe level. The bad news is that most of these on target countries were not on target for various important measures of human well-being. However, there were nineteen small nations, including Dominica and St. Helena, that were below the 2.6-ton carbon line and also had life expectancies of seventy years or higher.

Seven small nations have already overcome poverty and responded effectively to the global warming threat. These very successful small nation included two Latin American countries, Costa Rica and Uruguay; four Caribbean island nations, Santa Lucia, Saint Vincent and Grenadines, Dominica, and Turks and Caicos Islands; together with Cape Verde. These seven small nations were all above the $7,500 line, had carbon emissions below 2.6 tons/capita, had high life expectancies, and where reported did well on the HDI. One of these very successful countries, the Caribbean micro-nation of Dominica, was also among a group of twenty low-growth small nations whose populations had grown less than 25 percent from 1960 to 2008. Nicaragua, a Latin American small nation in the group of nineteen, experienced low economic growth from 1960 to 2008, and had a low GDP/capita of $3,760, but still achieved an over 70 years life expectancy and was even below the "likely safe" 0.92 emission target. Small nations demonstrate that it is feasible to lift people out of poverty, maintain high living standards, and respond to the climate change challenge.

THE ASHÁNINKA: CUSTODIANS OF THE TROPICAL ANDEAN BIODIVERSITY HOTSPOT

The Asháninka who I lived with in the 1960s were not yet self-conscious conservationists, and they were not "ecologically noble savages," but they were enjoying the benefits of life in an arcadian-like small nation. This was because they did not degrade their regional environments on a scale comparable to what commercially organized societies have done and are continuing to do. I was at first surprised to see that the Asháninka would readily cut down forest trees to collect the fruit, seemingly for convenience; and that they routinely hunted out highly sought game animals in the vicinity of their settlements. This was actually not a problem because nature was so rich, people could move, and go on foraging treks. They were a very small-scale society, placing extremely light demands on nature. The entire Asháninka system was designed to maximize their freedom to hunt, forage, fish, and garden in a sustainable way. This worked as long their basic culture remained intact, and outsiders, with their outsized demands, stayed away. Today, the Asháninka are making a promising transition to the demands of the commercial world in ways that deliberately seek to safeguard their natural environment. They are politically organizing against destructive invaders to protect their distinct cultures and communities, their territories, and the natural resources that sustain them. This means they are beginning to see themselves as a small nation in a world of large nation states, and they asking the international community to help them defend the rain forest.

In the twenty-first century many indigenous Amazonians like the Asháninka continue to exemplify small-scale, domestically focused, highly self-sufficient peoples who rely on local resources and ecosystems. Their ancestors developed diverse and highly successful cultural systems some 7,000 years ago using manioc cultivation, ceramics, the bow and arrow, and canoes in ways well suited to South American tropical forest and riverine environments.[10] Today most Amazonian peoples are engaged with the commercial world, and they continue to make a living from the rain forest, while conducting various commercial activities as citizens of modern nation-states.

The importance of Amazonian biodiversity is exemplified by Conservation International's designation of the Tropical Andes as a Biodiversity Hotspot, one of just thirty-four exceptionally rich biogeographic areas in the world which are especially threatened by human activities.[11] The Peruvian section of the Tropical Andes is home to the Asháninka as well as numerous other indigenous groups and is now blanketed by newly created national parks, protected areas, communal reserves, and titled indigenous community lands. The indigenous peoples who have always lived here are well equipped by their cultural heritage to be the best custodians of these biological treasures, and they now have legal authority to continue to protect their territories. However, overall, these regions are also threatened by uncontrolled logging, colonization, gold mining, the drug trade, anti-government militants, and contradictory support from the World Bank, the Inter-American Development Bank (IDB), and national governments for oil and gas development, large-scale timber concessions, new highways, and dam construction.[12]

Conservation biologists have characterized Amazonia as "the greatest tropical wilderness area on the planet," stressing its strategic benefits for the entire world. It is "the world's most important biological asset" because of its immense productivity and biodiversity.[13] Amazonian forests, rivers, and wildlife are all interconnected in a single vast ecosystem.[14] The biological productivity of tropical rain forest is three to five times that of most temperate forests, and the total biomass (weight of plants and animals per hectare) is among the highest of any terrestrial ecosystem. Worldwide, tropical forests potentially cover only 6 percent of the earth's land surface yet contain half of all species. The

Amazon is also the world's largest river system, and it accounts for nearly 20 percent of the world's freshwater flowing into the oceans. Conservationists designate much of the Amazon as "wilderness" in comparison to areas that have been more impacted by human activities. Conservation International, one of the largest and most influential conservation organizations in the world, officially defines "wilderness" as areas of 10,000 square kilometers or more, where at least 70 percent of the original vegetation remains and population density is under five persons per square kilometer.[15] By this definition most of Amazonia where indigenous people live can be considered wilderness and probably has been throughout prehistory, but it has also been extensively shaped by human activities. Classifications of anthropogenic biomes mapping human impacts on the global landscape show that most of Amazonia is still either "remote forests" with less than one person per square kilometer or "wild forests" with so few people that their presence is barely visible.[16]

Living successfully in the Peruvian tropical forest region means people must share the space with a truly amazing variety of other life forms. Overall there are 1,792 species of birds in Peru, and most live in the Tropical Andes hotspot and adjacent tropical lowlands.[17] There are 20,000 unique plant species and some 1,500 unique vertebrates in the Tropical Andes, and dozens of distinct habitat types. Surviving here requires that people have an impressive array of very specific environmental knowledge that must be produced, continuously verified, stored, and transmitted to each generation. I was introduced to a small sample of this knowledge one evening when I loaned my portable audio recorder to a small group of Asháninka who were visiting my camp. They immediately created a word game in which they excitedly passed the microphone back and forth, recording a steady stream of Asháninka words. They were spontaneously reciting a seemingly endless list of animal names, playing with their working knowledge of rain forest biodiversity.

Biodiversity is the foundation of the Asháninka way of life, and they treat nature as "natural capital." It is their investment in the future. The Asháninka not only know the names of the animals but they understand many details of their natural history and imbue many species with rich cultural significance. I later found that the Asháninka's knowledge of rain forest animals is matched by their knowledge of useful cultivated plants. I found dozens of named varieties of manioc and bananas in Asháninka gardens. People continually experimented with new varieties and were eager to discuss their different qualities. It is not surprising that rain forest peoples are interested in biological diversity, because it is the very source of their existence. Isolated Asháninka groups that I visited in the 1960s were entirely self-sufficient. With the exception of a few metal pots, knives, and axes, they found materials for everything they needed in their forest and gardens. They made their own houses, implements, food, medicine, and clothing directly from the raw materials that they extracted from their local environment.

The high biological productivity of the tropical forest does not automatically mean high human carrying capacity, because the forest puts much of its energy into the production of what for people is inedible wood and leaves. Except along the main rivers, soil fertility is often naturally very low and would be easily depleted by intensive cultivation. There is little readily harvested carbohydrate in the natural vegetation, and 90 percent of the animal biomass is composed of ants, termites, and other small invertebrates that can eat leaves and wood.[18] Large vertebrates are relatively scarce, and animal protein is difficult for hunters to secure because game is often nocturnal or hidden in the forest canopy. Natural food resources for people are so scarce that some authorities have argued that no one could live in the rain forest without access to garden produce.[19]

Manioc (*Manihot esculenta*) is the most important Asháninka food crop. It is an abundant source of carbohydrates, making it the key to successful human occupation of Amazonia. The productivity of manioc is truly impressive and readily explains its importance in the subsistence system. It provides more than two-thirds of their food by weight. I found that a single Asháninka household garden could produce some 30,000 kilograms of manioc in a year. This is five times a household's normal requirements and provides an important security margin.

Manioc production depends on a specialized system of shifting cultivation that minimally disrupts the forest ecosystem. It is the forest that ultimately maintains soil quality, regulates the local climate, recycles nutrients and water, and sustains the fish and game which are the crucial protein resources. With shifting cultivation food is harvested from small, temporary forest clearings containing mixed gardens. In comparison with the large monocrop farms and plantations that have recently been introduced in Amazonia for commercial purposes, Asháninka gardens rely on a diverse mix of plant species, thereby minimizing erosion and losses to insects and disease while making efficient use of the space. Asháninka gardens typically are about a hectare (2.5 acres) or less in size. They use a forest fallow system in which a plot usually would not be replanted for at least twenty-five years to allow ample time for forest regrowth. Full forest regrowth might require fifty to 100 years or more, but as long as gardens remain small and widely scattered, a twenty-five-year cycle can adequately protect the forest. Shifting cultivation works well until large-scale commercial agriculture invades tribal areas, displacing subsistence cultivators, and pushing them into marginal areas where they are forced to shorten the fallow cycle. Under these conditions shifting cultivation cannot be sustained, and people and lands are impoverished.

The Asháninka have very small, relatively impermanent settlements and very low-density populations, representing the extreme small end of the size scale. These scale features maximize individual freedom, access to natural resources, community autonomy, security, and overall sustainability. Because the Asháninka primarily live away from the major rivers and combine hunting and foraging with small gardens, their villages usually remain small, often only a dozen or so people in a few related families. People who chose to locate near missions, schools, and medical posts, or who want access to markets may live in larger, more permanent communities of up to a few hundred people. Small villages are relatively impermanent, as villagers can relocate every few years. In the 1960s, the Asháninka may have averaged only 0.4 persons per square kilometer, suggesting that the size, density, and permanence of human settlements were also determined in part by cultural factors such as beliefs about what constituted the good life. It seems likely that the human advantages of small-scale society encourage people to halt gardening, hunting, and fishing production at levels well below what would be theoretically sustainable. Cultural preferences for larger game animals, maximum leisure, and household-level autonomy seem to be more important objectives than supporting the largest possible villages. It seems that the tropical forest village way of life offers Amazonian peoples sufficient personal satisfactions that they choose to maintain and reproduce it as long as they have enough personal freedom to make that choice.

ASHÁNINKA REGIONAL ASSOCIATIONS
AND THE SIRA COMUNAL RESERVE

What do we want? . . . To recover to the maximum our ancestral territories as the only survival guarantee for our peoples and for the development of our future generations . . . . To protect our autonomous indigenous brothers that took the free determination of continuing with our ancestral customs, removing themselves from the large cities and remaining free within our Amazonian forests.—Alberto Pizango Chota, AIDESEP President, 2012-2014[20]

The Asháninka are now part of a federation of indigenous political organizations affiliated with the Inter-Ethnic Association for the Development of the Peruvian Rainforest (AIDESEP),[21] which was formed in 1980 by an alliance of tribal Aguaruna, Huambisa, and Asháninka political leaders. AIDESEP is a crucial organization because it links local indigenous communities to other organizations of indigenous peoples at national and international levels where they can press their claims for self-determination and defense of their territories and natural resources. By 2008 AIDESEP had become an organization representing 350,000 indigenous peoples living in 1,350 communities from sixteen language families. There were fifty-seven ethnic federations grouped into six regional organizations. AIDESEP is itself a member of COICA, the Coordinating Body for the Indigenous Organizations of the Amazon Basin, which is a network of representative indigenous organizations from all Amazonian countries. COICA is a member of The International Alliance of Indigenous and Tribal Peoples of Tropical Forests (IAITPTF), which is recognized by UN agencies such as the United Nations Forum on Forests. Indigenous groups also have access to the UN Permanent Forum on Indigenous Issues (UNPFII), and are being recognized within the United Nations Framework Convention on Climate Change (UNFCCC). This means that now even some of the most isolated indigenous groups can press their human rights claims through UN agencies, especially to protect their natural environment within the terms of the UN Declaration on the Rights of Indigenous Peoples (UNDRIP).

By 1985, sixteen years after I met Chonkiri, the Ashaninka big man, and his group in the Gran Pajonal, these formerly very isolated peoples had become the officially registered Native Community of Shumahuani with 358 people holding legal title to nearly 50 km^2 of territory within their traditional homeland. The Shumahuani community then became a member of the Gran Pajonal Ashéninka Organization (OAGP), which belonged to the Regional Organization of the Indigenous Peoples of AIDESEP-Ucayali (ORAU). This network of organizations for the first time ever gave them a global level voice that would have been unimaginable only a few decades earlier. This organizational hierarchy parallels similar organizations formed by other indigenous small nations such as the Inuit peoples of Nunuvat in the Canadian arctic and in Kalaallit Nunaat, both referred to in chapter 4.

After completing my dissertation research with the Asháninka in 1972, I proposed that the Peruvian government officially recognize the territories that the Asháninka occupied as their land, and allow them to control entry by outsiders as an exercise of their cultural autonomy. This would have acknowledged them to in effect be a small arcadian nation.[22] This was a realistic proposal given that most of this area was considered unsuitable for large-scale commercial agriculture, contained no important mineral resources, and was best maintained as a protected watershed. I also recommended that very large reserves be established on the best agricultural soils to give market-oriented Asháninka a competitive advantage. Later I called this approach the "cultural autonomy alternative" because it would allow tribal peoples the opportunity to maintain their independence. Cultural autonomy specified three key points:

1. National governments and international organizations must recognize and support tribal rights to their traditional land, cultural autonomy, and full local sovereignty.
2. The responsibility for initiating outside contacts must rest with the tribal people themselves: outside influences may not have free access to tribal areas.
3. Industrial states must not compete with tribal societies for their resources.[23]

More than thirty years later, these basic principles of cultural autonomy were at last fully incorporated in the 2007 United Nations Declaration of Indigenous Rights, especially as expressed in the provisions of Article 26[24] discussed in the previous chapter.

In 1996 with the passage of Peru's Law of Protected Natural Areas (Ley de Areas Naturales Protegidas, Ley No. 26834) it became possible for the government to establish specific protected natural areas whose natural condition would be "maintained in perpetuity" to conserve biological diversity as well as associated cultural values as part of the national patrimony. As of 2006 nine different categories of Protected Areas were recognized, including National Parks, Communal Reserves, and Reserved Zones that especially affected indigenous peoples in the Amazon. Protected Areas could also be surrounded by designated buffer zones to guarantee the conservation of the Protected Area itself. Communal Reserves are designed to conserve natural resources for the benefit of the indigenous residents and neighboring rural populations. Any commercial development of the resources must be according to management plans carried out by the beneficiaries themselves.

Much of Asháninka territory has been incorporated into this system of Protected Natural Areas. The El Sira Communal Reserve in the area where I had conducted my fieldwork in the 1960s was established in 2001 to protect the Sira Range between the Ucyali and Pichis-Pachitea Rivers for the benefit of all the indigenous people living in the region. Comprising more than 6,000 km^2 , the El Sira Reserve is the largest of four reserves established for the Arawak speaking Asháninka, Asheninka, Yanesha, and Machigenga peoples by 2004. The Asháninka and Machigenga Communal Reserves immediately south of the El Sira were situated on either side of the Otishi National Park which protected the Vilcabamba range. Altogether, these reserves, the park, and the San Carlos Protected Forest take up more than 15,000 km^2.

Creating this vast system of protected areas was an enormous effort involving many organizations and funding from many sources. IWGIA carried out some of the original planning for El Sira beginning in the early 1990s. The World Bank and the UN Global Environmental Facility, with 10 percent matching funds from the Peruvian government, contributed some $2 million dollars to fund the El Sira project over five years. The communal reserves are to be managed according to master plans developed by the indigenous peoples themselves with technical support from nonprofit, nongovernmental organizations including the Instituto de Bien Común[25] and CEDIA (the Center for Development of the Indigenous Amazon).[26] These NGOs have also supported indigenous land titling projects for many years. The master plans will detail how specific areas can be used sustainably to benefit local people. Some 14,750 indigenous people were living within the El Sira buffer zone, and some 25,000–30,000 people in 400 communities were living in the region.[27] These protected areas adjoin and sometimes overlap titled indigenous community lands, and in combination create a truly remarkable system for protecting peoples, their societies and cultures, and the natural ecosystems that sustain them. It is too soon to predict how this ambitious plan will unfold, but it can be hoped that it will optimize the ability of the Asháninka to continue to be effective custodians of their natural resources.

Until recently many tribal societies existed in Amazonia as still independent small nations with only minimal direct influences from the commercial world.[28] Anthropologists estimated in 2009 that 50 to 100 independent tribal groups were still living in voluntary isolation from the outside world in forested areas throughout the Amazon.[29] The new protected areas in Peru may afford them some continuing refuge. AIDESEP President Alberto Pizango Chota specifically includes protection for these people as "our autonomous brothers" in his above-cited "What do we want" statement.

DOMINICA: NATURE ISLAND OF THE CARIBBEAN

Although I had long been concerned with scale as a crucial sociocultural variable, most of my field research had focused on the scale extremes looking at either tribal societies or America and the global system. That changed when I visited the very small Caribbean micro-nation of Dominica in 2007 at the invitation of my colleagues at Washington State University, Robert and Marsha Quinlan, who were running our department's cultural anthropology field school in Dominica and who had conducted village level medical and ethnographic research there since 1993.[30]

Dominica (not to be confused with the much larger Dominican Republic) is a small volcanic island in the Windward Islands of the Lesser Antilles in the Eastern Caribbean, situated within sight of the French islands of Guadeloupe and Martinique. Dominica is about thirty miles long and twelve air miles wide at the widest points, but volcanic peaks reaching to nearly 5,000 feet dominate the rugged and heavily forested

interior. It is almost impossible to find enough flat ground to accommodate even a modestly sized commercial prop plane, and landing is always an adventure. Best known to outsiders as the place where *Pirates
of the Caribbean* was filmed, the island is also justly famous for having
the best preserved tropical forest in the Eastern Caribbean. Dominica
still supports two endemic, critically endangered wild parrot species,
one of which, the imperial parrot, *Amazona imperialis*, is featured on
Dominica's coat of arms. At the time of my visit the total population was
estimated at about 72,000 people, including 2,000 indigenous Caribs.
Its beautiful and well-protected natural environment, along with its
self-designation as the "nature island of the Caribbean," certainly qualify Dominica as an arcadian small nation.

When Columbus visited Dominica in 1493 he found it occupied by
village gardeners and fishing peoples known as the Kalinago, who spoke
Arawak and Carib languages and whose ancestors were from Amazonia.
Dominica was later visited by Spanish, English, and French adventur-
ers, missionaries, and colonists, and for a time it was treated as a neutral
territory and remained in Kalinago control. By the 1780s the British
were fully in control and established a plantation economy variously
based on coffee or sugar and imported African slave labor. The British
made Dominica a colony in 1805. Slavery was officially abolished in
1834, and although settlers attempted to maintain large estates, the
former slave population successfully gained control over the government and the land. The Commonwealth of Dominica has been a politically independent state since gaining independence from Britain in
1978.[31]

I was especially drawn to Dominica because it ranked number four
of 179 nations in the 2006 Happy Planet Index.[32] This super high score
was due to Dominica's high reported life satisfaction as well as its high
life expectancy of seventy-six years. This was amplified by a very low per
capita ecological footprint of under two global hectares, compared with
the average American footprint which approaches 10 global hectares.
Dominica also ranks "high" on the UN Human Development Index
which takes into account health, education, and income distribution.
What was remarkable about these very positive scores was that Dominica has a very small economy and was ranked by the World Bank as only
an "upper middle" income country with a PPP income of just $8,296
per capita in 2007. It is officially a relatively underdeveloped country. If

exchange rate GDP is used, per capita GDP drops to just $3,854. The PPP value gives Dominica credit for low prices for its abundant locally produced basic goods and indirectly for its strong subsistence economy, but when Dominican's engage in global trade the exchange rate operates to their disadvantage. A small nation like Dominica demonstrates that what matters is not how big a country's economy is, but how it is organized, and that if well distributed, even very small financial flows through households, businesses and governments can meet human needs and serve the public interest.

Although its local businesses are small, Dominica is certainly not unconnected from the global economy. The country has no stock market and thus no market capitalization ranking, but there were four publicly traded businesses headquartered in Dominica: Dominica Coconut Products Ltd, Dominica Electricity Services, the National Bank of Dominica Ltd, and Dominica Brewery & Beverages Ltd. These were listed on the Eastern Caribbean Securities Exchange on the island nation of St. Kitts. The largest commercial bank in Dominica had assets of US$246 million producing revenues of nearly US$22 million in 2007. Dominica is a member of the Organization of Eastern Caribbean States, and its currency, the Eastern Caribbean dollar, is shared with seven other Eastern Caribbean island governments linked by the Eastern Caribbean Bank which had total assets of a modest US$892 million in 2009.

The development paradox of Dominica is that although it ranks high for human well-being, according to a special report published by the Caribbean Development Bank in 2003, 29 percent of households and 39 percent of the population were officially "income poor" measured against a poverty line of an income of US$1,260 per adult per year.[33] Fifteen percent were considered "indigent" or "very poor" with incomes under US$740. The Bank report elaborated on the apparent paradox, noting that the people themselves ". . . speak of good infrastructure, housing and natural environment, adequate supplies of water, excellent access to health and education, and a tradition of well integrated, self-supporting communities. Many strongly decry the idea that they are poor indicating a clear lack of correlation, in this instance, between income poverty and well-being."[34]

Furthermore, the report noted that the country was a democracy, there was little crime, no human rights abuses, children were educated, food was plentiful, water was clean, and overall health was good. There were health clinics throughout the country, no access problems; free contraception; mass immunizations; and a low incidence, or nonexistence of poverty-linked health problems. The report also found that most people owned their own homes, and they noted that "traditional healthy diets of ground provisions [yams, manioc, and taro] and fish continue to be popular and there is little evidence of obesity or malnutrition." Nearly 90 percent of those considered "poor" owned their own homes, and nearly half owned televisions and phones; a third of those who were officially "not poor" owned vehicles.

My observations verified these upbeat descriptions, with some qualifications. I found Dominicans to be healthy, self-confident people, who seemed in control of their lives. Only about twelve men in the capital were considered to be "homeless." One of these homeless men who I chatted with in Roseau, the capital city, told me he had lost his job in New York and sometimes slept in the city park. Many Dominicans lived abroad and sent home remittances. Nevertheless, local businesses were thriving. There were virtually no fast food franchises and no shopping malls. The farmers market and street vendors were the major suppliers of fresh produce in the capital, and the entire island was a nation of small business owners and small farmers and fishermen. Rural families are strongly matrifocal, and women have an important role in the subsistence economy. Women also market their produce to other islands.

I thought that perhaps part of Dominica's success might be found in the country's founding documents and spent most of one morning in the capital city locating a print copy of the 1978 Dominican Constitution as amended through 1984. The preamble connected human rights and economic rights, social justice, and belief in God, declaring:

> Whereas the People of Dominica (a) have affirmed that the Commonwealth of Dominica is founded upon principles that acknowledge the supremacy of God, faith in fundamental human rights and freedoms, the position of the family in a society of free men and free institutions, the dignity of the human person, and the equal and inalienable rights with which all members of the human family are endowed by their Creator.

Part (b) of the preamble is so important that I quote it in full:

[Dominica is founded on principles that] "(b). respect the principles of social justice and therefore believe that the operation of the economic system should result in so distributing the material resources of the community as to subserve the common good, that there should be adequate means of livelihood for all, that labour should not be exploited or forced by economic necessity to operate in inhumane conditions but that there should be opportunity for advancement on the basis of recognition of merit, ability and integrity . . . ."

Clearly, Dominican people are very conscious of how their economic system is organized, and they want it to be fair and to serve human interests. It is not a deliberately ecodemia economy, but the effect is the same, because there are so few very large businesses. That economic rights and social justice were so strong is perhaps not surprising for a government controlled by the descendants of freed slaves. Governments have a major presence on the island and people are very politically engaged. There are ten local parish governments ranging in size from about 1500 to just over 10,000 people, in addition to three urban councils, the Carib Council, and thirty-seven village councils. Roseau, the largest city has fewer than 20,000 people. There is a president and prime minister and a thirty-member House of Assembly. There are four political parties, and political campaigns are intense.

Three years before visiting Dominica, I visited the Hawaiian island of Kauai, and now I can do some comparisons. Both are tropical islands with small land areas and small populations of similar magnitudes. Both have indigenous populations and similar histories of conquest and plantation economies with imported laborers. Both consider the development of nature tourism to be important goals. The big contrast is that as part of the United States, Kauai has a very large commercial economy. Both islands have high life expectancy, but Kauai represents America's position as 150th in the Happy Planet Index because of its high environmental footprint reflecting its large fossil fuel–dependent economy. Kauai has a $2 billion economy, measured as total personal income, twice Dominica's PPP GDP of under $1 billion, or just $279 million as measured in exchange rate dollars. Given their respective populations this gives Kauai a per capita income three to eight times greater than Dominica's. The annual budgets of each government are approximately the same, but on Dominica it represents 25 percent of the PPP GDP, or two-thirds of the exchange rate GDP, whereas on Kauai it is only 8 percent of total personal income. This means that the private commercial economy is much more important on Kauai.

Paradoxically, even though Kauai has a highly developed economy, a baseline report in 2000 found that more than a third of Kauai households were not making a living wage, allowing them to qualify as "economically needy."[35] This is about the same level of official poverty as in Dominica, but the crucial difference was that people on Dominica had land and were maintaining a viable subsistence economy. Much of Kauai's agricultural land was locked away in large privately held properties. The outlying seventy square mile island of Niihau is owned by just two families. The effects of Kauai's historic plantation era have not disappeared, whereas Dominica effectively redistributed its land to its residents. Development on Kauai has not benefited everyone.

Given the prevailing high property values and low wages, fewer than half of Kauai's households were homeowners in 2000.[36] Many housing units were second homes for nonresidents or were rented to tourists. This means that how money and resources are actually distributed in a regional economy may be more important than total income and wealth. Growth appears to be less important than the actual distribution of ownership and benefits. For example, although tourism is important in the economies of both islands, in Dominica hotels are primarily small and locally owned. The largest hotel has only seventy rooms. In contrast, there are many large hotels on Kauai, and the largest are likely to be owned by very large external corporations. For example, the Sheraton Kauai Resort on the south coast of Kauai has 394 rooms and is owned by Starwood Hotels & Resorts Worldwide headquartered in New York. Starwood owned fifty-three hotels with 18,000 rooms worldwide, and produced total revenues of nearly $6 billion in 2007. Its Kauai Resort produced an estimated $50 million in revenue, given its average returns per room. Starwood's largest owner was Fidelity Management & Research (FMR). This connects Kauai with the global plutonomy. FMR was the second largest owner-manager in the global stock market backbone discussed in chapter 12, and was dominant in thirty-two national stock markets and managed global assets of $1 trillion. It was itself privately owned and run by American billionaire Ned Johnson.

The size and ownership of retail establishments on each island also showed significant contrasts. For example, Dominica's largest retailer had revenues of just $20 million and was locally owned. The Walmart on Kauai produced estimated revenues of about $40 million, but 40 percent of its profits went to the five billionaire Walton families living in Arkansas, Texas, and Wyoming. Walmart's largest institutional owner, was again FMR, and it received nearly 3 percent of Walmart's profits. It is likely that very little of Walmart profit would have gone to Kauai residents, and many of Walmart's Kauai employees were likely among those receiving sub-living wages. These are significant cultural differences that represent very different ways of organizing a commercial system. Both Dominica and Kauai are "nature islands," but only Dominica can be called an arcadian small nation and that can make a huge difference for quality of life.

BOLIVIA: THE RIGHTS OF MOTHER EARTH

Bolivia is a remarkable example of a small nation (population just under 10 million in 2010) that elected an indigenous person, Evo Morales, an Aymara Indian, as president in 2005, and then strengthened its legal protections of nature. Given the strong indigenous perspective underpinning the new Bolivian Constitution, and the fact that approximately 60 percent of the population self-identifies as "indigenous," it is perhaps not surprising that in December of 2010 the National Assembly approved Law 071, the Law of Rights of Mother Earth[37] which obligates the Bolivian state and society to make sure that human activities are conducted in harmony with Mother Earth (*Pachamama*). The objective is for the earth and its life systems to be able to absorb and recover from the damages caused by people in order for present and future generations to *vivir bien* or "live well." Again this is the essence of the values we might expect in an arcadian small nation. The earth's life systems are not to be commercialized or privately owned, and the cultural values, knowledge, and practices that seek harmony with nature are to be respected.

The law declares Mother Earth to be a legal collective person of public interest, much like a commercial corporation. This is much in line with international laws recognizing business corporations as legal persons with specific rights, for example, the United States Supreme Court *Citizens United* decision in 2010 granted political rights of free speech to corporations. The Mother Earth law, in combination with the fact that Bolivia already has more than 20 percent of its territory in officially designated protected areas, makes it an obvious example of an arcadian small nation. It has one of the highest proportions of its territory in conservation areas of any country in the world. It is hard to imagine very many large nations having the political ability to reach a similar consensus to legally protect Mother Earth. Like its Peruvian neighbor, much of Bolivia is within the Tropical Andean Biodiversity Hotspot, so this makes legal protection for Mother Earth super important for the world.

Mother Earth is *Pachamama* for indigenous Andean peoples and is the earth's biosphere, the geochemical cycles that sustain life, organisms, and ecosystems. It is equivalent to the ancient Greek goddess Gaia and fits nicely with the Greek concept of arcadia. As a legal entity Mother Earth also specifically includes human beings and their cultural systems. In Article 7 of the Bolivian law, Mother Earth has the right to life, biodiversity, pure water, clean air, balanced natural cycles, the restoration of humanly disturbed systems, and to be free of toxic and radioactive wastes. The law requires the state to not only develop policies to protect the earth, but to also work at the international level for the adoption of similar measures.

Bolivia demonstrates that a broadly supported and nonviolent popular movement for social justice can also lead to political solutions to many human problems. Bolivia's indigenous majority is attempting to transform their country by drawing on cultural models from their national heritage in the tribal world and ancient Andean civilizations to help diagnose problems and find their own political path to sustainable development. Bolivia had the largest indigenous Amerindian population in South America in 2006. Nearly two million highland Bolivians speak Aymara and another three million speak Quechua, the language of the Inca Empire. There are also thousands of indigenous people living in small groups in the lowlands speaking some thirty-four other indigenous languages.[38] There are also other small little-known tribal groups living in voluntary isolation from the dominant society.[39] Bolivia is also rich in other natural resources including silver, tin, and fossil fuels, but paradoxically in 2006 it remained one of the poorest and most indebted countries in South America, even after following a vigorous IMF mandated structural adjustment program for more than two decades. Bolivia also faces serious threats from global warming, because

Andean mountain glaciers that supply critical water to its largest cities and irrigated agriculture are melting rapidly.

The World Bank and IMF consider Bolivia to be an HIPC (Heavily Indebted Poor Country). In 2006 the Bolivian government's external debt stood at just over $3 billion U.S. dollars, which represented about $317 dollars per capita. That may seem like a small amount, but it looms large in a country where more than a third of the population lives below the official poverty line and 75 percent do not have access to sanitation facilities. It is not irrelevant that in 2006 the world's 313 richest HNWIs had personal net worths of $3 billion or more, and were thus individually each worth more than Bolivia's debt.[40]

Contemporary Bolivian poverty can be understood as the heritage of a long history of exploitation by outsiders that began with the Spanish conquest in 1524. The indigenous imperial societies that preceded the Spanish were not totally benign, but the traditional rulers extracted labor from a largely self-sufficient rural population, who remained wealthy in their access to nature and culture and apparently did not feel unduly exploited. Even under Inca rule, local people remained in control of their local natural resources, managed their community affairs, and apparently believed the imperial system to be fair. The pre-Hispanic Andean rulers wisely constructed their empire to resemble a large family operated according to reciprocal exchange and carefully balanced complementary oppositions. Under Spanish rule, the new ruling elite confiscated local communally owned lands and concentrated them into vast privately held estates for the benefit of a handful of wealthy families. The indigenous people were impoverished and turned into landless serfs. Many were forced to work in the fabulously rich Potosí silver mines under inhuman conditions that caused horrendous mortality, as the wealth they produced was exported to Spain. There were many rebellions by Andean peoples, but they were unable to gain control over the political system. Formal independence from Spain in 1825 did not empower the majority and was followed by more than a century and a half of almost continuous political and economic turmoil. The government's external debt stood at over $5 billion (in constant 2005 U.S. dollars) by 1981 after a decade of military rule and political instability caused Bolivia's international credit rating to be downgraded and its currency to collapse. Per capita GDP dropped precipitously.

In response to the economic crisis, in 1985 the Bolivian government adopted severe structural adjustments called for by the IMF.[41] Structural adjustment in this case meant privatizing government-owned enterprises, selling off much of the nation's productive capital including its mining, railroads, communications, and oil companies to largely foreign investors who laid off workers. This was similar to what happened in Chile under Pinochet. Many angry and frustrated people began an intensive period of political mobilization and public demonstrations.

The turning point in Bolivian politics occurred in 1999 when the municipal government of Cochabamba privatized its public water system, signing a contract with a foreign-owned corporation, Aguas del Tunari. This decision inadvertently set off the "Water Wars" that helped people mobilize for the political transformation of their entire country. Cochabamba was then Bolivia's fourth-largest city with a greater metropolitan population of nearly a million people. People were outraged when they saw their water rates suddenly rise and when they learned that a new national law made local neighborhood and household water systems illegal. People believed that they could not even legally collect rainwater from their roofs. They also believed Aguas del Tunari had been granted an outrageously generous contract.

Aguas del Tunari was held by a consortium of corporate owners in Spain, England, Italy, and the United States, but at the top of the ownership hierarchy the principal owner of Aguas, and now Cochabamba's water system, was the Bechtel Group, a global engineering giant. At that time Bechtel was ranked as the fifth largest privately held corporation in the United States with revenues of $15 billion, which was nearly double Bolivia's GDP. By 2010 Bechtel's revenues had grown to $30 billion, and it was America's largest engineering company and third largest private corporation after Cargill and Koch Industries.[42] About 40 percent of Bechtel was owned by billionaire Stephen Bechtel Jr. and his son, and corporate CEO, Riley Bechtel, each worth $2.7 billion in 2007.[43] This suggests that the Bechtel Group itself was worth some $13 billion, more than five times the market capitalization of all the corporations listed on the Bolivian stock exchange. It is perhaps significant that Bechtel has been involved in numerous massive-scale energy and infrastructure projects worldwide. Bechtel built the Hoover Dam, the Trans-Alaska Pipeline, the Channel Tunnel, and one of China's largest petrochemical plants. Bechtel treats nuclear waste at the Hanford nuclear facility in Washington State, and took a major role in rebuilding Iraq after the war. Bolivian municipal water was a minor project for Bechtel.

It is not surprising that Bolivians sensed injustice and decided that they needed to change the political economy of their country and the terms of their relationship to the global system. All of this was an important precursor for passage of the Rights of Mother Earth. The Bolivian people understandably equated water with life, and the mass protests that followed the privatization of Cochabamba's water system quickly forced the government to renounce their contract with Aguas del Tunari in 2000. However, the protest helped fuel a larger social movement that by 2005 had catapulted one political party into national power, the Movement for Socialism—Political Instrument for the Sovereignty of the Peoples (MAS-IPSP).[44] This was the political banner that carried Morales to the presidency and changed the national agenda. Following the Morales election the people of Bolivia embarked on a vast transformation of their entire political economy.

Bolivia established a new Constituent Assembly in 2006 and approved a new constitution in 2009 that declared Bolivia to be a plurinational and communitary state. The new Bolivian Constitution is a remarkable document produced by people who adopted universal moral principles that they accepted as superior to the narrow economic goals, individualism, and market-based ideologies that had guided previous regimes. The new preamble declares:

> We build a new State. . . . A State based on respect and equality for all, with principles of sovereignty, dignity, complementarity, solidarity, harmony and equality in the distribution and redistribution of the social product, where the pursuit of the good life [*del vivir bien*] predominates; with respect for the economic, social, judicial, political, and cultural plurality of the inhabitants of this land; living together collectively with access to water, employment, education, health, and housing for everyone. [45]

Bolivia hosted a "World People's Conference on Climate Change and the Rights of Mother Earth" in Cochabamba in 2010 which endorsed a "Peoples Agreement" on climate change and called for alternatives to global capitalism that included a "Universal Declaration of the Rights of Mother Earth."[46] The Peoples Agreement advocates a new global de-

velopment model based on equity and "living well," and calls for cooperative international action to reduce carbon emissions to prevent global warming from rising above 2 degrees centigrade. The long-term
goal is to return atmospheric carbon dioxide levels to 300 ppm which
were last seen in 1909. At the urging of Bolivia and fifty other nations,
in 2011 the UN General Assembly proclaimed April 22 "International
Mother Earth Day," but many of the largest nations still resist making
the fundamental changes that protecting the earth would require.

In late 2010 the Bolivian Ministry of Economy and Public Finance
produced a "didactic" booklet showing that the country's New Model
was in fact already working even when viewed by standard economic
measures. Bolivia's international financial reserves increased significantly between 2005 and 2010. Bolivia's GDP was growing. Inflation
was down, and the government showed budget surpluses rather than
the deficits experienced between 1985 and 2005. The ministry also
noted that the World Bank moved Bolivia from its "low income" to
"medium income" ranking in 2009. Bolivia also received approving
comments from the IMF and the InterAmerican Development Bank in
2009, and saw its bond ratings elevated by the major bond ranking
agencies including Fitch, Moody's and Standard and Poors.

SMALL ISLAND NATIONS ON THE
GLOBAL WARMING FRONTIER

> Ultimately, the success of the island nations in responding to and
> combating the maze of modern environment threats and dangers will
> stand as a litmus test for the rest of the world. If we fail this test in
> our small island communities, I can guarantee you, we will fail the
> test on a global level. For our sake, and for the sake of future genera-
> tions, failure cannot be an option. —H.E. Tommy E. Remengesau
> Jr., president of the Republic of Palau [47]

Many small island nations quietly gained their independence from colonial rule after 1950 but remained off the world political stage until 1989
when the UN Intergovernmental Panel on Climate Change (IPCC)
issued its first report warning of the dangers of global warming. Recognizing their vulnerability to rising sea levels, small island nations immediately began forging a political identity for self-defense by forming an

Action Group at the "Small States Conference on Sea Level Rise" hosted by the Maldives. Their group became AOSIS, the Association of Small Island States, at the 1990 Second World Climate Conference where they advocated for the creation of the UN Framework Convention on Climate Change (UNFCCC), which was adopted in 1992 and came into force for 194 nations in 1994. AOSIS representatives played a major role as an intergovernmental organization in the negotiations that led to the adoption of the UNFCCC Kyoto Protocol in 1997. Facing the specter of being flooded into oblivion, small island nations understandably took an aggressive stance against the large greenhouse gas emitters. During negotiations in 1994 AOSIS proposed a target of a 20 percent reduction in greenhouse gases from the 1990 base by 2005, whereas the United States advocated simply returning to 1990 levels. AOSIS remains actively involved in post-Kyoto negotiations.

Small island developing states (SIDS) were singled out for special treatment in Chapter 17.G of *Agenda 21*, the UN global action plan for sustainable development in the twenty-first century drawn up at the 1992 Rio Earth Summit. *Agenda 21* recognized that small island nations are remote from the economic and financial centers of the global economy, their land and freshwater resources are often limited, and they rely heavily on coastal areas, reefs, and fisheries.[48] They were also special because "their small size, limited resources, geographic dispersion and isolation from markets, place them at a disadvantage economically and prevent economies of scale."[49] It was also recognized that small islands often had unique flora, fauna, and cultures. It was stressed that islands were especially vulnerable to sea-level rise and storms caused by global warming, and advocated the creation of special action plans supported by international organizations to help these small nations develop sustainably.

Small island nations quickly became the pioneer test case for sustainable development and the international response to global warming. Following the opening provided by Agenda 21, AOSIS helped organize a UN-sponsored Conference on the Sustainable Development of Small Island Developing States in Barbados in 1994 that was attended by representatives of 125 countries and territories, including forty-six small islands nations; fifty-three international commissions, UN bodies and programs, special agencies, and organizations; and eighty-nine non-governmental organizations. This was a remarkable mobilization of human effort and resources. The Barbados Conference developed a detailed Programme of Action, putting climate change and sea-level rise first on the their list of concerns, and proposing partnerships between governments, intergovernmental organization, and nongovernmental organizations (NGOs) to help small island nations achieve sustainable development.

The UN went even further in 1995 by setting up a special Small Island Developing States (SIDS) unit within the UN Department of Economic and Social Affairs (DESA). Fifty-one nations with 59 million people were designated as SIDS, and all but one, Cuba, were small nations with fewer than ten million people. Another international conference held in Mauritius in 2005 reaffirmed the original Barbados Action Plan and called for the establishment of a Global Island Partnership (GLISPA) which was established in 2006 as a program within the Convention on Biological Diversity. GLISPA networks fourteen island nations with 35 international agencies and organizations, and a dozen other governments including large wealthy nations such as Australia, the European Union, France, Germany, Italy, New Zealand, the United Kingdom, and the United States.[50] GLISPA is another addition to an expanding international network of networks promoting sustainable development. This is a headless, nonhierarchical web, or heterarchy, in which even the United Nations Secretariat itself, although a crucial hub, is not the director. No single great economic power is in control. This is truly a newly evolving form of global organization that can be a model for how a small nation world could be structured.

In confronting global warming and sea level rise small island nations and small nations generally help show what institutional functions are really necessary to maintain a high quality of life. For example, public health and formal education are certainly necessities, but very small nations may have difficulty providing a hospital and equipping it with expensive diagnostic equipment. Very small nations may not be able to provide post-secondary education to their citizens. Small governments are unlikely to maintain a military establishment, and they may have only a very small police force and limited legal system. They may have no central bank and currency, and government departments or ministries may have multiple functions. They may have only a very small private commercial sector, and the government may produce and distribute electricity, maintain telecommunications, and own and operate business enterprises to import, store, and distribute basic commodities rather than leaving this to private business.

As described above in their response to global warming, small nations have been quietly helping to create a vast network of nations, international organizations, and nongovernmental organizations that are dedicated to the spirit and practice of sustainable development overall. This "new global partnership"[51] is quite the opposite of the existing global commercial hierarchy of giant corporations which are solely dedicated to accumulating financial capital for the benefit of a few institutional shareholders and high net worth individuals. The sustainability issues that confront small island nations are dramatically obvious, but they are not fundamentally different from the issues that confront all nations, and the international network solutions that are working for small island nations can work for all nations. Small islands require sustainable development based on international sharing, and diffusing power and decision making, rather than concentrating power.

Perhaps most importantly, the emerging sustainable development network focused on small island nations is about promoting human well-being, rather than simply growing larger economies. Sustainable development requires social justice and in this respect is a direct challenge to the single-minded GDP-growth model that dominated twentieth-century development. What is needed is not increased material production, but better distribution of existing global resources, knowledge, and skills, and a rapid transition to renewable energy sources. This is sustainable development that can be applied everywhere, but it is small nations that are showing the way. The sustainability challenge facing small island states was thought to be particularly severe and complex, so what works here should work everywhere. Likewise, a major misstep, or the wrong development decision can fairly quickly have catastrophic effects on a small island, just as global scale reliance on fossil fuels can disastrously disturb global climate.

According to the Preamble of the 1994 Barbados Programme of Action, islanders understand the trade-offs they must make between the material versus cultural dimensions of development:

> Sharing a common aspiration for economic development and improved living standards, small island developing States are determined that the pursuit of material benefits should not undermine social, religious and cultural values or cause any permanent harm to

either their people or their land and marine resources, which have sustained island life for many centuries.[52]

The Barbados Declaration also stressed that small island nations are in position to protect both the world's oceans and global biodiversity, which are critical resources for them, as well as for the entire global community. The Barbados conference acknowledged that SIDS will be among the first nations to suffer the effects of global warming, but they have contributed the least to the causes of global warming. SIDS are also dependent on international trade but individually have limited capacity to influence the terms of trade in a global "free market" dominated by giant corporations and markets. The multiple vulnerabilities of SIDS are mirrored by the vulnerabilities of subnational regions and communities worldwide in the face of concentrated economic power that almost everywhere dominates production and distribution.

The following section looks at how this international concern for sustainable development and climate change looks from the perspective of the Cook Islands, a small Pacific island nation that was already dedicated to combining development with environmental protection.

COOK ISLANDS ENVIRONMENTAL CONSENSUS

The Cook Islands are a Polynesian arcadian small island nation, a self-governing country in Free Association with New Zealand since 1965. Its population was about 20,000 in 2006, and its people live on a dozen widely scattered small islands and atolls in the South Pacific. Cook Islanders have a solid consensus on their religion and their environment. To cover religion, they inserted a preamble to their Constitution in 1997 declaring, "We, the people of the Cook Islands, recognizing the heritage of Christian principles, Cook Island custom, and the rule of law, remember to keep holy the Sabbath Day."[53] At their 2004 National Environment Forum, Cook Islanders also pledged themselves to protect their environment as "E KURA" (The gift) "...that will continue to provide for successive generations of Cook Islands people the basic means of livelihood and the broadest of opportunities to lift their standard of living."[54]

Between 1971 and 2000 the government signed ten international conventions on environmental protection, including the 1992 Convention on the Conservation of Biological Diversity (CBD) the Biodiversity Treaty from the Rio Earth Summit. They have also approved numerous internal environmental laws. Environmental regulations are not controversial among the twenty-four members of Parliament and four cabinet ministers who constitute the very small Cook Islands government. The Cook Islands government is actively engaged with several international agencies concerned with climate change and sustainability funded through the UN Global Environment Facility (GEF), including the South Pacific Regional Environment Programme (SPREP) the Assessments of Impacts and Adaptations to Climate Change (AIACC) project, and the Pacific Island Renewable Energy Project (PIREP).

In 2001 the Cook Islands held a five-day National Biodiversity Workshop for some fifty local landowners from the islands, who represented about 80 percent of the entire national population to help draw up the Cook Islands Biodiversity Strategy and Action Plan.[55] The islanders had no difficulty endorsing the goals of the biodiversity treaty, which including conserving endangered species, developing a system of protected areas, sustainable use of biological resources, and equitable sharing of the benefits. An immediate practical application of the Cook Islands Biodiversity Strategy was the planned 2007 reintroduction of the IUCN RedList endangered Rimatara lorikeet (or Khul's lory, *Vini kuhlii*) from French Polynesia to the island of Atiu in the Cooks.[56] This lorikeet was prized for its red plumes which were used for chiefly headdresses, but it had disappeared before Europeans arrived. The returned lorikeets will share the ten square mile island of Atiu with 572 Cook Islanders, five villages, and three chiefs.

Cook Islanders can reach a political consensus on environmental regulations and biodiversity restoration in part because they have no giant fossil-fuel corporations lobbying against measures to reduce carbon emissions. They also have no billionaires or very wealthy super elites who might oppose any sort of government regulations on the free market. The 2001 census showed that barely 150 people had income above approximately US$46,000, which was the top income bracket, and incomes of the top earners were almost certainly less than US$100,000. Seventy-five percent of the population had incomes of less than US$15,000.[57]

Part III

How Small Nations Could Reshape the World

The success of small nations suggests that people in large nations could solve their own problems now by transforming themselves into federations of small, more functional and more democratic nations, and by adopting some of the crucial social and cultural structures already developed by small nations. Small nations demonstrate that economic growth is not the only pathway to prosperity and social justice. Zero carbon economies with stationary flows of energy and materials can be achieved. Transformed large nations could join with successful small nations to build truly democratic international and planetary-scale institutions that would effectively address planetary-scale problems in a newly reconstructed global system. Technology by itself will not solve global problems, because they are problems of scale, social power, and values, requiring an accurate perception of the realities of the physical world. We just need to look beyond the existing superpowers and their failed twentieth-century creations to find the models to follow. By building new twenty-first-century social institutions and new sociocultural systems based on small nations, we can create a truly sustainable global system that will safely take our descendants into the twenty-second century and beyond.

6

SMALL NATION SOLUTIONS FOR THE PACIFIC NORTHWEST, 2025

Decision makers in the Snohomish Basin can choose now to advance the economy for a sustainable, desirable future through sound investment decisions that strike the optimal balance between the production of built and natural capital. Improvements in social, financial and human capital will also flow from these investments. Using this new, "Whole Economy" model will lower costs, promote justice, improve efficiency, and advance the Snohomish Basin economy, while maintaining a suite of positive externalities through ecosystem services. —*Earth Economics, 2010*[1]

The Pacific Northwest (PNW) emerged as an early center for the environmental movement and futurist thinking in the 1970s. It was even the setting for Ernest Callenbach's 1975 *Ecotopia*,[2] a widely read countercultural novel of an imaginary PNW small nation environmental utopia. Callenbach described the region splitting off from the United States in 1980 and forming what was, in effect, an arcadian-style small nation as it might have appeared to an inquisitive journalist in 1999. Since then, Pacific Northwesterners have continued to evolve imaginative solutions to the growth mega-problem. If truly sustainable development can succeed anywhere in the world, it will work here, where per capita economic production is relatively high and natural resources are abundant. Pacific Northwesterners will not need to sacrifice their rivers, forests, and freedoms to live well, but they must recognize that sustainable development does not mean endless growth.

DIVERSE APPROACHES TO A SUSTAINABLE PACIFIC NORTHWEST

Today more than ten million people live in the PNW, and the region remains an ideal place in which to imagine possible applications of the small nation solution and to draw contrasts with the alternatives. The imaginary Republic of Cascadia, a long-proposed bioregion centered on the Columbia River Basin and including portions of Oregon, Washington, Idaho, Montana, and British Columbia, was included in a 2011 *Time Magazine* list[3] of the Top 10 "Aspiring Nations," along with Scotland; Tibet; the Basque Country; South Ossetia (Russian Georgia); Kurdistan; Quebec; Western Sahara; Padania (northern Italy); and the Second Vermont Republic. The Republic of Cascadia, partly inspired by Callenbach's *Ecotopia*, has been called a "far-off dream" and a "flight of fantasy,"[4] but some of its proponents envision it as a future "Bioregional Cooperative Commonwealth,"[5] suggesting that it might incorporate features of both ecodemian- and arcadian-type small nations.

By the 1990s organizations and governments throughout the real Northwest began to embrace sustainable development as an important goal. Sustainable development clearly enjoys widespread public support as a goal of public policy in the PNW, as illustrated by the State of Oregon's Sustainability Act of 2001 and Washington's Sustainable Practices Executive Order of 2002. Many local and regional businesses and organizations are dedicated to solving social and environmental problems. The nonprofit Sustainable Seattle, founded in 1991 to promote urban sustainability in the Puget Sound region, created a set of regional sustainability indicators in 1993 that became an internationally recognized standard.[6] The City of Portland created an Office of Sustainable Development in 2000. Oregon began forming local watershed councils in 1993 to restore healthy watersheds and salmon[7] and set up an initiative in 1998 to restore and conserve "the biological integrity and economic vitality of the Willamette River basin."[8] There are also research groups associated with regional state universities focused on PNW sustainability issues, such as the Pacific Northwest Environmental Research Consortium (PNW-ERC), the Institute of Sustainable Environment at the University of Oregon, Portland State University's Institute for Sustainable Solutions, and the Climate Impact Group (CIG) at the University of Washington. Many well-informed people know in general what needs to be done, but the most important changes will need to be much more fundamental than most people yet realize.

The PNW is also moving to the forefront of carbon-free renewable energy technology. A report by regionally based energy consultants Clean Edge and nonprofit Climate Solutions shows that Oregon and Washington have the potential for 75 percent of its electric power to be carbon-free by 2025.[9] Oregon's electric power was already nearly 64 percent renewable in 2010, making it the most carbon-free power-producing state in the country.[10] Washington's then-Governor Chris Gregoire even signed a bill in 2011 arranging a phase out of the last coal-powered electric plant in the state by 2025.

Some advocates of "sustainable growth" may be sending mixed messages. For example, the PNW has been identified as "Cascadia," one of twelve emerging American Megaregions envisioned in the Regional Plan Association's America 2050 project. This futurist planning project focuses on infrastructural improvements intended to accommodate a 50 percent increase in America's population by 2050, while proposing to keep the country prosperous and its economy globally competitive, while also providing employment to reduce poverty, protecting the environment, and reducing carbon emissions.[11] This is as much of a utopian project for the entire country as Callenbach's original *Ecotopia* was for the PNW, but the America 2050 planners would take the country further along its present path predicated on continuous economic growth and globalization.

The Regional Plan Association is a nonprofit urban planning organization founded in 1922 to plan for the growth of New York, New Jersey, and Connecticut. Its infrastructure planning approach to urban growth helped produce the virtually continuous urban megalopolis of more than 52 million people that we now see stretching from northern Virginia to southern Maine. This Northeast Megaregion had achieved a regional tera-economy of nearly $3 trillion in GDP by 2010. Historically, this kind of planning is quite the opposite of the small nation solution and has been called the "Metropolitan Tradition" which originated with the Chicago School of Sociology.[12] The Cascadia Megaregion branch of the America 2050 project is funded by the Rockefeller Foundation; the Discovery Institute, a conservative Seattle-based think tank; Talgo, a private Spanish light-rail manufacturer; and CH2M Hill, an employee-owned engineering firm with multi-billions in revenues in 2010. The centerpiece of the Cascadia proposal is for the creation of a high-speed light rail system to connect the region's major urban centers. This new infrastructure is expected to boost regional productivity and deal with a wide range of urban growth problems.

An even more influential regional organization dedicated to growing an even larger population and economy in the greater PNW is the intergovernmental Pacific NorthWest Economic Region (PNWER) formed in 1991 by Idaho, Montana, Oregon, Washington, Alaska, British Columbia, and Alberta. Like the Northeast Megaregion, this greater Pacific Northwest region has a tera-economy of more than $1 trillion. PNWER's mission is to "achieve continued economic growth while maintaining the region's natural resources, while drawing on resources from Ottawa and Washington, D.C.," to "enhance the competitiveness of the region in both domestic and international markets."[13] PNWER sees its role as promoting public-private partnerships and includes representatives from many of the largest private sector corporations in the region. It provides a forum for the Cascadia America 2050 project. PNWER promotes the idea that the region is "China and East Asia's gateway to North America"[14] and is facilitating development of transport infrastructure to support the shipment of western coal to China.

There are many good reasons for regional economic cooperation and for supporting an improved rail system in the PNW, but there are even more compelling reasons for making the more fundamental transformations that the small nation solution would mean, but first, an overview of regional ecology, history, and native people will provide some important background.

BIOLOGICAL POTENTIAL AND CULTURAL DEMAND IN THE PACIFIC NORTHWEST

> We have within our borders all that is needed to sustain a vast population. . . . our magnificent resources . . . the wealth of our state in mine, in forest, and in stream . . . . —Washington Governor John H. McGraw, Inaugural Address, 1893[15]

Forests are among the most conspicuous natural resources in the PNW, and this is reflected in their symbolic importance in regional popular culture. Forests provide jobs for people, they generate revenue, and they regulate water flows, build and protect the soil, store carbon, and of course provide habitats for many plants and animals, including the salmon. Forests help define the PNW as a natural region. Washington adopted "the Evergreen State" as its official nickname in 1893, and Oregon's upper Willamette basin is the "Emerald Empire." However, the scale at which the region's forest and water resources were historically allowed to develop and the way timber ownership and production has worked to concentrate economic and political power and accelerate timber harvest far beyond sustainable limits illustrates the problematic effects of elite-directed growth in action and shows why the small nation solution is so badly needed in the PNW.

When Washington Governor John H. McGraw confidently declared in 1893, "We have within our borders all that is needed to sustain a vast population," as quoted above, there were fewer than 500,000 people in the state, and the future looked bright indeed. Four years later, Governor John R. Rogers claimed that Washington had "the largest body of valuable timber" and the best harbor (Seattle) in the country, and affirmed, ". . . it would appear that everything necessary to man's prosperity has been provided with a generous hand. . . . Nature has here lavished her bounties, and nothing is lacking to complete a perfect picture of God's favor to man."[16] Paradoxically, Governor Rogers spoke next of "the existence of want and involuntary poverty among us" and warned darkly of "the organized aggressions of the privileged few . . . a poorly concealed plutocracy . . . and "the oncoming forces of despotism." He was warning the state of the danger of elite-directed growth. Shortly after Governor Rogers' inauguration, the railroads transferred vast tracts of the best PNW forest lands in their federal land grants to a handful of timber barons, whose descendants still reap a disproportionate share of the benefits of northwest forests.

The PNW is an amazingly dynamic, wonderfully rich natural region. At its center is the greater Columbia River watershed which drains a vast area of hundreds of square miles stretching from the crest of the Canadian Rockies in British Columbia to the continental divide in Glacier National Park and Yellowstone in Wyoming and Montana to the fringes of the Great Basin in southeast Oregon, Nevada, Utah, and Idaho. In 1850 the PNW was a biological treasure. It was home to spectacular old-growth coniferous forests, and the world's greatest salmon runs ascended the mighty free-flowing Columbia River. This is still a highly diverse natural region where fifteen terrestrial and sixty-six freshwater ecoregions have been distinguished. There are thirty-two distinctive habitat types and 593 wildlife species in Oregon and Washington alone.[17] The Columbia and Fraser Rivers were famous for enormously rich salmon fisheries.

In 1750, on the eve of Euro-American colonization, the PNW was home to perhaps 200,000 tribal world people living in tribal societies and small chiefdoms representing eight language families and seventeen cultural subareas. Many groups lived in permanent villages, and all depended on fishing, hunting, and collecting wild plant resources. Their ancestors entered the interior Columbia Basin at least 10,000 years ago, and their cultural system proved to be highly sustainable.[18] My careful assessment of their aggregate subsistence demand suggests that native peoples were using less than 1 percent of the potential annual biological product of this vast region. Just as in Amazonia, such a small cultural demand made it possible for people to maintain the entire ecosystem in prime condition as natural capital providing natural services. Everything had changed by the end of the twentieth century when the commercial economy was consuming more than the region's entire biological potential, thanks to imported fossil fuels and global trade. This new system of resource use was completely unsustainable.

The practical monetary value of nature's services for PNW indigenous peoples became overwhelmingly clear to me after my work in British Columbia with the St'at'imc Nation (Lillooet) in 2003–2005 in support of their negotiations with BC Hydro, the provincial power company. The St'at'imc are a Plateau people, for whom the salmon are sacred, much like for the Yakama, although their language is different. They live along the Fraser River, which still maintains healthy salmon runs, except for the Bridge River, a Fraser tributary at the center of traditional St'at'imc fishing grounds.

The St'at'imc were negotiating for compensation for damages because no fish passage was ever constructed at BC Hydro's massive Bridge River Dam, and those salmon runs were completely destroyed. BC Hydro is owned by the British Columbia government and is the primary electric utility in the province. The Bridge River complex is the source of most of Vancouver's power, but the salmon are the foundation of St'at'imc culture and society. The St'at'imc fed me salmon and took me to ancient fishing sites where I saw fish drying racks and people fishing from rocks their ancestors had used for millennia. The value to the St'at'imc people of salmon, other natural resources, and nature's services in the watershed went far beyond the monetary value of salmon as food. Salmon were central to their negotiations with BC Hydro, which dragged on for eighteen years, until a final settlement was reached in 2010. The monetary agreement totaled nearly $500 million and included specific provisions to be paid out over a hundred years to protect the salmon and other natural resources (see further discussion in chapter 7).[19] This settlement does not mean that the St'at'imc political struggle for full control over their territory is over because they still had not signed a formal treaty with British Columbia to recognize their local sovereignty as a Canadian First Nations tribal nation.

In contrast to the demonstrated sustainability of PNW tribal cultures, the cultural demands placed on the PNW's natural resources by Euro-American settlers in the 150 years after 1850 was a biological catastrophe that occurred in the blink of an eye in comparison with the length of time that Indian people had occupied the region. I am a fourth-generation Oregonian, and my ancestors and I were part of that cultural and biological transformation. My great-great-grandfather Barnes walked the 2,000 miles over the Oregon Trail from his home in Missouri to settle his family in the Willamette Valley, Oregon, in 1865. When the Barnes family reached Oregon there were only about 75,000 settlers in the state, and Portland, the largest city, had fewer than 8,000. My other great-grandparents came to Oregon by ship and rail, via San Francisco, shortly after the completion of the first transcontinental railroad in 1869. Within my lifetime the population of Oregon more than tripled from just over a million in the early 1940s to over 3.4 million by 2000. The population has become two orders of magnitude greater since 1865. This demographic transformation is reflected in dramatic scale-related changes in the organization of Oregon's political system, and in the distribution of its wealth and income. By 1880 the immigrant population exceeded the native population, and by 1900 there were a million people in the region, and the population exceeded 10 million by the year 2000, when people were extracting the equivalent of 131 percent of the 1750 baseline biological product.

A major dam-building project begun on the Columbia River in the 1930s, along with intensive commercial fishing quickly devastated the once massive salmon runs. Seemingly endless stands of centuries-old,

250-foot-high trees in the coastal forests were almost totally cut down within the first five decades of the twentieth century.[20] The former Palouse Grasslands, one of the regions fifteen terrestrial ecoregions, where I currently live in southeast Washington, was virtually destroyed and replaced to make way for wheat farming. By 2000, 98 percent of the wild salmon runs in the Columbia drainage and 80-90 percent of "old growth" forests in western Oregon and Washington were gone. Salmon were listed under the Endangered Species Act in 1991 and expensive efforts were underway to "save" them, but by 1997 the annual harvest of farmed salmon exceeded the wild catch.

A remarkable transformation accompanied the loss of the Columbia River salmon. Salmon mature in the ocean and formerly deposited as much as 100 million kilograms of marine energy and materials throughout the Columbia Basin in their biomass when they returned to spawn in the headwaters. Less than 1 percent of this now reaches the interior.[21] In place of the salmon, barges now transport wheat downstream and fertilizer and petroleum products upstream. PNW forests, rivers, and soils contributed to the ten-fold increase in the national economy between 1938 and 2004. Northwest wheat, cattle, and fruit helped to feed the country and the world. PNW hydroelectric power and nuclear facilities helped win World War II and helped pull the country out of the Great Depression. PNW lumber and plywood supplied the nation's postwar building boom. By 2005 there were a dozen resident billionaires collectively worth some $95 billion, thanks largely to the success of regionally based software and telecommunications industries. However, the PNW's growth has also been accompanied by persistent poverty and has contributed to global warming.

THE COLUMBIA RIVER INTER-TRIBAL FISH COMMISSION: WE ARE ALL SALMON PEOPLE

The people of these tribes have always shared a common understanding—that their very existence depends on the respectful enjoyment of the Columbia River Basin's vast land and water resources. Indeed, their very souls and spirits were and are inextricably tied to the natural world and its myriad inhabitants. Among those inhabitants, none were more important than the teeming millions of anad-

romous fish enriching the basin's rivers and streams. — Columbia
River Inter-Tribal Fish Commission (CRITFC)[22]

We are all salmon people. All people of the Northwest. We, who call
the Pacific Northwest our home, have the privilege of living amongst
the great salmon nation. Like the salmon, we take comfort and suste-
nance from the mountains, forests, valleys, high plains, rivers, and
the ocean that is their home. For thousands of years, and especially
the past few hundred years, we have taken much of what was and is
theirs. For countless years our salmon brothers and sisters returned
without question to nourish us, sustain our cultures, our economies,
our society and our spiritual well-being. Today, they barely survive.
Without us, they cannot survive. We must find balance. Today and
from this day on, it is our time to give to them. . . . —Paul Lumley,
executive director, CRITFC[23]

Four Plateau tribes who relied on the main Columbia River fisheries in
Oregon and Washington organized in response to a time of crisis for the
salmon caused primarily by the construction of eleven major dams between 1937 and 1971. Overfishing by commercial fishermen, pollution,
and habitat destruction were added threats to the salmon. The Nez
Perce Tribe in Idaho, the Confederated Tribes of the Umatilla Indian
Reservation in Oregon, the Confederated Tribes of the Warm Springs
Reservation also of Oregon, and the Confederated Tribes and Bands of
the Yakama Indian Nation, representing different languages and cultures, all came together in 1977 to form the Columbia River Inter-
Tribal Fish Commission (CRITFC) to re-assert their traditional authority over fisheries management in the Columbia River.[24] They shared a
common goal: "Unity of action in service of the salmon."

The Yakama and allied tribes take a holistic approach to salmon
restoration. They call this "gravel to gravel," meaning that they want the
salmon to be able to complete their life cycle by beginning in natural
spawning gravels and returning to spawn in those same gravels. Ideally,
people would not need to intervene with salmon hatcheries and expensive barging operations to move salmon through the dams. The
CRIFFC tribal members have a full understanding of the place of salmon in the ecosystem and of how human activities are making it difficult for salmon to survive and thrive. They also understand that if the
salmon don't survive, our existence will also be in jeopardy. CRITFC

works with the Northwest Power and Conservation Council and other state and federal agencies all concerned with salmon recovery.

Here is where the importance of the great depth of the shared Plateau culture comes to the forefront. Tribal nations can succeed as ecodemia-style small nations, or economic democracies, because there is no conflict between economic activities and environmental protection. In practice this also makes them arcadia nations and means that growth ideology is not the prime directive for their decision makers. There are elite directors here, the members of the tribal council, but their powers are limited by the people, and they are unlikely to be self-interested economic elites. They must remain public servants. Unlimited growth is not seen as the way to avoid a fair distribution of economic benefits. There is also no conflict between tribal people's spiritual beliefs and scientific realities. The above-quoted statements on behalf of the salmon by contemporary Indian leaders combine spiritual understandings with solid science.

Even more importantly, these tribes share a common and very profound cultural understanding of the meaning of salmon that goes far beyond their obvious material importance as food. This is stated emphatically in the two-volume formal proposal for salmon restoration produced by CRITFC in 1996 entitled "Wy-Kan-Ush-Mi Wa-Kish-Wit Spirit of the Salmon."[25] When presenting the case for salmon restoration to outside agencies Indian people immediately point out that salmon are part of their spiritual and cultural identity. Salmon have specific roles in religious ceremonies such as the first salmon feast, celebrating the annual return of the salmon. This deep spiritual connection between people and animals that is virtually universal among indigenous people helps explain why they are fighting so hard to protect and restore the salmon. The motivation for Indian people is not primarily economic; it is in reality spiritual. It is also a profoundly different way of understanding nature and the relationship between people and nature than the purely instrumental understanding that has prevailed under the free market ideology that has predominated in the contemporary commercial world. Tribal nations such as the Yakama Nation have the kind of "environmentalist" value system that advocates of the "Great Transition" are calling for as the basis for sustainability.

To speak of human souls and spirits being connected to nature and to say that people are salmon is not empty metaphor. I heard the

Asháninka and other Amazonian peoples speak the same way, as do indigenous people worldwide. They all apply kinship terms to important animals, treating them as family. Such concepts must have utility, or they would not appear in so many cultures and be so continually reproduced. The Lillooet people (St'at'imc Nation) also told me that they were salmon, and I realized that this was literally true. Archaeologists can identify salmon eaters by the ratios of carbon and nitrogen isotopes incorporated into their bones from eating salmon. Salmon eaters are also salmon in the sense that as long as salmon runs are healthy, all other natural resources will be intact, along with the salmon eaters. In the language of science, salmon are an "indicator species." Likewise, the Asháninka speak of spirit guardians of important animals and consider the Amazonian giant otter to be their brother who brings fish. This makes sense. The giant otter is at the top of the aquatic food chain and requires a vast area of river and forest to support a viable population, just as the salmon require marine and freshwater ecosystems. There is a moral argument here.

The soul concept as understood by indigenous people calls attention to striking contrasts between tribal world and commercial world ways of knowing and relating to the physical and metaphysical worlds. Considering the invisible, or metaphysical aspects, of people and animals, we assume that only people have souls and make that the major difference between us and them. Natural scientists assume that people are physically animals. Indigenous peoples see the physical differences between people and animals, but they imagine how other animals also see the world, assuming they have minds and souls like us. This leads to some interesting and useful ways of relating to nature. All life forms, animals and plants, or their spirit masters, as well as spirit beings are transformed human persons and still have human-like spirits or souls. Animals are spiritually humans on the inside with animal exteriors, or "clothing," on the outside. The modern scientific view of course is the opposite, that humans were originally animals, and in effect remain animals wearing cultural clothing. Thinking of animals as transformed people makes it natural to treat them with respect and to imagine that they are reciprocating by allowing us to eat them. This of course means that we have a duty to provide animals suitable conditions for their well-being.

Attributing human-like souls to animals is also a "framing" technique that environmentalists might find useful to adopt in their political campaigns. Cognitive linguist George Lakoff reminds us that saving the environment is first and foremost a moral problem involving our values. Speaking of the environment or the salmon or polar bears as objects that need protecting, or dealing with them only in monetary terms, says that these objects are external to us, and they face external threats. The reality is everyone is part of nature and totally dependent on it. As Lokoff says, ". . . we are the polar bears. Human existence is threatened, as is the existence of most living beings on earth. When we see the polar bear struggling on the ice floe, that is us."[26] This is quite literally true.

RAIN-ON-SNOW: A PACIFIC NORTHWEST GROWTH, SCALE, AND POWER PROBLEM

The ecological and sustainability catastrophe that befell the Pacific Northwest can be attributed to the now familiar problem of elite-directed growth, and it can be reversed and prevented by applying the small nation solution. Only certain forest-related aspects of this problem will be detailed in this section, but the overall environmental problem resulted from a political maldistribution of costs and benefits that did not fully take into account the value of nature as capital, or the needs of future generations. The catastrophe would very likely not have happened if small nations had continued to control the PNW after 1850, and especially if they were organized as arcadia-style small nations. Neither agoria nor ecodemia small nations would have allowed such a rich ecosystem to have been destroyed for the short-term benefit of a few. When a resource is democratically managed by owner-beneficiaries as a commons according to the subsidiarity principle, we would not expect it to be destroyed. This is how Native Americans treated the resources of the PNW when they were in charge. The scale, power, and complexity issues at stake can be illustrated by the rain-on-snow problem.

Rain-on-snow (ROS) refers first of all to a local and regional environmental phenomenon that can cause sudden flood disasters in the Pacific Northwest when too many trees are cut on steep hillsides. Rain falling on snow exposed on bare ground causes it to melt too quickly, and when the ground is still frozen, rain and snowmelt drain off together in a sudden flood. Loggers understand this problem. Rain-on-snow is also a broad metaphor for the global mega-problem of unlimited growth causing global warming and unsustainable use of natural resources and human problems generally.

The phrase "rain-on-snow" appears in the State of Washington's Administrative Code (WAC 222-22-100). This section of Title 222 describes how the state Department of Natural Resources (DNR) is required to assess the effects of logging practices on fish, water, and capital improvements on 9.3 million acres of state and private forest lands within the state. The ROS rule[27] was established in 1991 by the Forest Practices Board, an independent state agency. The rule requires the state Department of Natural Resources (DNR) to set the maximum size of a forest clearcut when a landowner wants to remove an entire stand of trees in a lumbering operation. The rule applies under certain conditions in specifically defined "rain-on-snow zones." The rule is intended to minimize the rain-on-snow problem, but when forests are managed by giant corporations and government bureaucracies, each procedural detail must be spelled out in writing, and the ROS rule becomes excruciatingly complex and difficult to implement and monitor on the ground. For example, the DNR Forest Practices division manager needed a forty-eight-page memo to explain the rule to regional managers.[28] The rules in WAC Title 222 Forest Practices Board are spelled out in fifteen chapters and require some 150 general definitions. They were elaborated to implement the 1993 revisions to the legal requirements of the state Environmental Policy Act (SEPA) of 1971 (RCW 43.21C).

The question is, why such legal complexity? Historically, rain-on-snow became a problem in the PNW because of decisions made by a handful of corporate business leaders, the principal owners and directors of giant lumber corporations, seeking to maximize the short-term timber cut on both private and public lands. Profit-driven overcutting was supported by compliant government officials, until the situation had reached a crisis in the state by the late 1980s. The ROS rule recognizes the need for locally specific production limits, but it does not get at the root of the problem, which is concentrated economic and political power in the hands of directors who demand continuous economic growth to satisfy their shareholders. Many of the beneficiaries of this process have no direct interest in either trees or forests, or particular animals or people who depend upon them for their long-term well-being. ROS-type regulations are part of a broader effort to find policies and technical solutions that will allow economic growth in general to continue by minimizing the local damage it may cause.

Rain-on-snow is of course a natural process that occurred forever in the PNW but on a very small scale that would cause only limited damage. The Department of Natural Resources did not implement the rain-on-snow regulation until 1991. Indeed, there were no state forest practice rules of any kind in Washington until 1945, when the state began requiring loggers to reforest their cutover land. Postwar economic expansion placed enormous pressure on forest resources, but it was not until 1974 that the state of Washington passed a comprehensive Forest Practices Act requiring the state to regulate logging practices to protect "forest soils, fisheries, wildlife, water quantity and quality, air quality, recreation, and scenic beauty," while at the same time maintaining "a viable forest products industry." Prior to 1974, nature did the job of protecting and restoring the forest, but even by 1945 large-scale logging was clearly overwhelming natural recovery processes.

The rain-on-snow rule recognizes the need for locally specific production limits, but it is also part of the state government's broader effort to find policies and technical solutions that will allow growth in general to continue. Of course the broader problem is that growth does have natural limits and exceeding them can have disastrous and unpredictable boom-and-bust effects. The American timber industry clearly illustrates this boom-and-bust nature of unlimited growth, as well as the crucial role of historical circumstance, and the decision making of elite individuals with disproportionate power. The most crucial decisions affecting PNW forests were made by very remote political and economic elites in Rock Island, Illinois, New York, and Washington, DC, who did of course not follow subsidiarity principles. Quirks of nineteenth-century American history, political influence, and personal deals involving New York financier J. P. Morgan (the second richest American at that time), investment banker Jay Cooke, various compliant congressmen, and lumber magnate Frederick Weyerhaeuser set the stage for the first harvest of the Pacific Northwest's seemingly endless expanse of giant trees west of the Cascade Mountain crest. Many of these centuries-old trees on the most accessible and commercially valuable old-growth

Northwest forests were in Weyerhaeuser's hands by 1899, and were almost totally cut down within the first five decades of the twentieth century.[29] The federal government transferred these prime forest lands from the public domain to the Northern Pacific Railroad Company during the Civil War as part of the government's 38 million acres railroad land grant giveaway of 1864. By 1911, the Weyerhaeuser Timber Company owned nearly 2 million acres of forest, and Frederick Weyerhaeuser had amassed a personal fortune worth some $2.5 billion in 2000 dollars.[30] In 2005 the Weyerhaeuser Corporation still owned 2.2 million timber acres in Oregon and Washington, and many of Weyerhaeuser's descendants were still shareholders.

After 1945, timber harvesting action shifted to the marginally productive and less accessible lands that had been reserved by the federal government in the National Forests since 1891, precisely because they were less productive. With the prime timber in private hands mostly cut, the timber magnates persuaded the Forest Service to shift from its historic role of forest conservation to a major new effort to increase the harvest, building some 65,000 miles of new roads into previously inaccessible forests over the fifteen years from 1945 to 1960. By the early 1990s there were 342,000 miles of roads in the national forests, compared with only 50,000 in the federal highway system. This road-building effort was a staggeringly costly public subsidy for the timber companies, who had already depleted their private forest holdings, especially because many timber sales did not produce enough revenue to cover the Forest Service's costs.[31]

The Forest Service controls massive holdings of federal forest land. Its total national acreage was 187 million acres in 2000, including some 25 million acres in Oregon and Washington,[32] but not all of this was harvestable timberland. The Forest Service is an agency of the U.S. Department of Agriculture and is saddled with a contradictory "multiple-use" mission of increasing the timber harvest and supporting livestock grazing, while at the same time conserving forest resources and protecting the forest environment for wildlife, aesthetic values, and recreation. After 1945 an "irrepressible march toward maximizing harvests" was encouraged by professional incentives within the Forest Service agency that rewarded managers for treating forests like agricultural crops that would respond to intensive harvesting with increased growth. This was seen as a technological fix for declining harvests. In a "conspiracy of optimism" foresters were apparently convinced that they could steadily increase the allowable cut without damaging the forests by following their scientific management practices.[33] This progrowth technocratic belief was understandable, given that Forest Service administrators gained budgets, personnel, and decision-making autonomy by increasing production, and their primary staff consisted of professional foresters, not conservation-minded forest ecologists and wildlife biologists. Forest directors were also able to retain a substantial portion of revenues from timber sales for internal use and turned 25 percent over to local counties, thereby gaining local political support for increased cutting. Budget allocations for the Forest Service are determined by the executive branch and congress, both of which have an incentive to favor increased production over conservation for political reasons.

With two-thirds of Washington's timberland controlled by large corporations and the Forest Service, it is not surprising that serious overcutting occurred. By the 1930s it was already estimated that forest cutting was exceeding the replacement rate by four to one.[34] Nearly two-thirds of the original stand of prime commercial timber in Washington had been removed by 1947, and nearly three-fourths was gone by 1995. Between 1945 and 1970 another 1,000 square miles was permanently lost to roads, reservoirs, pipelines, farms, and urbanization.[35] Total lumber production in Washington had peaked in 1925 at some 7 billion board feet, but by 2002 the annual harvest had declined to 3.5 billion. Decision making by a handful of business leaders and their government partners succeeded in converting a great natural resource from a rich, self-maintaining ecosystem into tree farms within a few decades. This process resembled in many respects what happened in Chile, which is the PNW's southern hemisphere ecological counterpart. All of these forests could have been treated as capital and harvested sustainably, for much broader public benefit, but that would have required a different decision-making structure.

By 2003, Weyerhaeuser and its descendent companies, Potlatch, Plum Creek, and Boise-Cascade, still controlled nearly 4 million acres of prime forest land in the PNW, approximately equal to all the productive forest lands owned by the state governments of Oregon and Washington.[36] The holdings of these companies were mostly in second or third growth, and much of it had been converted to intensively managed tree farms. Tree farms can be highly productive, at least over the short run, but they are also costly to maintain because people must take on many functions that nature would otherwise do for free. It is also not certain how long tree farms can remain productive, and no one knows the full costs of these highly simplified artificial forests. As in the Chilean case, tree farms can have numerous unanticipated negative social and environmental consequences. The prime beneficiaries of this great transformation of Northwest forests into tree farms were the principal shareholders of these four companies which were all still producing billions and tens of billions in annual revenues, and hundreds of millions in profits for their shareholders. Historically, the members of a few prominent PNW families were among their largest individual shareholders and served for decades as directors on corporate boards interconnecting the railroads and the great timber companies.

Since 2000, ownership and management of private forest lands has become increasingly concentrated in the hands of bankers, mutual fund managers, timber investment management organizations (TIMOs), and real estate investment trusts (REITs), who treat forests as marketable investment opportunities. The managers of REITs and TIMOs are selling ownership shares in PNW forests to superwealthy investors and the right to access forest lands and harvest trees to logging companies, lumber and paper mills. For example, in 2004 Boise-Cascade, the fourth largest forest products company in the country, sold its northwest timber holdings to a TIMO, Forest Capital Partners, who buy, sell, and manage timber lands for an anonymous few wealthy foundations, endowments, and families. Georgia-Pacific, the second largest forest products company in the country, with more than $20 billion in revenues in 2003, was purchased outright by Koch Industries in 2005 for $21 billion. This purchase made Koch Industries the largest private company in the world at that time. Georgia Pacific was then owned by two brothers, Charles and David Koch, who between them were worth $8 billion at that time and were among the world's wealthiest 400 individuals. The environmental organization Greenpeace devotes an entire report to the role of Koch Industries, also discussed in the next chapter, as one of the most influential climate deniers, pouring tens of millions of dollars into what Greenpeace calls the "denial machine" of right-wing think tanks, advocacy groups and political candidates opposing reductions to carbon emissions.[37]

HOUSEHOLD WELL-BEING, WEALTH, AND INCOME IN WASHINGTON STATE

Rain-on-snow, as in "rain on a parade," is also a metaphor for any unexpected and undesired outcome that dampens what should otherwise be a happy social event. In this case, the happy event is the promised enrichment of everyone's life by economic growth and material progress. This is the positive side of growth, and it is what we all want to happen. This was beginning to happen in the 1950s and '60s in the PNW and in the United States generally. Since then, the reality is that too much badly managed growth in the PNW is making a few people very rich, while the relatively impoverished majority falls further behind, and many people, an increasing number, remain absolutely poor. The negative social consequences of misguided growth can be as disastrous as growth's environmental effects.

Washington State is a good example of the problem of badly distributed wealth and income. Washington had 6.7 million people in 2010 and a $340 billion economy, making it the equivalent of one of the world's richest countries with a Gross State Product (GSP) per capita of more than $50,000. Washington's growth between 1972 and 2010 caused per capita GDP to double, adjusted for inflation; but this growth did not fairly benefit the majority. Washington is home to six billionaires and some of the most influential corporations of the digital age, including Microsoft and Amazon, yet over 800,000 people were living in official poverty in the state in 2009. Many more were financially distressed, because the poverty threshold represented only a third of the "living wage." The official unemployment rate reached 10.8 percent in 2010. Nearly a million people had no health insurance. Poverty and unemployment are distribution problems in the state, not production problems, because Washington's citizens produce enough income from their labor and capital to provide everyone a living wage, with billions to spare.

There is enough current diversity in Washington State to imagine that people could plausibly devise several variations of small state solutions in different regions of the state to solve these problems by 2025. Applying proven small nation solutions, this chapter does a "what-if" thought experiment to see what problems could be solved if Washington's citizens could reach a consensus to remove costly growth subsidies, to right-size their businesses, restore and protect their common wealth, and to bring much of their financial capital home from the national and international speculative markets.

The growth subsidy in Washington, the cost of growing things larger, is huge, and the benefits of "right-sizing" are equally huge. For example, half of the electrical energy in large-scale power grids is lost in transmission.[38] At the national level in 2004 it has been estimated that only about 40 percent of GDP is "genuine progress" or goods and services that actually benefit people.[39] Nationally, 80 percent of food costs go to processing and large-scale marketing, not primary farm production.[40] These figures suggest that some $200 billion of Washington's GDP goes to kinds of economic growth that might not be needed in a successful small nation. Bringing capital home is a small nation solution which could produce a vast "structural adjustment" in the system. Bringing capital home means adding "invest local" to the "buy local" strategies that Washingtonians have already widely adopted. Investing locally would add further support to small businesses and would keep more money circulating in local communities. The truly outrageous goal of this thought experiment is to see if the citizens of a future small nation Washington State could prosper with a very low growth (VLG), or even stationary, economy based on social justice and protection of and widespread access to all forms of wealth.

When I began to study the connection between growth and power in Washington State in 1996, rather than thinking about social class, I decided to focus on the actual distribution of household income and wealth, as well as on the distribution of business revenues and assets, and how these were affected by change in the scale of urban places. In my part of the state, where I looked first, the biggest individual property owners were located not surprisingly in the largest urban places, but the smallest places had the best distribution of property, the highest proportion of home-owners, the least poverty, and the widest participation in local government. Smaller places seemed to have a ceiling on wealth, but this did not appear to detract from most people's well-being. The ceiling may have actually enhanced well-being, because it was accompanied by a floor below which people did not fall. Very quickly I was able to connect the value of individual property holdings in specific urban places with income levels to distinguish a four-level ranking of households by material well-being.

It was almost unbelievable how closely the power law matched the distribution of real property ownership in the two Washington counties where I first tested it. Wanting further confirmation, I immediately set out to see if the power law also applied to all 273 urban places in Washington State.[41] This time I was not totally surprised to find that throughout the state larger urban places not only produced more total wealth and more wealth per capita, but income, wealth, and economic power all appeared to become more concentrated as growth occurred. The concentration of economic power was also apparent in the distribution of revenues to businesses. With each order of magnitude step up the urban scale, larger businesses became a declining proportion of total businesses, yet they received an increasing share of total revenues. In Washington's largest metropolitan centers with populations of 100,000 or more, I estimated that at the top of the business hierarchy a handful of businesses with billion dollar revenues were receiving nearly half of business revenues. A tedious computerized inspection of the state's business license files showed that business ownership also tended to become disconnected from the place of business as urban places grew larger. This meant that business profits were more likely to be removed from local communities. This seemed to be another negative effect of growth, at least from the perspective of local people, but economic elites would certainly benefit from this increased complexity.

I ranked households by well-being from the bottom up as: poor, maintenance, elite, and superelite. Poor and maintenance level households were everywhere the majority. The households that I ranked as "poor" in Washington State, generalizing from Federal Reserve data,[42] had incomes under $10,000 in 1998 dollars and were generally below official poverty levels. Median net worth for poor households in the state overall was only $3,600, showing that poor households had little wealth, as well as very small incomes. In large urban areas this would ordinarily make it difficult for the poor to meet their basic needs for food, shelter, clothing, and health care. However, in small places with fewer than 2,500 people, the poor on average held more property value than the poor in larger places. Furthermore, the lower property values in small places, and the social support network that family and neighbors provided to each other, appeared to soften the effects of wealth and income poverty. With wealth more equitably distributed there was likely to be a reduction of competitive emulation and feelings of relative depravation. Maintenance level households had larger incomes, but they did not exceed $100,000, and their median net worth averaged $60,000, which was primarily in a house and car. These were better-off households with enough income and wealth to comfortably meet basic needs, but there was not enough left over to be saved for capital investments that would produce significant unearned income.

The elite were the modestly wealthy upper 8 percent of American society with income and net worth of more than $100,000 each. It quickly became apparent that elite and superelite households were the effective directors of American economic growth and were the economic "winners," whereas the poor and maintenance level households were relatively passive producer-consumers. The heads of elite and superelite households were owners and managers with high enough incomes to save and invest to produce significant unearned income from their accumulated capital. This made it possible for them to be elite directors actively promoting local and regional economic development. Some elites were millionaires with enough financial wealth to qualify as High Net Worth Individuals (HNWIs). The superelite were the top 0.5 percent of households with annual *incomes* in the million dollar-plus range and wealth in the hundreds of millions to billions, making them national and global-level elite directors. The lifestyles of these superelite Americans have been well described,[43] but their real significance is how as individuals they both direct and benefit from the growth and power cycle.

It turned out that these household wealth ranks proved to be broadly applicable to households throughout the country and were extendable to the global system with a global economy. Together poor and maintenance level households represented more than 90 percent of American society at that time, and this majority were primarily wage and salary earners and small entrepreneurs with small, if any, directly managed capital investments. This pattern of wealth distribution closely follows Pareto's power law, but it does not apply everywhere in the world, and especially not in many small nations.

WASHINGTON STATE'S BIG BOX STORES

When I put together my findings on scale and power in Washington State with related findings from throughout the country and looked closely at the significance of the scale of businesses and various regional economic measures, I was astounded at how quickly and how dramatically economic power had become more concentrated as things grew larger. I saw this first when I looked at the scale of business enterprises in Washington State and found that in 2004 the big box retail businesses overshadowed smaller retail business to a degree that I could not have imagined. Big box stores are giant nationally branded chain stores with national revenues of $1 billion or more. They include Walmart, the largest publically traded corporation in the world, a company that in 2011 had global revenues of $421.8 billion, profits of $16 billion, and 2.1 million employees. Target Corporation, a more representative big box also operating in Washington, is one of the largest chain store retailers in the country with 1,750 stores in the United States and global revenues of $67 billion in 2010. A single typical Target store occupies a footprint of more than 10 acres, with 179,000 square feet of retail space, plus 300,000 square feet for on-site parking. One Target store produces annual revenues of about $50 million. In contrast, comparable small retailers produce revenues of about $1 million and use only 1800 square feet. This means an average big box store takes up nearly 100 times more space and produces about 50 times more revenue. [44]

Big box stores matter, because their great size allows them to take a huge bite out of the retail sector in the local markets where they operate, and a higher proportion of their revenues do not circulate in the local economy, as they do with smaller businesses. According to my estimates based on average per-store revenues for these chains nationwide, the $15 billion in revenues that may have flowed through the 477 stores belonging to the ten largest "big box" retail chains in Washington in 2004, including Walmart, Home Depot, Costco, Target, Safeway, Kmart, and other well-known chains, might represent as much as an astounding 79 percent of the total of the $18.8 billion in the retail trade component of Washington's Gross State Product.

A series of studies comparing locally owned retail businesses with big box retail chains selling similar merchandise in New Orleans in 2009 dramatically showed that local businesses recirculated about twice as much of their revenues than the big boxes: 32 percent for locals versus 16 percent for the chains.[45] In Washington this suggests that the chains exported more than $2 billion dollars out of the state that would have otherwise been retained by locally owned independent businesses where it would have produced local jobs and modest profits. The difference is that local businesses pay better wages, retain their profits, purchase more goods and services locally, and give more to community charities. The ten chains whose Washington operations were included in my sample produced *national* revenues of more than $500 billion in 2004. Revenues of this magnitude are reflected in the high salaries and bonuses paid to their top executives and in outsized returns to their remote HNWI shareholders, including multi-billionaire families such as the Waltons. Chain stores are not a new phenomenon in the United States, but the big boxes are relatively recent, with the first Walmart opening in 1962. National big boxes require national markets, and they thrive in a growing economy. The rise of the big boxes corresponds to the period of especially rapid economic growth that occurred after about 1950. The big boxes are part of the vicious cycle of growth and power because they take business revenues away from smaller businesses and create amazing concentrations of economic power.

A PACIFIC NORTHWEST SMALL NATION TEST-MODEL: THE SNOHOMISH BASIN

The Snohomish Basin is a small bioregion north of Seattle and the Puget Sound metropolitan center. At 1,856 square miles it is about the size of the state of Delaware. It is offered here as an ideal small nation test model to explore what this natural region might look like restructured by different policy alternatives designed to increase sustainability for people and the environment. Alternative policy approaches will be projected onto an existing baseline of population, business, and government, taking into account the various forms of natural and cultural capital to make this exercise both as realistic and as plausible as possible. The purpose here is to consider what possibilities the small nation solution might present when applied to a real place in the PNW. In theory, people in such a small place could conceivably reach a consensus to make really dramatic changes and transform their territory into an agoria-, ecodemia-, or arcadia-style small nation. A special challenge of this example is that the basin is not currently a single political jurisdiction. We have to suspend disbelief and imagine Snohomish as a free-standing small nation.

Recognizing the existence of ecosystems immediately makes things complex, and shows why giant, centrally directed management systems are unlikely to succeed unless lower-level units have power and authority to make decisions based on local knowledge following subsidiarity principles. Any bioregion is part of a natural hierarchy. The Forest Service works with an eight-rank nested aquatic ecosystem hierarchy of zone, subzone, region, subregion, river basin, subbasin, watershed, subwatershed.[46] The state Department of Ecology recognizes the Snohomish Basin as Water Resource Area No. 7 of 62 WRAs. In 1994 the state identified the central issue in the basin as ". . . the potential conflict between increased human water demand and the desire to maintain and enhance fish productivity."[47] This is surely an environmental problem for a small nation to deal with.

The Snohomish Basin is the natural watershed of the Snoqualmie and Skykomish Rivers which originate in the Cascade Mountains and empty into Puget Sound. The total population of the basin was about 500,000 people in 2010, which represents about two-thirds of the population of Snohomish County. Part of the basin is also in King County, but the population of that part of the basin represents less than 10 percent of the basin's total population. Three-fourths of the basin is forested with more intensive land use concentrated on the lower river valleys and the coastal lowlands. Nearly half of the land area of the county is privately held, and the federal government owns more than a third. State and municipal governments own only about 13 percent, and tribes less than 2 percent. The basin's forests are under intense pressure for conversion to other uses, but the greater Puget Sound Basin is a hotspot of regional biodiversity with more than 4,000 animal species and 1,500 plants, nearly a 1,000 of which are considered imperiled.[48] Habitat pressure is the biggest immediate threat to biodiversity in the region, but that threat is being overshadowed by global warming.

Researchers at Earth Economics in Tacoma, Washington, have produced an analysis of the "whole economy" of Snohomish Basin from an ecological economics perspective taking into account all forms of capital—natural, built, financial, human, and social.[49] Their analysis fits well with the small nation solution because it starts with a small region, and follows four guiding principles that are assumed to be the foundation of a healthy economy: good governance, sustainability, efficiency, and justice. This corresponds to the small nation principles of scale, justice, political and economic democracy, and sustainability.

Earth Economics conservatively estimates that the existing natural ecosystems of the basin provide residents the equivalent of between $383 million and $5 billion in annual, otherwise-unpriced, benefits. This includes the value of nature's services for flood control, waste treatment and maintaining water supplies; stabilizing climate, fisheries, food production; and protecting critical habitats, but this does not include all of the regulating, habitat, provisioning, and information services that the basin provides its residents. The range of values is wide because there are many different methods of measuring ecosystem service values, including costs avoided, as from flooding, and replacement costs, as for a municipal water purification system. Increases to income can also be counted, as when naturally pure water improves fishery returns, and the amount people are willing to pay to enjoy a given natural service, such as the view. For example, snowpack melt provides some 70 percent of drinking water to greater Puget Sound residents annually. Replacing the natural snowpack water supply with an artificially constructed reservoir system would cost up to $39 billion annually for the greater region. Wetlands in the Snohomish Basin are high valued at $7,025 per acre, which at 26,444 acres yields a high annual value of more than $2 billion.

The value of annual natural services, or ecosystem services, is in effect measuring income. The $5 billion high estimate for the basin is nearly one-fourth of the $21 billion in personal income received by basin residents in 2010. The net present value of natural capital viewed as wealth, rather than income, is sometimes calculated as a declining value over a period of future time. Valued at a 2.7 percent declining value over a hundred years, the basin's $5.2 billion in currently produced natural services would represent annual natural capital worth $180 billion. If we assume that the basin's nature doesn't depreciate because it is used sustainably, then its future value would be $522 billion. Such valuations are starting points for how to think about the value of nature, and can help guide policy makers, but they necessarily leave out many important human values. Significantly, by any of these calculations, the value of nature as capital is an order of magnitude greater than the net value of the built capital and financial assets held by all the residents of the region. Just as in the Asháninka example considered in chapter 5, nature is overwhelmingly important to people whether or not it is valued by the market.

Snohomish County is overall relatively prosperous by conventional economic values. The county's 2011 median household income of $63,685 was somewhat above the $57,742 figure for Washington State as a whole and well above the national figure of $50,502. However, income and wealth were not equitably distributed in the county, and nearly 12 percent of families with children were below the official poverty level. I estimate that in 2010 the residents of the hypothetical Snohomish Basin Small Nation held in the aggregate approximately $75 billion in net worth in privately held, human-made tangible capital assets, such as cars and houses, and financial assets such as stocks, bonds, mutual funds, and retirement funds, discounted assets for debts. This figure is arrived at by first sorting the residents into my standard four household well-being categories (superelite, elite, maintenance, and poor) based on an updated version of the ranking system that I developed in 1997 for my study of property ownership in the Palouse. Taking household income distribution figures from the 2011 Census figures for Snohomish County in combination with the Federal Reserve's Consumer Finance Survey[50] for 2007 showing assets and debt holdings by income rank,[51] I was able to construct a reasonable approximation of actual income and wealth holdings for Snohomish Basin. My estimates may be conservative, but they are the right magnitude when cross-checked by other means. I estimate $42 billion in residential property in the basin, which compares well with the equivalent of $45 billion in property valuations by the county assessor.[52] These estimates would of course change completely if Bill Gates with his personal net worth of $61 billion in 2011 were to move into the basin from his home next door in King County.

My household finance analysis model suggests that there would be 6,661 superelites, the top 4 percent of households, who would hold 30 percent of net worth in the basin, and a third of all financial assets. Superelites were millionaires with average net worth of over $3 million and average incomes of $396,400. Average elite net worth would be $614,470 and their average incomes $116,000; maintenance households would hold $209,878 in net worth and have incomes averaging $57,900; poor households would average $105,833 in net worth and $12,300 in income. Maintenance and poor wealth levels modeled by this method feels much too high but will nevertheless be used for the present exercise because relative values and magnitudes are more useful than precise figures.

The maintenance level income threshold would allow most households to meet typical monthly expenses in Snohomish County as calculated by the Poverty in America Living Wage Calculator.[53] In order to meet basic needs for food, child care, medical, housing, transportation, taxes, and other expenses totaling $42,711 a year, a single adult with one child would need to earn an hourly wage of $20.53 in a full-time job. My figures suggest that nearly one-fourth of households would be poor by this definition, and this conclusion is reflected by their relatively small average holdings of tangible assets, which are mostly in houses and cars. Only the superelite have two-thirds of their tangible assets in investment properties and business equity. Their higher wealth levels would allow the elite and superelite to save significant amounts and invest in income-producing assets.

One way of restructuring to reduce poverty and obtain a more equitable distribution of wealth and income in this wealthy small nation would be for the citizen democratic majority to legislate a progressive wealth tax. Every wealth distribution is in effect a political decision, and the nation would need to reach a values- and justice-based decision on how to restructure capital allocation in the small nation. Taxes on various sorts of property, including of course real estate, but also on farm machinery, supplies, and materials, already exist in Snohomish County, but a broader wealth tax would be innovative to say the least. A wealth tax could take many specific forms, but it would need to be progressive enough to make accumulation beyond a certain point much less appealing for naturally aggrandizing individuals. Such a wealth tax that effectively reduced the average net worth of the basin's superelite to the level currently enjoyed by the more modestly situated elite would yield a "surplus" of over $18 billion for local reinvestment.

If nature in the basin is treated as capital, and if we take the high-end value of $522 billion for sustainably managed nature, then each household's equivalent share of that natural wealth would be $2.7 million. Nature's value is of course nonmarket, so it would need to be

represented in novel ways, such as rent value levied on those who benefit from natural resources. Even a modest 5 percent annual return on
that capital would be more than $135,000 per household per year. The
point here is not the exact amount, but that there is plenty of wealth in
nature and in "surplus" superelite wealth that an economic democracy
might choose to re-allocate to its citizens in more locally beneficial and
sustainable uses. Citizens might decide to place revenues derived from
the wealth tax or nature rent into special trusts funds modeled after the
Norwegian government's pension, or petroleum funds. The $18 billion
could finance new public infrastructure, including community-owned
business enterprises, such as renewable electric power cooperatives, or
help to restore degraded ecosystems.

A regional wealth-restructuring program might also inspire wealthier
people to bring home their personal capital and re-invest in their own
small nation. The amount of such "foreign" invested capital is significant. The Snohomish Small Nation is currently situated within the Seat-
tle-Tacoma-Bellevue Metropolitan Statistical Area, where according to
Civic Economics 2011 Indie City Index, about 40 percent of retail revenues are extracted by big box retailers. This represents some $2.5 bil-
lion in lost revenues to the basin at least some of which could be recovered when investors bring home their investments in the big boxes and
turn them into shares in local businesses. There is also a recoverable
loss in the higher proportion of retail revenues that recirculates in the
local region when local merchants in turn buy local for their goods and
services. Such local revenue recirculation would represent another
$850 million.

The question is, how much capital could local investors return to the
small nation of Snohomish? It is important to note that raising wealth
levels in this way would give more people access to income-producing
wealth. This would raise incomes, but would also mean that more local
people could be engaged in investment decision making. It would be
reasonable to estimate that as much as 80 percent of the $24 billion in
tangible assets in real property and business equities held by residents
of the Snohomish Small Nation are in local and regional investments.
This is based on my research on business licenses in Washington State,
which showed that about 90 percent of businesses in Washington municipalities were locally headquartered, but corporations were much
more likely to be nonlocally headquartered and were probably also

remotely owned. The $21 billion in directly held stocks, pooled invest-ment funds, including retirement accounts, and other managed assets also held by local residents can be estimated to be invested 90 percent nonlocally. In total this suggests that about $24 billion in capital in-vested outside of Snohomish could be brought home. This could be invested in many ways to create employment opportunities, more per-sonal income, and more local tax revenues.

Additional scale subsidies could of course also be recovered from the gap between the national "genuine progress" index value and GDP as discussed in the next chapter. This might be estimating at some $10 billion per year as the per capita share of basin residents for things like lower costs for national advertising, fossil fuels, national defense, crime, and social inequality that local residents would gain by forming a small nation. Some of these recovered costs would also be realized in environ-mental restoration. Aside from the obvious loss to depleted forests, eroded hillsides, dwindling farmlands, and disappearing salmon, unbal-anced growth in the PNW has produced a badly skewed distribution of income, wealth, and social power. Fixing all of these problems would bring enormous benefits to the citizens of the new small nation of Snohomish Basin.

7

UNITED SMALL NATIONS OF AMERICA

Why and How

[U]nder our current operating system, the rights of capital trump everything else. The rights of workers, communities, nature, and future generations—all play second fiddle to capital's prerogative to maximize short term gain. This hierarchy isn't the doing of God or some inexorable law of nature. Rather, it's a result of political choice. —Peter Barnes, *Capitalism 3.0,* 2006[1]

How do you revise a system as vast and complex as capitalism? And how do you do it gracefully, with a minimum of pain and disruption? The answer is, you do what Bill Gates does: you upgrade the operating system. —Peter Barnes, *Capitalism 3.0,* 2006[2]

Profound improvements will unfold when people living in America's existing economic areas, large metropolitan areas, small states, and large counties make the gradual shift to thinking of themselves as small nations and then acting accordingly in their best interests. America was a small nation, with fewer than 10 million people until about 1825, when it crossed the line to large-nation status by expanding to more than 10 million people. It reached mega-nation status with more than 100 million people by 1915. American's economy grew to $100-giga ($100 billion in $2005 dollars) by 1860, and became the world's largest economy by 1872. By 1916 America passed the $7,500/GDP per capita poverty threshold, the minimum level of economic development for a country to in theory escape material poverty, assuming a well-distributed national income. Thanks to continuing economic growth, Americans became a $tera ($ trillion) economy by 1925 and a $10-tera economy by 1998. By 2010 America was a mega-nation of over 300 million people that dominated the world with its $14 trillion dollar, $42,000 per capita economy, its great financial wealth, giant corporations, great military power, science, and technology. America was also using more than its share of the world's energy and resources, and producing 18 percent of global carbon dioxide emissions, second only to China.

In 2010 there were some 308 million people in the United States. America had the fourth largest land area in the world after Russia, Canada, and China and was the third largest population in the world after India and China. America had the world's largest economy at $14 trillion in 2008, which was about one-fourth of global GDP. In 2007 it was responsible for about 20 percent of global carbon dioxide emissions from energy consumption, reflecting its consumption of 21 percent of the world's primary energy.[3] America also had the world's largest market capitalization, the world's largest corporations, the largest military expenditures, and the largest share of the world's billionaires, but it ranked only thirteenth on the UN Human Development Index in 2009, and was twentieth best on the 2011 Failed State Index, which placed it in the "needs watching" category.

The biggest beneficiaries of America's amazing economic growth were the three million High Net Worth Individuals (HNWIs), Americans who held total investment assets of more than $10 trillion in 2010. These are precisely the top 1 percent identified by the Occupy Wall Street movement and certainly qualify as the primary elite directors of American growth. As the theory of elite-directed growth predicts, recent American economic growth has not been accompanied by significant poverty reduction. In 2009 more than 56 million Americans were living below 125 percent of the official poverty threshold. This was higher in absolute numbers than at any time since the Census began tracking poverty in 1959. Between 1979 and 2007 the top 1 percent of households' after-tax incomes grew 275 percent and the top 20 percent by 65 percent, whereas everyone else's income share declined. American poverty is now expanding into formerly affluent middle-class suburbia. The question explored in this chapter is why the small nation solution needs to be applied to the United States, and how it might be done to achieve a more beneficial and more sustainable distribution of wealth and power.

A VERMONT INTERLUDE

In the summer of 2000 I was invited to teach a summer anthropology course at the University of Vermont. This was a welcome opportunity to visit one of the smallest states in the country and test my findings on the power-concentrating effects of growth that I had found earlier in the much larger state of Washington. Vermont then had a population of just over 600,000, about the same as my hypothetical Snohomish Basin small nation and just ahead of the smallest state, which was Wyoming with about 500,000 people. At that time the state of Washington had about six million people, making it ten times larger than Vermont. This meant that Washington was still the equivalent of a relatively "larger" small nation, but Vermont was in effect a mini-nation on the scale of Luxembourg. A careful comparison would be expected to reveal significant scale-related differences between the two states. That summer I traveled throughout Vermont collecting comparative data on property ownership and businesses and assessing at sidewalk level the overall well-being of households and communities.

The small size of Vermont made my research an absolute pleasure. I could readily arrange personal interviews with government officials at all levels of government, and town officials were happy to share their computer databases. What I found mirrored precisely my findings in Washington State and showed that in part because Vermont was so much smaller than Washington, wealth and power was much more widely distributed in Vermont. The critical factor was that Vermont had been a small nation for a very long time, at least since it became the independent Vermont Republic in 1777. It did not join the United States until 1791, as the fourteenth state. This meant that elite-directed growth was much less likely to be a problem in Vermont, and I expected that genuinely sustainable development with social justice would have a much better prospect in Vermont than in Washington. Events since then seem to confirm this prediction and provide strong support for the importance of the small nation solution.

More than a decade after my summer in Vermont, the contrasts between the two states remained really clear. Washington added nearly a million people between 2000 and 2010, but Vermont added fewer than 3,000 people. Both economies grew by roughly the same percentage (about 15 percent) in real (constant 2005 dollars), with Washington growing slightly faster and increasing from $259 billion to $305 billion. Vermont's GDP added about $3 billion, growing from $20 billion to nearly $23 billion, but because its population barely changed, its GDP per capita actually increased substantially. Both states would be considered high income countries by World Bank per capita GDP rankings, although Washington's per capita was higher in 2010 at $45,225 versus $36,518 and both have roughly equal income Gini ranks. Vermont's per capita GDP added $3,765 in comparison with Washington's $1,381. More significantly for the well-being of its population, Vermont's median household income increased dramatically, adding $5,812 in comparison with Washington's $2,412. Vermont also had a lower percent of its population below the 125 percent of the official poverty line (14.6 versus 16.1) in 2010. In real numbers this meant that Vermont had 90,000 poor people and Washington over a million. This suggests that Vermont's economy was actually working better for its citizens.

Vermont's Burlington–South Burlington Metropolitan Statistical Area (MSA) also ranks near the top of the Indie City Index released in 2011 by Civic Economics. This is another indication that independently owned local businesses are thriving in the state, because they are not overpowered by giant externally owned corporations. In 2010 there were only two businesses with revenues of more than a billion dollars headquartered in Vermont.[4] In comparison there were 23 billion-dollar companies headquartered in Washington State in 2008.[5] As will be discussed later in this chapter, billion-dollar corporations represent concentrated economic power that is associated with the kind of elite direction that can disempower the majority of smaller businesses in a particular region. The alternative is that a state that incorporates relatively fewer billion-dollar businesses can be expected to have a more equitable distribution of economic power, especially if relatively few externally headquartered billion-dollar businesses are also operating in the state.

The Burlington–South Burlington MSA (hereafter simply Burlington) was the largest urban area in Vermont, with over 200,000 people, but by population it was only the 201st largest MSA in the country in 2010. In order for the Census Bureau to qualify an urban area as an MSA, it needed to comprise at least 50,000 people. At that time there were fifty-one MSAs in the country with more than a million people, and two that exceeded 10 million. The relatively small size of the Burlington MSA, combined with its location in a very small state, helps explain the success of its local businesses. Civic Economics ranked it twenty-third out of 324 MSAs, with an index value of 123.6. The index is calculated from a baseline of 100 representing the average market saturation by billion-dollar retailers. The higher the index value, the lower the market share taken by the big boxes.

Civic Economics is a consulting firm formed in 2002 to help governments, businesses, and civic organizations promote sustainable local and regional economies and communities. Based in Austin and Chicago, Civic Economics researchers look at development issues holistically, like anthropologists, and they correctly assume that healthy communities require healthy, sustainable economies. The Indie City Index measures the vitality of independently owned businesses in all MSAs. The Civics Economics researchers used a method similar to my earlier estimate of the impact of big box retailers in Washington State. Drawing on more extensive marketing research data bases, they were able to include every billion-dollar giant retailer in the country, operating in every sector of the retail economy except groceries and automotive such as car dealerships and service stations. There were only 107 such parent companies, with familiar names such as Walmart, Costco, Home Depot, Target, Walgreen's, Lowe's, Rite Aid, and Staples. These were typically big box chain stores each with revenues of a billion dollars or more that were operating store-front retail businesses at some 122,000 locations in MSAs throughout the country. These giant corporations averaged more than 1,000 retail outlets each. They ranged from taking 20 to more than 80 percent of retail sales, averaging 45 percent, with their impact apparently greater in smaller MSAs, where they saturated the market and could be simply overpowering.

THE GREAT WEALTH AND INCOME SHIFT
TO THE TOP, 1950–2010

The effects of the vicious cycle of elite-directed growth can be seen at the national level in the United States where changes in government policies from 1950 to 2010 caused business revenues and assets to shift dramatically away from small proprietorships and partnerships and become concentrated in a very few super-large corporations at the top of the business hierarchy. This shift in the economic power of businesses was paralleled by a shift in wealth and income from the middle and lower household ranks to the top 1 percent of households. These were political changes that disempowered the middle and lower ranks in America and allowed top corporate directors and the super-wealthy to exercise ever greater power over the national and global economy. The statistical evidence for the reality of this huge transformation in the distribution of American political and economic power is outlined below, drawing on data collected by the Census Bureau and the IRS. These changes in power underscore the importance of restoring political and economic democracy in the United States by means of the small nation solution.

Sole proprietorships, mom and pop stores, are the most numerous form of business in the United States and almost certainly in the world. For much of the twentieth century they were the heart of neighborhoods and small towns. Businesses organized as proprietorships are also relatively small and uncomplex, short-lived businesses, legally existing only during the lifetime of their proprietors. These intrinsic features limit the amount of capital assets proprietorships can accumulate, and they create a practical upper size limit to their growth. Most proprietorships are stable, stationary, no-growth businesses that are successful when they allow a family to maintain itself and build modest capital. As a result of the natural ceiling on the size of proprietorships, their revenue size ranks do not follow the Pareto power law distribution. In fact, at least in 1960 when 16 percent of all business revenues flowed through proprietorships, the overwhelming majority (97 percent) of proprietorships were small, with revenues under $500,000 (in 2005 dollars), and small proprietorships produced the overwhelming majority of proprietorship revenues.[6] These facts make it easy to imagine how a small nation based entirely on small proprietorships might do just fine, producing and distributing everything the country needed.

For businesses to escape the limits of proprietorship and grow larger, their owner-managers must adopt different organizational forms. Business partnerships are the simplest way to raise the upper limits. Partnerships are larger, more complex businesses, although still somewhat impermanent. Unlike with proprietorships, it is the middle revenue size range of partnerships that are the most numerous. In 1960 a third of partnerships were mid-sized (revenues of $250,000 to $500,000 in 2005 dollars) and had most (78 percent) of partnership revenue.

It is large, complex corporations that can grow without limit. Fewer than half of corporate businesses were in the top revenue rank in 1960, but even then the top rank had an astounding 98 percent of corporate revenues. This reverses the distribution seen in proprietorships and follows Pareto power law expectations for concentration. Corporations are a form of business that concentrates economic power, whereas proprietorships do so only to a lesser degree. It is also remarkable that among corporations the power law works to dramatically concentrate power. This power-concentrating effect is seen most strongly in the distribution of corporate assets. This is seen clearly in the way that corporate assets shifted to the largest corporations over the nearly six decades between 1950 and 2008. The elite, top-ranked corporations, constituting less than 1 percent of all corporate businesses, held only 58 percent of corporate assets in 1950, but by 2008 they held an astonishing 90 percent. This means that the top gained a much larger slice of a much larger asset pie. Over that time *average* elite corporate assets grew from under $1 billion to over $7 billion in constant 2005 dollars, but even within the top rank, assets shifted to the super-elite at the very top of this powerful group of businesses. For example, at the tip top of American corporations, Walmart's market value stood at $202 billion in 2012. This sudden growth of elite and super-elite corporate business power is probably more the result of a cycle in which business power becomes political power, then becomes more business power, than of the market processes that Adam Smith imagined operating in a world of small businesses and small markets.

One of the "vicious" aspects of this elite-directed growth process is that the shift toward more complex forms of business organization, which raised the scale threshold and produced higher levels of economic growth, also caused a qualitative change in American business that had negative economic effects for smaller businesses and most Americans. The rise to power of larger-scale and more complex businesses may not have been the only way to increase the total economic product of the country, but it apparently did cause sole proprietorships to lose a significant share of business revenues. The percentage of business receipts received by proprietorships dropped from 16 percent in 1960 to 5 percent in 2008.[7] In contrast, partnership businesses doubled their share from 7 to 14 percent, but corporations continued their relentless climb, increasing their share from 77 to 81 percent, even though by 2008 corporations only constituted 18 percent of all businesses. The putative loss in proprietorship business revenues to partnerships and corporations between 1984 and 2008 was about $60 trillion dollars (in 2005 dollars) in comparison with what they would have had if they had kept the 16 percent share of revenues that they were receiving in 1960. Total business revenues more than doubled from $14 trillion in 1984 to more than $30 trillion in 2008, again in constant 2005 dollars, but *average* proprietorship revenues actually declined by nearly 30 percent over this period (1984 to 2008) from $76,513 to $53,633, again in constant 2005 dollars. This is serious revenue lost to real communities and is a reflection of the degree of economic disempowerment experienced by local business people as big box corporate businesses invaded their neighborhoods.

The economic loss to most small businesses caused by this gigantic shift of business power to large corporations since 1960 is also seen in the equally gigantic shift in personal income from poor and maintenance level households to the elite minority of households between 1950 and 2009 as revealed by a careful look at IRS statistics of individual income and its sources.[8] In 1950, 99 percent of tax filers were the poor- and maintenance-level majority of Americans, and they reported receiving 87 percent of income. This meant that most people were doing reasonably well, and even the poor were on average not too badly off. By 2009 this majority had dropped somewhat to 88 percent of tax returns, but now they had only 51 percent of revenue. This was a huge loss of household maintenance income, which was reflected in the new reality that it was now almost impossible for a single income earner in a household to be an adequate provider for anything larger than a single-person household. Both parents would now need to seek outside employment just to stay even. At the top of the household income hierarchy, the elite expanded their proportion of filers from just over 1 percent with 1 percent of income in 1950, to 12 percent with nearly half of all income. This was a seismic shift in economic power that can readily be accounted for by a combination of factors related to the overall growth in the economy and the rising dominance of super-elite corporations. These factors included the loss of manufacturing to lower-wage overseas producers and the increasing importance of the financial sector. As larger volumes of money began to flow through the economy and as globalization became a stronger force after 1980, managerial and executive salaries began to soar, especially for those in finance. People with money also began to gain large returns from speculative finance.

Virtually hidden in the economic transformations that accompanied growth during the post-1950 Great Acceleration era (see chapter 1) was a massive transfer of new wealth, especially financial wealth, from the majority producers to the super-elite directors. Everyone surely contributed to the production of this new wealth, and it might have been more equitably distributed if the organization of business had not also changed in a way that favored the interests of the owners and directors of large corporations over the millions of small proprietorship businesses that were flourishing in 1950.

Most people are understandably concerned with employment and wage and salary income, because that is now the source of most of our income, but what really matters now is income from wealth, and this is most important at upper income levels where elite-directors are located. It was this transfer of wealth to the top that greatly amplified the influence of elite directors over all aspects of the global culture, but it was the positive feedback of great masses of new wealth that especially put elites in a position to promote their particular form of growth and the political policies that propelled the great increase in mass consumption and the concentration of wealth that led to still more growth. In this growth process most people fell behind in wealth and their income stagnated, whereas a few raced ahead.

Wealth redistribution to the super-elite can be seen in the fact that individual *unearned income* (from dividends, interest, royalties, rents, estates and trusts, and capital gains) increased at a faster rate than income from wages or business from 1950 to 2009. The elite also took a much larger share of unearned income, increasing their take from over half in 1950 to 85 percent by 2009. After 1950 the mathematical average unearned income for all tax filers approximately doubled in constant 2005 dollars reaching $50,000 by 2009, but the average super-elite unearned income rose to $2.8 million, up from $2 million in 1950. Such figures are understandable given that the super-elites have millionaire incomes by definition. Unearned income for average maintenance-level filers remained relatively flat at around $1,000. The crucial point here is that this distribution of income and wealth is not inherent in nature and it is not universal. As noted above, sole proprietorship income and wealth did not concentrate at the top in this manner.

The great wealth and income shift that occurred from 1950 to 2010 was a particular *political distribution* resulting from human decisions to impose particular rules and to favor particular forms of business organization. Income from wealth shifted to the top in the United States at this time in part as a result of a political change to impose less progressive income taxes, and much lower tax rates at the upper ranks. In 1950 the effective income tax rate for a single maintenance-level person with an income of $25,000 was 35 percent, and an elite with a $500,000 income paid 79 percent. In 2009 individuals at the same rank would pay an effective rate of 13 and 30 percent, respectively. The highest unadjusted rate was 35 percent, less than half of the 1950 rate. The tax rate on capital held over a year and for most dividends was just 15 percent, which was a huge incentive for investors. The highest tax rate on corporate income was 42 percent in 1950, and it reached 53 percent in 1968-69 during the Vietnam War, but it stood at 35 percent in 2009.[9] There were also many new ways that corporations could avoid being taxed.

GOLDMAN SACHS: WHY TOO BIG IS NOT THE RIGHT SIZE

Why the seemingly unlimited growth of corporations contributes to global problems is well illustrated by a recent high-level resignation in a giant American investment bank. Greg Smith, a London-based executive director for Goldman Sachs' equity derivatives in Europe, the Middle East, and Africa, resigned very publicly in 2012, detailing what he saw as serious moral problems with the "toxic and destructive" cultural environment at Goldman.[10] His primary issue was with the way Goldman's top executives allowed short-term profits to be placed ahead of the interests of its own clients, who he repeatedly saw Goldman managing directors denigrating as "muppets." Smith was immediately mocked and savaged by opinion leaders in the finance community, and his accusations drew a quick denial from Goldman CEO Blankfein, but this case nevertheless highlights what can go wrong when businesses grow too large. In making the case for why small nations are places where businesses, markets, and economies can be the right size, and to establish what the "right size" is, it is important to know why premier, world-class businesses like Goldman are not the right size.

It turns out that Goldman Sachs is not just a very successful, very large corporation. It is also one of the largest, most important global corporations according to Forbes Global 2000 list of the largest publicly traded corporations in the world. In its 2011 list Forbes used a composite ranking that only considered corporations with revenues of at least $3.3 billion; profits of $207.9 million; assets of $6.59 billion; and market value of $4.14 billion. Only 3,400 corporations of the world's 37 million corporations, or the top 0.009 percent, met at least one of these criteria. Goldman Sachs ranked thirty-seventh in the Forbes list with revenues of $46 billion; profits of $8.4 billion; assets of $911.3 billion; and market value of $90 billion.[11] More significantly, recent analysis of worldwide ownership and control of transnational corporations, both publicly traded and private, conducted by a team of physicists and network analysts at the Swiss Federal Institute of Technology in Zurich, found that Goldman ranked eighteenth in a group of transnational corporations that collectively controlled more than 25 percent of the entire network of more than a million ownership connections among more than 600,000 large corporations worldwide in 2007.[12] Control refers to the amount of a given corporation's value that an owner can influence.

Goldman is at the very heart of the American and the global economy, and its top executives are closely connected with the highest levels of the U.S. government. Like the Koch brothers, Goldman officials have actively worked to shape the laws. According to public records Goldman spent more than $27 million dollars lobbying the federal government between 1998 and 2011, and somewhat more, $28 million, on political contributions to federal candidates and political parties during election cycles from 2000 to 2010. This counts contributions by Goldman to its political action committee (PAC), and individual contributions by Goldman and individual officers, employees, and immediate family members. This is more than $55 million and must surely have purchased a substantial return in political favors. Such lobbying helped maintain the "favorable" regulatory environment for Goldman's interests which contributed to the global financial crisis of 2008.

Smith was handling assets for clients who in total had investments of about a trillion dollars, including sovereign wealth funds. He resigned because he believed that Goldman's official corporate culture that had emphasized trust and integrity and put the interests of the client ahead of short-term profits changed rather abruptly when Lloyd Blankfein took over as CEO in 2006. A crucial trust issue was Goldman's betting that certain securities that it sold to its own clients would fail, which was among the criminal fraud charges brought against Goldman by the Securities and Exchange Commission in 2010 following the financial meltdown. Although the criminal charges were dropped in late 2012, other business experts confirmed some of Smith's accusations, noting significantly that business culture and the incentives for managers did change when the company transformed itself from a partnership to a publicly traded corporation in 1999.[13] This further reflects the scale effects of business organization that I discussed above. The CEO of a very large publicly traded company has a strong incentive to show growth in profits to raise share value, and as is well known, the heads of the very largest companies are rewarded with outrageously high levels of compensation. This surely creates a perverse short-term incentive to promote growth at whatever the long-term cost.

THE ULTIMATE SOLUTION FOR TOO BIG TO FAIL BANKS

The Dallas Fed has advocated the ultimate solution for TBTF [too big to fail]—breaking up the nation's biggest banks into smaller units. —Harvey Rosenblum, VP, Federal Reserve of Dallas, 2011[14]

For there is scant chance that managers of $1 trillion or $2 trillion banking enterprises can possibly "know their customer," follow time-honored principles of banking and fashion reliable risk management models for organizations as complex as these megabanks have become. —Richard W. Fisher, president, Federal Reserve of Dallas, 2011 speech at Columbia University's Politics and Business Club[15]

The global financial crisis was very much a product of tera-scale economies led by the United States. Countries with the world's largest economies also hosted the biggest financial institutions, encouraged their
growth, and then bailed them out when they failed in 2008. Their
failure is also a failure of the ideology of perpetual economic growth.
Some of the strongest evidence that gigantic piles of money, as in trillions or hundreds of billions, cannot be safely managed by individual
human beings comes from the financial sector of the American economy where some of the world's very largest stacks of money can be
found. Goldman Sachs, discussed above, is just one example of this
problem. In view of the great importance of financial capital in the
contemporary global system it is relevant to further consider the significance of the size of financial corporations measured by the assets they
command, and to ponder in what sense any concentration of capital can
be considered too large. This is especially the case now that the largest
American financial institutions have been singled out for primary responsibility for the global financial collapse of 2008.[16] There is abundant evidence that the largest financial corporations grew too large
because their executives chose to use their great power to, in effect, buy
political influence by lobbying for favorable legislative rulings that removed their limits to growth and encouraged them to gamble with the
capital they controlled.[17] When these giant corporations took too many
risks and began to fail, the government declared them to be "Too Big to
Fail" (TBTF) or "Systematically Important Financial Institutions" (SI-
FIs) and propped them up with public funds to presumably prevent
even greater financial disaster.

Compelling arguments that banks can indeed be too large have
come from such authoritative sources as economists associated with the
IMF, the U.S. Federal Reserve, and from investigations conducted by
the U.S. House and Senate. In its 2011 annual report published in
March of 2012, Harvey Rosenblum, executive vice president and director of research at the Federal Reserve Bank of Dallas, issued a scathing
warning about the dangers of financial institutions that were TBTF,
calling them "a clear and present danger to the U.S. economy."[18] Rosenblum placed blame for the great financial disaster of 2007-2008 on
human complacency, self-delusion, or "willful blindness," and greed
that became especially problematic during the "Great Moderation" of
steady economic growth that occurred from 1983 to 2007. Human

greed, "the human desire for material gain," gave financiers perverse incentives to take advantage of lax regulations and enforcement to game the system, gambling with huge risks on the assumption that government would bail them out if they failed. This was the "moral hazard" that richly rewarded financial institutions for writing and selling loans, rather than keeping them on their books. They then made even more money by betting that the risks would fail.

Concentration in the American financial sector caused the global financial crisis to unfold much more quickly and made it much worse than it might have been otherwise. Rosenblum points out that the country's *top five* banks grew dramatically and dangerously larger from 1970, when they held only 17 percent of financial assets in the financial sector, to 2010 when they held 52 percent of a much larger total. In 1970, 12,500 "smaller" banks held 46 percent, but by 2010 the number of smaller banks had shrunk to only 5,700, and their share had declined to just 16 percent of assets. This of course mirrors the general trends in American businesses discussed above.

The actual quantities of financial assets held by different size ranks in the American banking sector are astounding. When 2011 began, all 15,218 U.S. commercial banks, U.S. branches of foreign banks, thrifts, and credit unions held total assets of more than $16 trillion in the United States, but the *top 50* banks held more than 90 percent of these assets, and the *top five* had a commanding 53 percent. The largest bank, JPMorgan Chase, had $2.2 trillion, 14 percent of the total. JPMorgan Chase's assets are so huge that the loss of $2 billion due to "errors, sloppiness and bad judgment" at a trading desk in its London branch in 2012[19] would technically have a trivial balance sheet impact, given that $2 billion is a mere 0.1 percent of $2 trillion. Nearly half of the total number of American banks was represented by the 7,339 credit unions, which had just over 5 percent of total assets.[20] Credit unions serve ordinary people, who also own them. They were more reasonably sized, with assets that averaged barely $125 million, several orders of magnitude less than the $295 billion average of the top 50. Credit unions are ideal models of how financial services would be handled in a small nation.

Rosenblum argues that the big banks grew by taking advantage of the complexity and confusion that accompanied growth, relying on deceptive accounting techniques and use of novel investment instruments that were poorly understood and loosely regulated. The big banks also turned to proprietary trading, using bank money to make profit for themselves directly. This was a practice that was banned by the 1933 Glass-Steagall Act which attempted to keep commercial banking separate from speculative securities trading in response to the banking crisis that led to the Great Depression. Rosbenblum is in effect describing the vicious elite-directed cycle of growth and power that I describe in chapter 1, and which would hopefully be prevented by the small scale of financial institutions in small nations.

It has often been argued that "scale efficiencies" both explain and justify growth in the size of businesses, and this has certainly been argued in the case of the biggest banks. However, there are prominent economists and bankers who stress that scale efficiencies are hard to prove for the very largest banks, and even if they exist, whatever benefits they might yield may be outweighed by the implicit and actual subsidies that the largest banks receive from government, and thus indirectly from tax payers. Investigations commissioned by governments and by the banking industry itself often claim to find little persuasive evidence that corporate size, or degree of concentration, are in themselves necessarily problems. However, a broader view, especially considering subsidies to the big banks, long-term economic stability, and fairness to people at large, reaches different conclusions. For example, Andrew G. Haldane, executive director for Financial Stability of the Bank of England, cites figures showing that from 2007 to 2010 global banks received annual subsidies averaging $242 billion.[21]

This discussion of financial scale is not to demonize money and markets; it is about getting them the right size and getting decision making at the best levels for capitalism to function in a more beneficial, just, and sustainable way. As anthropologists Sol Tax[22] observed decades ago, and Keith Hart[23] more recently, the solution to contemporary problems will require a combination of governments and markets in which both can function democratically at regional, national, and global levels. That is the essence of the small nation solution. For democratic processes to function effectively, decision-making power over wealth needs to be widely distributed, not concentrated in a few hands.

LOOK AT THE MONKEY: THE GDP DELUSION
AND THE ALTERNATIVES

> What we measure affects what we do; and if our measurements are
> flawed, decisions may be distorted. Choices between promoting
> GDP and protecting the environment may be false choices, once
> environmental degradation is appropriately included in our measure-
> ment of economic performance. —*Report by the Commission on the
> Measurement of Economic Performance and Social Progress*, 2009[24]

Two poorly trained monkeys, a large howler and a very frisky squirrel
monkey, had free rein at a small rustic hotel where we frequently stayed
during one of my research projects in the Peruvian Amazon in the mid-
1970s. My son Brett was only four years old at the time, but the antics
of these monkeys were so outrageously distracting and so memorable
that, as an adolescent, Brett began saying, "look at the monkey" as a
joking way to divert my attention. By the late 1990s the phrase entered
popular culture after an episode of South Park used "look at the silly
monkey" in a parody of a nonsensical phrase used to distract and con-
fuse a jury into reaching an improper acquittal. It became known as the
"Chewbacca defense," in reference to the tall hairy Wookie in Star
Wars. I now recognize that GDP is the distracting Chewbacca, "look at
the monkey," defense of elite-directed growth.

In the present context, I suggest that in the United States and in
much of the world, Gross Domestic Product (GDP) is a similar "look at
the monkey" distraction, because it is likewise nonsensical and equally
distracting, but in this case it is leading us toward an improper judg-
ment on the necessity of endless economic growth as the best measure
of human well-being. Many distinguished economists now recognize
that GDP is a flawed measure because it does not actually measure our
well-being, but I would add that worse yet, it draws our attention away
from the dual problem of elite direction and concentrated power. This
makes it more difficult for a very large nation like the United States to
get things the right size and wealth and power sustainably distributed.

GDP is part of the elite-directed growth problem for the United
States because it is elite directors who continually point to GDP growth
as our primary goal and the primary measure of the effectiveness of our
economic system. This distraction makes it harder for the majority to
understand how the vicious cycle of growth actually works. GDP is an

illusory and distracting measure because it ignores wealth *distribution* and the multiple *forms of wealth* which are the real sources of GDP. Even more fundamental, many people have come to imagine that infinite growth is a realistic possibility.

The modern concept of GDP originated with American economist Simon Kuznets' work on national income during the Great Depression.[25] Measures of national income date back to English economist William Petty's writing in the seventeenth century at the dawn of capitalism, but economic growth as *a good in itself* has only become a distracting national obsession since about 1950. Kuznets wanted a measure of economic goods that would apply to a "highly developed national economy" such as the United States, so he intentionally disregarded "primitive tribes" along with the goods and satisfactions that an active life might generally provide, and instead he measured the money value of "economic goods" defined as "commodities, services, arrangements, etc. that are dealt in on the market. . . ." Although Kuznets did extensive research on *wealth* and *wealth distribution* in the United States, GDP measures only the flow of money, not the wealth behind it. It does not measure human well-being, and it only counts aspects of nature that are "on the market." Kuznets' concept of GDP excludes not only nature, but also unpaid domestic labor within the home, such as cooking, cleaning, and childcare. A broader concept of human well-being that would apply to "primitive tribes," as well as small and large nations, calls for measures that include all forms of income, including nature's services and domestic human services that would not be part of the market; and that count as wealth, or capital, all sources of income: individual humans, society, culture, and nature.

National policies that narrowly focus on increasing GDP delay the urgently needed transition to a more sustainable relatively steady-state economy with costs and benefits fairly distributed, which of course defines the small nation solution. American economist Herman Daly and the Center for the Advancement of the Steady State Economy (CASSE) have long advocated for the establishment of such an economy, following the lead of eighteenth- and nineteenth-century economists Adam Smith and John Stuart Mill. These pioneers, at the dawn of the industrial age, already foresaw a time when growth in material production and consumption would necessarily end.

Daly defined the steady state economy as "An economy with constant stocks of people and artifacts, maintained at some desired, sufficient levels by low rates of maintenance 'throughput', that is, by the lowest feasible flows of matter and energy from the first stage of production to the last stage of consumption."[26] This does not mean that all economic growth would stop, but both population and per capita material consumption would stabilize. Services, knowledge, culture, and human leisure and well-being could continue to expand, and to the extent that these less tangible things were measured by an improved GDP, GDP could also grow.

Researchers at the public policy "smart economics" American think tank, Redefining Progress,[27] founded in 1994, developed a now widely accepted alternative economic measure, the Genuine Progress Indicator (GPI)[28] to address many of the deficiencies of GDP. Unlike GDP, the GPI is concerned with accounting for the benefits of consumption that actually promote human well-being. These are things that everyone would recognize as benefiting households, communities, society, and the environment. GPI starts with personal consumption expenditures adjusted for inequality and adds the value of unpaid household work, services provided by household appliances, community volunteers, and public infrastructure, but deducts as costs the effects of crime, family breakdown, the loss of leisure, unemployment, consumer durables, commuting, pollution, auto accidents, and the loss of public goods such as wetlands, old-growth forests, farmland, depletion of nonrenewable resources, and long-term environmental damage. Graphed between 1950 and 2002 in constant dollars Genuine Progress remained relatively flat, even as total GDP soared to more than three times higher than GPI. This is clear evidence that progress measured by growth in GDP is illusory. Similar conclusions about the deficiencies of growth as a measure of human progress were reached by Nobel laureate economists Joseph Stiglitz, and Amartya Sen, who co-chaired the 2009 Commission on the Measurement of Economic Performance and Social Progress (CMEPSP), which was commissioned by French president Nicolas Sarkozy.[29]

BELLIGERENT BILLIONAIRES: WHY PLUTONOMY FAILS

The world is divided into two blocs—the plutonomies, where economic growth is powered by and largely consumed by the wealthy few, and the rest. . . . In a plutonomy there is no such animal as "the U.S. consumer" or the "UK consumer," or indeed the "Russian consumer." There are rich consumers, few in number, but disproportionate in the gigantic slice of income and consumption they take. There are the rest, the "nonrich" the multitudinous many, but only accounting for surprisingly small bites of the national pie. Consensus analyses do not tease out the profound impact of the plutonomy on spending power, debt loads, savings rates (and hence current account deficits), oil price impacts etc., i.e., focus on the "average" consumer are flawed from the start. —Citigroup analysts Ajay Kapur, Niall Macleod, and Narendra Singh, 2005[30]

It is commonplace to recognize that money buys political influence, but super-wealthy individuals can influence whole sectors of the culture in ways that ramp up and perpetuate the costly forms of production and consumption that subsidize unsustainable growth. Since the 1990s it has become increasingly obvious that we live in a global *plutocracy*, rule by the rich; and we have a global *plutonomy*, an economy run by and for the rich.

This is not some outdated Marxist critique of capitalism; it is an interpretation shared by sober investment managers such as the Citigroup analysts cited in the above quotation from 2005. Citigroup was the third largest bank in the United States, and one of the world's largest financial services corporations in 2011, reporting that it was managing assets of $12 trillion.[31] This was after being bailed out as an institution that was "too big to fail" by the U.S. federal government following the global financial crisis of 2008. Citigroup's Global Transaction Services division is by itself absolutely central to the daily operation of the global plutonomy, moving $3 trillion daily between the world's largest corporations, producing $10 billion in annual revenues in the process.

In crafting their stock investment strategy Citigroup's analysts, as noted in the above quotations, concluded that ordinary consumers were now virtually irrelevant. Only the truly wealthy and their money actually mattered, as they declared: "The earth is being held up by the muscular arms of its entrepreneur-plutocrats, like it, or not."[32] This also means that decisions being made by the plutocrats are a primary cause of global problems. If plutocrats are running the global economy, and global production and consumption is being so badly misallocated that the entire system is now unsustainable, then plutonomy and plutocracy are monumental failures. This is also an opinion shared by some members of the international banking community. In 2012 analysts at Barclays Capital, a branch of Barclays, a top tier global bank, called the recent boom in building "the world's tallest buildings" a "bubble" that was a reflection of a "widespread misallocation of capital" that pointed to another financial crisis.[33] Maybe the world really doesn't need another world's tallest building.

This is a culture scale and power problem, not just a problem of personal greed. The rich in effect "rule" because great wealth gives them too much power in the market, whether it is deciding what to put on the market and what sells, in what to invest, in using their influence to set the rules, or in defining what people will believe to be unquestionably true. Great wealth gives individuals more power than anyone could wisely and safely handle. For example, multi-billionaire Rupert Murdoch, as CEO and 40 percent owner of News Corporation, directs a global media entertainment company that reported $60 billion in assets in 2008. News Corp claimed to reach an audience of 4 billion people speaking the world's ten most-spoken languages in the hundred largest countries where 97 percent of the global population lives. Its audience in the United States and Europe was enormous, but it may be even bigger in Asia. Murdoch has been widely perceived to have significant political influence as an advocate of conservative and free market causes. Wanting more power, he successfully lobbied in the United States for passage of the 1996 Telecommunications Act to permit greater concentration of media ownership. News Corp was enmeshed in an ethics scandal in the UK in 2011 but also promoted a "Global Energy Initiative" to help reduce global warming as "good business practice."

The specific phrase "belligerent billionaires" was applied to superwealthy Australian mining magnates who have shrilly condemned the Australian government's efforts at introducing a carbon tax to reduce carbon emissions and a super-profits tax on minerals in response to global warming. China's economic boom has created a super-lucrative export market for Australian minerals, causing mining profits and car-

bon emissions to soar. Australian professor of public ethics Clive Hamilton attributes much of the acrimonious political controversy over climate change in Australia in 2011 to financial backing and organizing by
a handful of mining tycoons such as Gina Rinehart and Andrew Forrest.
They ranked 29 and 173, respectively, on Forbes global billionaires list
for 2012 and were able to bankroll their antigovernment campaign with
over $100 million. Their employees shook their fists at an antitax rally in
Perth and were able to win concessions from the government. Angry
protests from the extreme right helped bring down Prime Minister
Kevin Rudd in 2010, shortly after his government ratified the Kyoto
Protocol. Mining industry–promoted protests further escalated from
abusive public speech against government officials to open threats of
violence against scientists who took global warming seriously.[34]

In the United States, Koch brothers Charles and David, ranked individually as the twelfth wealthiest on the Forbes global billionaire list for
2012 with $25 billion each, are a parallel example of plutocratic influ-
ence over the American political system and over public understanding
of the realities of contemporary world problems. The Koch brothers'
fortune was derived from Koch Industries, a giant petroleum-refining,
commodities trading and shipping, petro-chemical, plastics, minerals,
lumber, paper, and cattle conglomerate. Koch was the second largest
privately held corporation in the United States with revenues of $100
billion in 2008. As a private corporation Koch can keep a low public
profile, but the brothers have financed and orchestrated a vast network
of think tanks, lobbyists, foundations, funding organizations, political
and public policy advocacy groups that support their interests in reducing government regulation of their business. Between 2008 and 2011
Koch Industries spent more than $54 million on federal lobbying and
$8 million on political campaign donations.[35] The Kochs have given
millions of dollars to progrowth, antiregulation organizations such as
the Americans for Prosperity Foundation (AFP), Heritage Foundation,
and Cato Institute, and Tea Party activists, news commentators, and
bloggers willing to support their business interests.[36] AFP describes
itself as "an organization of grass roots leaders who engage citizens in
the name of limited government and free markets. . . ."[37] One of its
specific goals is "removing regulatory barriers and keeping energy taxes
low."[38]

An antigovernment regulation and especially antienvironmental regulation stance makes sense for Koch Industries, which was ranked number ten in the toxic 100 list of air polluting industries in the United States by the Political Economy Research Institute (PERI) in 2010.[39] Koch had 129 polluting facilities in twenty-nine states, releasing 33 million pounds of some seventy toxic materials into the air and transferred nearly 2 million pounds to incinerators, according to data compiled by the Environmental Protection Agency (EPA). Among its toxic emissions was more than 10 million pounds of ammonia, which is considered to be one of the most hazardous compounds to ecosystems. Koch Industries does not release figures on its carbon emissions, but based on figures for comparable corporations, it is likely to be about 300 million tons per year, which would make it responsible for an astounding 5 percent the U.S. annual total.[40]

WHO OWNS THE SKY? CAPITALISM 3.0 AND THE NEW COMMONS

After trying for many years to find a balance between left and right political perspectives on the relative size and roles of government and business in the United States, American environmentalist and entrepreneur Peter Barnes concluded that *the way capitalism operates* in America is "the central problem of our day."[41] In the language of computer software, he argues that we need a new operating system, Capitalism 3.0, which would reclaim capitalism by bringing our commonwealth, especially nature, into balance with corporations. Treating nature as capital and as a commonwealth is exactly how the tribal world proved to be so durable, and it is proving to be a key element in how the most successful small nations work. Barnes' proposed Capitalism 3.0 operating system fits so well with the small nation solution that it merits careful consideration.

The central concept behind Capitalism 3.0 is the commons, or the commonwealth. In general our commonwealth is our shared wealth of nature and culture that everyone depends on for survival. This includes what the Cook Islanders (chapter 5) referred to as "the gift," because no one individual single-handedly created this gift. It is what we inherit and pass on to the next generation, but it also includes important aspects of our shared culture such as knowledge and language that are produced by society.[42] Even billionaire Warren Buffet acknowledged that "society is responsible for a very significant percentage of what I've earned."[43] The basic idea is that there are things in the world that are the common heritage of humanity, like water, air, or the sky. When the commons is used for private gain the user should pay rent which can offset damage done, help to restore the commons, or provide a shared benefit to society. A more detailed "map" of commons includes many categories such as hospitals and public health, public infrastructure, the electromagnetic spectrum, and mass communication.[44]

Barnes explains that before about 1950 America was operating under Capitalism 1.0, which was *shortage capitalism*. Poverty was common, wages were low, capital and consumer goods were scarce. After 1950 postwar America shifted fairly quickly into Capitalism 2.0, *surplus capitalism*, where capital and goods were so abundant that they exceeded our needs. Advertising was needed to create a serious consumer economy. This was what Galbraith hoped would create the *Affluent Society*.[45] Easy credit and lots of advertising persuaded people to buy things, but as we have seen, the system was skewed toward corporations at the expense of our commonwealth.

Closely paralleling my earlier analysis of the concentration of power in American corporate business in the present chapter, Barnes refers to the "Ascent of Corporations," calling them "automatons" that relentlessly externalize costs in pursuit of their sole purpose of maximizing profits for shareholders. Externalized costs mean environmental destruction. Furthermore, the corporate automaton is unable to decide that "This is enough. Let's stop here."[46] Corporations simply keep growing larger and more powerful, as was shown above, where I tracked the growth of corporate power from 1960 to 2010. Barnes uses a "Wall Street versus Main Street, 1953–2000" bar graph to show the same process.[47] Single-minded profit seeking and environmental destruction is the first problem with Capitalism 2.0. Unlimited growth in corporate power is the second problem with Capitalism 2.0. Under surplus capitalism there is plenty of finance capital, large piles of which are being misallocated on the tallest, ego-satisfying buildings, or purely speculative finance. What is in short supply is income for consumer needs, nature, nature's services, community, and human well-being. Barnes lists three specific pathologies of Capitalism 2.0: "destruction of nature, the widening of inequality, and the failure to produce happiness despite the pretense of doing so."[48]

The failure of economists to distinguish between wants and needs is clearly expressed in the elevation of market demand to a desirable goal in itself, quite apart from the consequences of meeting all market demands. Barnes reminds us of the Lorax in the Dr. Seuss story and his objection to the Once-ler's promotion of *thneeds* as something that "all people need." Real needs like food, shelter, transportation, and healthcare do not require branding and marketing, because they are needs, whereas, *thneeds*, like Coca-Cola, must be branded and are much less obviously connected to the satisfaction of human needs. In a market economy where only money can produce effective market demand, people without money can produce no demand. Barnes maintains that ignoring damage to nature, the poor, and future generations is a fundamental failure of the present "operating system" of the capitalist economy. The system needs an upgrade to Capitalism 3.0.

Barnes notes that Garrett Hardin originally argued that there were only two possible ways of averting the "Tragedy of the Commons"— either government regulation, or by turning the commons over to private owners operating in a free market. The first question is, should protecting the commons be primarily the responsibility of government? For the best outcome, we might add, "democratic government protecting public resources." The problem with this ideal model is that private economic power distorts democracy through a process that we readily recognize as political corruption. Unlike democracy, which assumes an open society, capitalism is, in effect, a "gated community," to which only the economic elite have meaningful access. The elite have every incentive to use their unequal power to direct government to their private ends.

In the United States, government may have the legal authority and the agencies to regulate business for the public good, but in practice American government authority can be readily subverted by powerful business interests. The revolving door between business and government, business presence on advisory committees and commissions, business lobbyists, think tanks, and foundations, combined with business influence on political campaigns can exercise overwhelming power over government decision making to favor private business interests over the public good. For example, writing in 2006 during the Bush administration, Barnes noted that the head of public lands in the Interior Department was formerly a lobbyist for mining, and at the Environmental Protection Agency, the second in command, the head of the air division, and the head of the Superfund to clean up toxic waste all had compromising prior connections with corporate business.

Industry groups are large enough to hire tens of thousands of lobbyists and pay them billions to write favorable legislation for congress to approve. This is not a conspiracy. It is legal and mostly readily observable, but the public remains ill-informed, unaware, and seemingly unconcerned about this corruption of the democratic system. This is primarily due to the power imbalances involved. Ordinary citizens do not have the time or energy to keep track of political corruption, or to do anything about it. Furthermore, according to the logic of collection action theory,[49] it is easier for a small organization, such as a coalition of large corporations, to lobby government for their interests than it is for the public at large, because the individual payoff is very small in relation to the cost of lobbying. The losers in this unequal power struggle are all those "stakeholders" remaining outside the market economy, such as the poor, future generations, and nature.

Unfortunately, in the United States, public agencies are widely criticized for doing a poor job of managing public resources, because their policies are skewed by political influence to favor the industries that exploit those resources. Many of the management decisions made on public resources are highly politicized and kept intentionally outside of the public view. In contrast, some 155 million acres of state-managed lands held in trust for public education are more open to public scrutiny, less politicized, and more likely to be better managed. The states of Texas and Alaska both have permanent funds based on oil revenues from state lands that are used, respectively, to support public education or to provide an annual dividend to individual citizens.

Barnes points out that nature is different from impermanent commercial goods because nature is an irreplaceable and invaluable gift. It is both morally wrong and economically unwise to treat nature like ordinary merchandise. No single corporation or super-wealthy individual should be allowed to own the sky. The problem is that, under standard capitalism, capital is automatically given priority over workers, nature, local communities, and the future. This is not only immoral and irrational, but it is a dangerous political choice. Regardless of the ruling ideology of our time, giving to privately managed capital the right to maximize short-term returns at public expense is not inevitable, it is a political choice. Unfortunately, in the United States this choice has become a legal imperative in multiple situations. For example, the managers of shareholder-owned corporations and mutual funds are legally required to give top priority to maximizing profits for shareholders. Only the Endangered Species Act gives clear priority to nature, but then only when it is almost too late. Even this small concession to nature is under constant political assault in the United States. The solution to these problems is to expand and strengthen the common property of all Americans.

A UNITED SMALL NATIONS OF AMERICA

Restructuring the global tera-economy United States of America into a United Small Nations of America would require reconvening the Constitutional Convention. It would of course also require that many contending interest groups reach political consensus at many levels. We would need consensus on the need to restructure in the first place, then on how to do it, and finally on what a restructured America would look like. In the current political climate any of this seems both unthinkable and inconceivable. However, times of deep political division and increasing economic insecurity present opportunity and could stimulate movements to reconfigure and reboot our current operating system. As a creative thought experiment a reconstructed America can be imagined as a possible future. Restructuring would emphatically not be a "down-sizing" of America as some have proposed.[50] It is also not about a go-it-alone secession of states from the Union, as suggested by the flurry of secession petitions that circulated when President Obama was reelected. Restructuring is about "right-sizing" by getting decision making as close to the people as possible and working together to solve the country's central problems of injustice, inequality, and environmental degradation.

It is an open question how many small nations might emerge in the United States. Many of the 3,142 county-level governments would be obvious candidates for small nation status, because only Los Angeles County was pushing the ten million population threshold in 2010. However, thirty-four counties had fewer than 1,000 people in 2010 and 664 had average populations of under 10,000, which would at best qualify them as nano-nations. Forty-three of the fifty states are also below 10 million in population. Most of these existing political jurisdictions could reconfigure themselves as small nations if their citizens could reach a political consensus for major change. Reconfiguring would also be an opportunity to draw more rational boundaries in regard to natural, cultural, and/or economic geography. For example, analyst Joel Garreau identified *The Nine Nations of North America* as emerging economic and cultural regions in 1981.[51]

America is so culturally diverse that it has been called a "Patchwork Nation" in a recent analysis designed to understand voter behavior.[52] Political scientist James G. Gimbel found that it was useful to sort America's 3,142 counties into just twelve categories based on a series of social and economic characteristics. The twelve national "patches" in descending order by aggregate population size were labeled Monied Burbs; Boom Towns; Industrial Metropolis; Service Worker Centers; Immigration Nation; Evangelical Epicenters; Minority Central; Campus and Careers; Emptying Nests; Military Bastions; Tractor Country; and Mormon Outposts. Each of these patches represents county-level communities of people who share enough of the same values, culture, and experiences that they are likely to vote in predictable ways. Blocks of adjacent counties of a given patch type would be an obvious basis for drawing small nation boundaries.

All together the 329 "Monied Burb" counties represented the largest patch type by population with nearly 69 million people in 2006, approximately 23 percent of the U.S. population. They were scattered across the country, but were most densely represented in the urban Northeast and California. Monied Burbs had median household incomes of $51,234 and highly educated people with little cultural diversity, and they tended to vote Democratic. Some 385 Boom Town counties were also scattered throughout the country and covered about 20 percent of the population. Their fast-growing economies were severely impacted by the downturn spawned by the financial crisis. Boom Town populations grew twice as fast as the national average between 1996 and 2006, and they voted Republican in 2008 by a small but firm margin. The Industrial Metropolis patch consisted of higher than average income and dense urban centers that tended to vote Democratic. Collectively

Monied Burbs, Boom Towns, and Industrial Metropolises were 60 percent of the population. Most people in these community types were likely to share an interest in economic growth, but otherwise were politically quite diverse. People living in Evangelical Epicenters and Mormon communities might have a political consensus on several very contentious cultural issues, yet together they constitute only just over 5 percent of the American population.

There might be difficult choices over whether to draw small nation boundaries in relation to natural areas such as watersheds, or ecosystems as in the hypothetical example of Snohomish Basin explored in chapter 6, whether to use market or economic areas, or to go with the "patch." One possibility would be to start with Rand MacNally's mapping of 487 basic and forty-seven major trading areas focused on 1,492 ranked market cities. Trading areas are drawn with respect to county lines but disregard state boundaries.[53]

A good compromise might simply be for each of the 179 Economic Areas defined by the Bureau of Economic Analysis (BEA) in 2004[54] to be granted small nation status. The BEA Areas account for commuting distances in relation to major economic centers and would make sense as small nations if economic considerations are primary. Only three of the BEA Economic Areas, centered on New York, Los Angeles, and Chicago, had populations of more than 10 million in 2003, but there were huge economic disparities between areas. The Los Angeles Area approached the trillion dollar threshold for aggregate personal income, and twenty other areas had hundreds of billions in personal income. The median was about $20 billion. The maximum per capita personal income was the New York Area with $40,627, and the median was $26,628. BEA Economic Areas have a close parallel in the European Union's 279 Basic Regions where similar economic disparities exist, but the EU is already working hard to reduce disparities among its member nations and regions as a matter of political policy (see chapter 8).

Interesting possibilities emerge if we consider what a serious restructuring of wealth and power would look like in a United Small Nations of America. Such restructuring would be the opposite of the recent epidemic of leveraged buyouts in which large corporations grew larger by swallowing up smaller corporations in a redistribution process that concentrated power. The present thought experiment is basically a scaled-up version of what I attempted with my model of the Snohomish

Basin small nation of 500,000 people in the previous chapter. Restructuring America would be democratically directed *development*, not elite-directed *growth*. This would be problem-solving restructuring, not primarily intended to produce economic growth.

Restructuring America, whatever specific form the project might take, would reflect a recognition that elite-directed growth has not only not solved problems but has inflicted a vast backlog of costs on the majority that must be redressed. These negative externalities would be removed by means of a negotiation process between the elites and the majority stakeholders. The negotiators would be the democratic representatives of the small nations and corporate wealth holders and rule setters, including larger governments and corporations. We can imagine that such negotiations might take place in a new Constitutional Convention. The objective would be to reallocate power and thereby solve problems, not to simply grow a larger economy. Such restructuring would depend on a democratic negotiation process to fix existing wealth and capital misallocations, because any alternatives to negotiation would risk destroying the commonwealth, the capital that everyone needs for survival.

Again, restructuring could be implemented in many other ways, and might include many new forms of taxation, including progressive income, or corporate taxes, individual and corporate wealth taxes; or by other novel taxes such as on financial transactions. Current very large property owners might be persuaded to transfer their holdings to other institutional owners, as with agrarian reform programs, or nationalization of businesses that many countries have practiced. For example, the State of Washington's Utilities and Transportation Commission negotiated a transfer of the electric power distribution assets of Pacificorp to the Yakama Nation, as described in chapter 4. The point here is that capital reallocation of the sort anticipated by the small nation solution is in reality not a particularly radical concept. It is already happening.

I was inspired in part to think about the capital reallocation component of the small nation solution and how it might be accomplished as a result of my work with the St'át'imc Chiefs Council for the St'át'imc Nation during 2003–2005. I referred to this example briefly in the previous chapter in regard to the importance of salmon, but it is a real-world example involving nearly half a billion dollars, making it important enough to be described here in more detail. The St'át'imc are some

5,000 indigenous Canadian "First Nations" members of ten band communities in the Fraser River region of British Columbia. They have been working to gain full recognition for rights to their land, economic, and political self-determination since seventeen St'át'imc chiefs submitted a formal petition to the Canadian government in 1911 laying out their claims.[55] The historical record showed without a doubt that the St'át'imc and their natural resources had suffered almost continuous exploitation and abuse following the occupation of their territory by outsiders. In my view, the injustice was that the St'át'imc lost the opportunity to independently manage and benefit from their own natural resources. For example, I visited a St'át'imc community at the end of a sixty-mile gravel road that had to run a diesel generator for their electric power, even though BC Hydro's power lines passed directly overhead.

The negotiations I was involved with addressed the past and ongoing St'át'imc grievances that could be attributed directly to the presence of BC Hydro's hydroelectric facilities on traditional lands that the St'át'imc had never surrendered. In 2010, after eighteen years of negotiations a settlement agreement that acknowledged the damages, but not the injustice, was finally reached. The agreement took numerous specific steps to mitigate damages, set up a working relationship between the St'át'imc and the company for managing water to protect the salmon, and for the St'át'imc to benefit from the company's hydroelectric operations. This was a negotiated revenue sharing agreement, resembling the outcome of collective bargaining between labor and capital in a workplace. The Agreement contains a provision that neither BC Hydro nor the Provincial government admits any wrongdoing or liability, and at the same time there are no restrictions on the St'át'imc pursuing further claims to aboriginal title, or other rights over water, land, and resources. Those claims are being pursued separately and when completed would constitute a transfer of wealth to the St'át'imc from the Crown.

The final agreement with BC Hydro involves an initial monetary payment to the St'át'imc Nation and the ten participating St'át'imc communities of approximately $60 million, followed by annual payments that would bring the total to about $100 million over the first six years. Payments do not go directly to individuals, but a small part goes directly to the individual communities either for specific projects affecting individual communities or for communities to use as they see fit.

The rest goes into a trust fund and must be used in support of the St'át'imc Nation as a whole, for St'át'imc heritage and culture, and for education and training. These payments will be followed by annual payments of $6.6 million until 2051, and $880,000 annually for environmental management and administrative costs until 2111. The grand total of payments over a hundred years would total some $500 million or more, given the built-in adjustments for inflation. These payouts are small amounts relative to BC Hydro's reported 2012 revenues of $4.6 billion and profits of $558 million and their anticipated future revenues.

After working with the St'át'imc I realized that many American communities have also suffered similar injustice as well as economic, social, natural, and cultural damages resulting from the operations of large corporations. The St'át'imc settlement was an implicit acknowledgement that the St'át'imc commonwealth had been damaged by the power company. It is significant that payments were made for training, heritage, and culture, as well as for the salmon. It would not be unreasonable to imagine similar negotiations to be brought on behalf of American small nations against corporations, even if their most powerful owners could escape liability. It is unfortunate that BC Hydro and the BC Provincial Government were able to avoid the injustice issue, because ultimately exploitation and injustice are moral issues that go far beyond the monetary values that may be negotiated. Injustice is just plain immoral and is an issue that must be addressed, especially in a world where power is so concentrated that monetary penalties for immoral acts may be trivial to the corporations and their owners involved.

To further pursue economic restructuring, for simplicity's sake, I imagine that, much like the European Union using its Structural Funds to support its Cohesion Policy of improving opportunities in the Regions, or the Council of Europe's provisions for "financial equalization," the new United Small Nations of America would institute a similar policy and put in place a steeply progressive wealth tax. As in the Snohomish Basin example, the goal would be to reallocate capital in a way that would have the overall long-term leveling effect of raising the average wealth of poor households to average maintenance wealth levels, and reducing the super-elites average wealth to elite levels. I make the same assumptions as described previously. The rank averages are the same, modeled after averages from the Federal Reserve's 2007 Survey of Consumer Finance.[56] This time, however, I use Census Bureau figures for 2011 household income distribution to calculate the number of households in each wealth rank.

Modeling the entire country gives huge numbers, but of course the assumption is that the restructuring would occur independently in each small nation as a democratic process. There are 231 million American households, with nearly $50 trillion in tangible and financial assets and nearly $40 trillion in net worth. These wealth estimates compare with an aggregate household *income* of $8.4 trillion in 2011, from the Census. I must stress that my figures are conservative, "back of an envelope" estimates based on estimates and do not pretend to great precision. The magnitudes are plausible, however, and closely approximate the estimate of $54 trillion in net worth for American adults in 2010 appearing in the Credit Suisse wealth report.[57] They are also lower than the asset value estimates based on macroeconomic national accounts data used by the Federal Reserve to calculate GDP.[58]

As in the Snohomish model, by my estimates the American super-elite are holding an average of about $3 million in net worth, elite households $614,000, maintenance households nearly $210,000, and the poor $105,000. By these calculations, the American super-elite would be holding more than $9 trillion, or nearly one-fourth of total household net worth. If an effective wealth ceiling were established this would yield a surplus of $7.5 trillion for reinvestment according to the principles of economic democracy. An effective ceiling on corporate and individual wealth accumulation would produce a large enough surplus to in effect elevate all poor households to maintenance level and significantly reduce the wealth gap between top and bottom. Most significantly, it would reduce the political influence of the wealthiest and increase political democracy in the country. How capital reinvestment would ultimately shape income distribution is uncertain, but the restructuring process would provide strong incentives for movements to shop local and "bring capital home" which would create new employment opportunities.

Natural capital or the wealth of nature would also be reallocated to the new small nations as part of a general movement to return the benefits of the new commons to local and regional citizens. How much natural capital actually exists at national levels is uncertain. The World Bank has developed its own set of measures for the wealth of nations, which includes natural capital,[59] but there is no universal method calculating a dollar value for natural capital. The Bank uses an estimated rent value of natural capital in the United States in 2005 and comes up with a figure of $43.6 trillion. This includes aggregate net present values for crops, pasture land, timber, nontimber forest, protected areas, oil, natural gas, coal, and minerals calculated using various discount rates, but making allowance for some sustainable use.

Another estimate of the value of America's natural capital uses an ecosystem services approach based on satellite-measured light emissions and ground cover analysis to measure GDP and biological productivity, respectively. This indicated that the annual value of nature's services in the United States was over $2 trillion in 1995.[60] Barnes converted this to a capital value by using the average annual price/earnings ratio of 16.5/1 since about 1950, to obtain a value of $33 trillion. Alternatively, discounted at 2.7 percent over 100 years as in the Snohomish example, $2 trillion in natural services would represent the equivalent of $72 trillion in natural capital, or more than $208 trillion over 100 years if all natural services were managed sustainably, and not discounted. Calculated either way, this makes natural capital much more valuable than financial and conventional tangible wealth.

The magnitude of the potential savings in energy and dollars that might accompany a transformative restructuring of the United States into a federal system of small nations can be estimated by several measures. For example, the Genuine Progress Indicator suggests that perhaps as much as 60 percent of the American GDP in 2002 was wasted in social and environmental costs.[61] This can be compared with the estimate that 56 percent of the country's energy flow was wasted in 2005 in thermodynamically inefficient processes.[62] Half of the thermodynamic loss was in the fossil fuels used in thermal electric power generation and in transmission. The rest of the loss was in the transportation sector. Any cultural changes that reduced thermal electric production and long-distance transmission and transportation requirements would be a huge energy savings. Here is where investments in efficient light rail systems as envisioned by the America 2050 project would pay off.

Other potential savings do not involve energetic or technological inefficiencies. For example, combined American expenditures on national security, including the Defense Department ($495 billion) and domestic advertising ($271 billion) in 2005 nearly equaled the $827 billion spent on all forms of education in the 2003–2004 academic year.[63] A substantial part of the $654 billion spent on transporting, warehousing, and manufacturing chemical products, food, and beverages can be attributed to national-scale marketing.[64] How much of these costs are scale-related processing and distribution costs rather than primary production is indicated by the fact that in 2004 only 20 percent of consumer expenditures on food went to the farmer (as noted in chapter 5). Only 15 percent of the foodstuffs and animal feed by weight in the American food system is actually consumed by people.[65] Any shifts toward vegetarian diets and local, rather than national and global food provisioning, and toward less processing would further reduce costs. Consuming less processed food would produce immediate savings on health care, which cost $626 billion in 2004. Water is so heavy that carbonated soft drinks, alcohol, fruit drinks, and bottled water made up nearly 40 percent of the weight of all inflows of food and beverages into an American city in 1997.[66] Consuming locally produced, rather than nationally advertised, transported, and warehoused, beverages would be an enormous savings. These cultural changes in diet would stimulate local producers, creating employment, and might dramatically lower the consumption of corn syrup, which is implicated in obesity and diabetes.

8

UNITED SMALL NATIONS OF THE WORLD

Confronting Poverty and Global Warming

We assert that the key to social justice is the equitable distribution of social and natural resources, both locally and globally, to meet basic human needs unconditionally, and to ensure that all citizens have full opportunities for personal and social development. —*Charter of the Global Greens*, 2012[1]

International conflict, many economic and political causes of poverty, and climate change are all global-scale problems that can only be effectively addressed at the global level based on an international consensus on global justice and a restructuring of social power. This is the irreducibility principle and means that small nations by themselves are not complete solutions to global problems. Several newly created nonprofit organizations such as the World Social Forum, Alternatives International, the Transnational Institute (TNI), the Center for Global Negotiations, Association for the Taxation of Financial Transactions and Aid to Citizens (ATTAC), The International Forum on Globalization, the New Economics Foundation (NEF), Share the World's Resources (STWR), and the Global Marshall Plan, and numerous networked coalitions of organizations are proposing major changes in the international political economy. The goals of these organizations often overlap with the small nation solution, but they often do not specifically take into account the scale dimensions that the small nation solution addresses.

The inescapable conclusion of a power and scale perspective on the development of nations is that large nations and the global system need to be restructured. The necessity for this was first proposed in 1957 by Leopold Kohr in his book, *The Breakdown of Nations*, but at that time Kohr could not imagine how it could be done. Since then, the Soviet Union's breakup showed that it was possible for very large nations to disintegrate, but in this case the process was elite directed and chaotic. The British Empire came apart more slowly and gracefully, and Spain and the UK are currently undergoing a similar decentralization process. The worldwide emergence of indigenous nations is also a very helpful model that is nudging all of these great cultural transformations along. The European Union's Committee of the Regions is a very useful example of an institutionalized mechanism for operationalizing the subsidiarity principle for subnational units within the European Union federalist system that will be examined in this chapter.

A world system based on democratic representation by small nations has the potential to loosen the stranglehold over global affairs held by the giga- and mega-nations and the transnational corporations and financial institutions they support. A small nation world would be less likely to promote a global arms race, would be more open to global level social justice and environmental protection, and would place sustainable *development* ahead of economic *growth*. The benefits of greater knowledge, prosperity, and security can be gained in the contemporary world by continuing to integrate small nations into federations and international organizations of various sorts operating according to the subsidiarity principle. This means getting decision making at the right level and will require deliberate mechanisms to prevent the negative effects of elite-directed growth.

There are many examples of this small nation integration process already in place. Indigenous people have for example the Inuit Circumpolar Conference (ICC) and The Coordinating Body for the Indigenous Organizations of the Amazon Basin (COICA). In Siberia there is the Russian Association of Indigenous Peoples of the North (RAIPON). Six Celtic nations are united in the Celtic League. Eight nations form the Nordic Council. The Association of Small Island States (AOSIS) is a network of thirty-nine small, mostly Pacific island nations, which is primarily concerned with environmental protection and sustainable development. AOSIS is very active internationally. There are also numerous small nation intergovernmental regional organizations (IGOs) such as the Pacific Islands Forum and Council of Regional Organizations in the Pacific (CROP). Nine small Caribbean nations belong to AOSIS and to the regional Organization of Eastern Caribbean States (OECS). They also share a currency system and a central bank, some legal functions, and they are connected by the Caribbean Electric Utility Services Corporation (CARILEC), a nonprofit utility support corporation. The EU's Committee of the Regions will be discussed further in a later section.

Small nations solutions to global problems are also supported by other international organizations such as the Community of Democracies and the Commonwealth of Nations that are not exclusively for small nations. There are numerous other organization seeking to democratize the United Nations, or to create new world parliamentary forms, or federalist systems, that would give small nations a larger voice in world affairs.

Small nation international organizations are strikingly different in form and function from other intergovernmental organizations dominated by big nations such as the Organization for Economic Co-operation and Development, the Group of Nine, the World Bank, the IMF, and the World Trade Organization. The UN Security Council is presently structured in a way that gives five tera-economy (tera for trillion) big nations veto power over decision making. These big nation organizations largely exist to promote globalization in the interests of the HNWIs and giant transnational corporations, which as we have seen do not always coincide with the interests of the global majority.

One of the largest global problems is the reluctance of the governments of rich, high-consumption countries like the United States and very large, but poor countries, such as India and China, to accept responsibility for their primary role in causing global warming, even as they have enjoyed the early boost that fossil fuels gave to their economic development. This is a global political problem that could be resolved in an international system in which democratically organized small nations had the political ability to neutralize the disproportionate elite-directed power of large nations and the influence of giant corporations.

The repeated failure of international climate summits to reach a consensus on effective emission reductions to mitigate climate change demonstrates the shortcomings of existing global political institutions.

At the same time nearly two billion people are languishing in "multidi-mensional poverty." The global consumer class must force their govern-ments to accept responsibility for global warming, adopt a zero carbon economy, and systematically shift their economies to sustainably used renewable resources to help reduce climate change. New global institu-tions are also needed to implement a fair distribution of the remaining conventional oil to meet human needs while easing the transition to a zero carbon future. Under a small nation regime, each nation would agree to act in proportion to its responsibility for warming and its eco-nomic capacity. This is a global political problem that can best be solved by politically disarming the great transnational corporations, especially in energy, food, and finance, because their overwhelming influence presently stands in the way of social equity and justice for the global majority.

TERA-ECONOMIES AND RESTRUCTURING THE WORLD'S WEALTH

Thinking about how big an economy should be is a good place to start on the way to arriving at the "right size" for everything else—busi-nesses, markets, and governments, because everything in our commer-cial world is situated in an economy. Economies have become so large and play such a dominant part in our lives that it is now reasonable to say that we are living in a global economy, rather than a global society. Given that "the economy" is an imaginary construction and not a physi-cal thing, we will of course need to consider the proper size of an economy in relation to many other "things" that we value. Establishing the optimum size of an economy is absolutely a question of values, especially in reference to the ultimate purpose of an economy, which must be to provide the goods and services that people need to be successful human beings in a particular society and culture. We can accept money as a unit of value, and money can measure the size of the economy, but it would not be prudent to treat money as an ultimate value in itself, and we must therefore have a balanced view of the economy in relation to other things that people value. As we have seen, these other "things" to be valued surely must include wealth in the larger sense to include humans and their knowledge and skills, institutions, the built environment and of course the natural environment, along with money and financial instruments generally. Aggregate values of wealth at global and national levels involve very large numbers, and large numbers lead immediately to the problem of scale. We cannnot avoid these big numbers and the issue of scale because this is precisely why small nations are a solution to global problems.

A useful way to think about scale as a problem in itself is to first consider things that can be measured by the very largest quantities of money in the world. Perhaps the largest aggregated "thing" is the entire world's wealth in every form, which I suggest could be worth as much as $1.5 quadrillion dollars. This inconceivably large quantity can be derived by starting with the World Bank's estimates of $708 trillion for the total "wealth of nations" in 2005."[2] The Bank's figure included $125 trillion as the value of *produced capital* such as all the tangible machinery, structures, urban land, and equipment in the world; then counted $43 trillion for the value of *natural capital* counted as "rents" derived from all the crop land, pastures, timber, nontimber forests, protected areas, fossil fuels, and subsoil minerals in the world; and then added $541 trillion for the estimated value for all the world's intangible assets such as human, social, and institutional resources, as well as net foreign financial assets. This of course all totals less than a quadrillion dollars.

The World Bank's final figure of $708 trillion doesn't feel right because it counts nature as worth only 6 percent of global wealth, and makes intangible capital, including money, more than 75 percent of total wealth. If the value of nature is increased based on the value of the services that it provides humanity such as production of soil, water purification, and climate control a much higher dollar value for global wealth emerges. The value of nature's services is gaining wider recognition as GDP is increasingly proving inadequate as a measure of progress.[3] Nature is clearly worth much more than most economists have thought. Ecological economists estimated that nature provided us with the equivalent of $33 trillion in services in 1997 (within a range of 16 to 54 trillion), which would be $39 trillion in 2005 dollars.[4] That amount actually exceeds the $36 trillion (in 2005 dollars) in global GDP in 1997.

The value of natural services is a flow, like GDP, and the figure we need is a value for the underlying ecosystems which constitute the wealth or natural capital that produces these services. Using the Barnes'

method of calculating nature's wealth value based on an average price/
earnings ratio on the stock market of 16.5/1 gives a figure of $211
trillion. At the $54 trillion highest estimate for the value of nature's
services nature would be worth $891 trillion. This exceeds the Bank's
$708 trillion figure for the total wealth of nations which attributed only
$43 trillion to nature. Replacing the Bank's rent-based figure with the
much higher nature's service-based capitalized figure gives the astounding figure of $1.5 quadrillion as the total wealth of nations. This higher
figure makes natural capital more than half of the wealth of nations.
This "feels" like a more realistic value balance between nature and
conventional humanly constructed forms of wealth. It is also the kind of
balance that will no doubt be required to produce a sustainable commercial world. It is remarkable that this is also closer to the apparent
value that tribal peoples place on nature.

A quadrillion dollars of global wealth is of course a totally unimaginable quantity, but this higher figure does help put nature in proper
perspective in relation to the scale of our standard economic values.
This also helps us understand the irrationality of allowing an infinitely
expanding monetary system to distort our sense of the importance of
nature. Equally problematic is the distortion of human values and the
threat to the sustainability of our sociocultural systems that are caused
by allowing individual people to manage unimaginable but ever-grow-
ing sums of money. The real problem is that nature cannot expand
infinitely and is in fact being degraded to produce the physical flows of
energy and materials that allow our monetary values to expand. We
need to grasp what trillions of dollars actually mean, especially if a few
people actually make decisions over quantities of such magnitudes.

Very few dollar amounts that people deal with can be measured in
trillions, and nothing on the market is priced in trillions, but there are
some quantities valued at more than $100 trillion and several in the tens
of trillions of dollars. Perhaps the biggest regularly accepted dollar
amount in the world is the World Bank's estimate of $708 trillion for
the aggregate wealth of nations discussed above. Even though it deval-
ues nature, the Bank's figure is substantially greater than the $197 tril-
lion in net worth that Credit Suisse, the giant Swiss financial services
corporation, estimated was held by all the world's 6.4 billion people in
2010.[5] The Credit Suisse figure was based on adults and includes personal financial assets, nonfinancial assets in house and land, and sub-

tracts debts. This figure in turn still thankfully exceeds the total value of assets held by the world's 2000 largest publically traded corporations which was listed by Forbes at $138 trillion in 2011.[6]

Regardless of which global wealth figure we take, the Credit Suisse's $197 trillion for personal wealth the World Bank's $708 trillion for the wealth of nations, or $1.5 quadrillion for the wealth of nations with maximum value for natural capital, a bit of math shows that there is plenty of wealth in the world to end poverty by improving its distribution according to human moral values of justice and fairness. That is precisely what we would expect a world of small nations would do based on economic and political democracy. Opening the political discussion to all forms of capital and recognizing that much of social, cultural, and natural capital is commonwealth property a gift held in trust and earning rent makes the redistribution task much easier and much fairer.

As a thought exercise, leaving to the small nations the details of exactly what capital would be restructured, or how it would be accomplished politically, the arithmetic shows the magnitude of the capital that could be shifted by restructuring. The reality is that the global per capita wealth averages of $30,000, $104,000, or $220,000, depending on which global wealth baseline is used, are in every case more than sufficient to lift every household out of poverty. The different base line figures simply use increasingly broader concepts of what constitutes the commonwealth. We can imagine that the $2 trillion, $7 trillion, or $15 trillion, respectively, in super-elite holdings, which the super-elite accumulated in the previous restructuring of global capitalism from 1950 to the present, can be restructured to benefit the majority maintenance and poverty level households. The result would be a two-ranked world, in which elite per capita wealth would average either $165,000, $568,000, or $1.2 million, respectively; and maintenance per capita wealth would average either $18,500; $64,000 or $135,000, depending on the baseline.

To put these figures in perspective they can be compared with the figures that Lester Brown, founder of Worldwatch Institute and Earth Policy Institute, used in his "Mobilizing to Save Civilization" Plan B 4.0.[7] Brown's plan calls for spending just under $2 trillion over a decade to restore the environment and end poverty. This assumes that two energy revolutions would occur to stabilize climate—the first based on technological fixes to greatly improve the efficiency of energy use, the second a shift away from fossil fuels to renewable energy sources to produce a global zero-carbon economy. Among the political changes recommended by the "Great Mobilization" required to implement Plan B are removal of subsidies to agriculture and fossil fuels and damaging activities, especially in the wealthiest countries.

In addition to the technological fixes, Plan B would require government expenditures of an additional $187 billion annually through 2020 ($77 billion to meet basic social goals for education and health in the impoverished world and $110 billion to restore damaged ecosystems). Brown emphasizes that the world needs a "new" economy and makes tax restructuring and budgetary priorities the economic centerpieces of the plan. However, Plan B relies on international aid from wealthy nations and debt relief to end poverty by promoting public health and education and to restore the environment, and it advocates a "Great Mobilization" to bring this all about.

The problem with Plan B is that it would leave untouched the super-elite directors and the unbalanced international political economy that produced the problems in the first place. Furthermore, simply providing education and health care to the poor would not eliminate global poverty. The healthy and educated poor would still be dependent on global super-elites to provide them with jobs. Education and health would improve their human capital, but they would still need access to material and financial capital to gain control over the conditions of their lives, and they would need a significant political voice over their governments. The small nation solution is a political mechanism for the full mobilization of the wealth of nations that is needed to "save civilization."

On the face of it, one trillion dollars is probably too much money for any person to even keep track of, or to reasonably conceive of, but a brief thought experiment can help to put such a quantity in perspective. A hundred $100 bills can be bundled into a neat stack half an inch thick to make $100,000 dollars, which was more than half of the median sale price of a home in the United States in 2011.[8] A hundred of these half-inch-thick bundles of $10,000 in hundred dollar bills would make a million dollars which one person could fit into a briefcase or a large grocery bag and carry to the bank. Working eight hours a day, five days a week for forty-seven years, at a wage of $10.23 per hour, which is above minimum wage in many U.S states, a dedicated worker would earn a total of a million and eighty-five dollars in a forty-seven-year working lifetime. At that rate the worker would not of course be able to *accumulate* a million dollars, because most of the $21,278 in annual earnings would be expended every year on basic subsistence. However, according to Credit Suisse's estimates, some 24 million people world-wide had accumulated at least a million dollars in net worth by 2010, and in the aggregate they held nearly $70 trillion. The total held by the world's wealthiest is more likely to be more than $90 trillion and maybe more than $100 trillion, if the Tax Justice Network's 2012 estimate of $21-$32 trillion in "missing" offshore holdings in 2012 is correct.[9] So, a million dollars is maybe not an impossibly, or unimaginably huge amount, and there are many houses, cars, yachts, and airplanes on the market in that price range.

A *billion* dollars is qualitatively different. It is a *thousand* million dollars and is not so easily imagined, transported, or spent. Even *one hundred* million dollars is too much money for anyone to carry about single-handedly. A hundred million is 10,000 bundles of hundred dollar bills and would fill a cargo pallet. A forklift would be needed to hoist it onto a pickup bed. The ten pallets of a hundred million dollars each that make one billion dollars could only be transported on a very large flat-bed truck. According to Forbe's ranking, in 2011 there were 1300 global billionaires worth a collective $4 trillion.[10] It is grotesquely excessive for any one person to literally have a semi-truck and trailer full of money in a world where nearly two billion people are living in "multi-dimensional" poverty. Yet in 2012, at least ninety-two people in the world had at least *ten* billion dollars or more. Maybe ten truckloads of money is too much for any single person to accumulate, especially considering that there are so few single items that a private citizen might buy for a billion dollars. However, the world's most expensive house, the new twenty-seven-story skyscraper built in Mumbai for Indian multi-billionaire Mukesh Ambani, the nineteenth-richest person in the world, may cost more than $2 billion.

So, a billion is a lot, and ten billion is an obscene amount of money. A *trillion* dollars is a totally inconceivable amount. No one person is yet worth that much, but there are people who manage trillions of mostly other people's dollars, and as we noted above, there are wealth aggregates of that magnitude. One trillion dollars would require 10,000 pallets of $100 million to store and move. Stacked two high, in a hundred rows of fifty pallets, these 10,000 pallets would more than cover an American football field. It would take a fleet of 192 semi-trailer truck rigs, each pulling fifty-three-foot trailers, to transport a trillion dollars. This is why the global financial system must be satisfied with accumulating and moving digital money, rather than paper money, or other physical proxies such as gold. The quantities of money changing hands in twenty-first-century global financial and commodities markets would simply not be possible without computerized exchanges.

Among the trillion dollar figures are the world's GDP of $61 trillion in current exchange rate dollars in 2008, or $72 trillion in current purchasing power parity (PPP) dollars. The market capitalization value of the companies listed on all the world's stock markets peaked at $65 trillion in 2007 before plunging to $35 trillion in 2008, all in current dollars. Market values actually exceeded global GDP in 1999 and 2007 and reflect the hyper development of the global financial sector. The 2000 largest publicly traded corporations reported profits of $2 trillion in 2011 from their $32 trillion in revenue. Their market capitalization was $37 trillion, but their assets stood at $138 trillion.

To make these trillion dollar figures relevant to the small nation solution they need to be contextualized in reference to specific economies. In 2009 there were just fourteen countries with economies of a trillion dollars or more: Brazil, Canada, China, France, Germany, India, Italy, Japan, Mexico, Russia, South Korea, Spain, the United States, and the United Kingdom. These fourteen countries can be characterized as tera-economies. They illustrate the problems of economies that are too big and failing, because the costs that sustain them undermine the sustainability of the global system. The aggregate exchange rate GDP of the tera-economies in current dollars was $46 trillion dollars, which was a staggering 74 percent of global GDP, even though the tera-economy countries were only 55 percent of global population. These fourteen countries are dominating the world's decision-making forums including the United Nations, the World Bank, the IMF, and NATO in clearly undemocratic ways, because of their preponderant economic power, even though they represent only 6 percent of the world's countries. Subgroups of the tera-economy nations, such as the Group of Eight (Canada, France, Germany, Italy, Japan, Russia, the UK, and the United States), also have enormous influence in global affairs. The problem with this sort of concentrated economic power is that it responds primarily to financial interests and remains focused on promoting ever more costly economic growth.

Using figures for 2010–2011 tera-economy countries have concentrated from 72 to 85 percent of a whole range of economic values, including 74 percent of global market capitalization, 77 percent of global billionaire wealth, and 82 percent of total household wealth. They are home to 1,453, or 73 percent, of the 2,000 corporations in the Forbes Global ranking of the world's largest corporations, and these corporations account for 75 percent of the profits, 78 percent of the market capital, 81 percent of the assets, and 82 percent of revenues in the Global 2000. The cities that command global business and finance are likewise situated in just eight tera-economy countries.[11] As might be expected, the tera-economy nations are also responsible for 72 percent of cumulative global carbon dioxide emissions from fossil fuels and cement production from 1990 to 2005,[12] and 72 percent of the $9 trillion expended globally on four readily measured growth-related variables in 2010: fossil fuels ($4.6 trillion), Forbes Global 2000 corporate profits ($2.4 trillion), military costs ($1.6 trillion), and national-level advertising ($465 billion). These expenditures can be considered scale costs or subsidies because they are strongly correlated with the economic scale in GDP and everyone else pays for them directly or indirectly.

THE WORLD FUTURE COUNCIL AGENDA: ENERGY, ECOLOGY, AND EQUALITY

The World Future Council (WFC) is one of the new NGOs whose objectives are very compatible with the small nation solution. The WFC's fifty councilors are part of an emerging global network of individuals and organizations that are moving the world toward social justice and sustainability. WFC councilors set the agenda for this organization whose overall objective is promoting genuine sustainability to safeguard the planet for the benefit of future generations. The WFC vision calls for "a sustainable, just and peaceful future, where the dignity and rights of every living being and the connectedness of human beings to all life are universally respected."[13] Councilors and Honorary Councilors are "respected personalities" from all over the world, and include prominent activists such as Jane Goodall, Frances Moore Lappé, founder of the Small Planet Institute, and Vandana Shiva, critic of large-scale, energy-intensive agriculture and founding member of the International Forum on Globalization. Sustainable Chile program director Manfred Max-Neef is also one of the councilors, along with Ashok Khosla, president of the International Union for the Conservation of Nature (IUCN), who also serves as co-president of the Club of Rome. It was the Club of Rome's 1972 *Limits to Growth* report that first drew widespread attention to the problem of global sustainability. WFC councilors also include indigenous leaders, environmentalists, people associated with various UN agencies, corporate business leaders, and politicians, as well as representatives of many other NGOs concerned with sustainability and social justice. The WFC fills a vital niche between national-level sustainability organizations and think tanks like Chile Sustentable and the Insituto de Ecología Política in Chile and political parties that promote specific sustainability candidates in national elections such as the Partido Verde de Chile (Green Political Party of Chile, PEV) formed in 2002 and the Global Greens network of Green political parties. The WFC is a nongovernmental, nonprofit charity founded in 2007 and headquartered in Hamburg, Germany. It was designed specifically to develop public policies for governments to adopt that will solve global sustainability problems.

The diverse organizations that are linked via World Future Council directors reflect a global consensus that connects social justice with environmental sustainability. For example, in his introduction to the World Future Council report, *A Renewable World*, published in 2009, WFC Councilor Ashok Khosla declared that a renewable world requires that natural resources, energy, and materials must, by definition, be used sustainably, but for this to happen the world must also be fair.[14] It is the affluent "very rich" who are driving the overconsumption of irreplaceable resources such as fossil fuels and old growth forests, whereas the world's poor are forced to survive by overusing basic natural resources such as soil, water, and biomass. This understanding is also presented in the IUCN vision of "A just world that values and conserves nature" and the IUCN mission "To influence, encourage and assist societies throughout the world to conserve the integrity and diversity of nature and to ensure that any use of natural resources is equitable and ecologically sustainable."[15]

The WFC *Renewable World* report lays out a clear and plausible pathway to a sustainable world that merits close attention in relation to the small nation solution. This report is about how the changes necessary to produce sustainability can actually happen—what political and economic policies will be needed to bring them about. It begins by explicitly acknowledging that human activities have reduced the earth's biological capacity to store carbon. It is simply unacceptable and unsustainable for humanity to burn in a single year a quantity of fossil fuels that nature spent two million years to produce, as was the case in 2001. It is also unacceptable to try to replace natural biological carbon storage with expensive CCS (Carbon Capture and Storage) technology in order to reduce global warming, when nature does the job better and less expensively. This means that the solution to global warming requires a global effort to restore depleted soils, forests, and aquatic ecosystems, and in the process protect biodiversity. A sustainability strategy that sees connections between the health of ecosystems and climate change is what we would expect from someone like Ashok Khosla, who leads the World Future Council as well as the International Union for the Conservation of Nature. Connecting the needed changes with the problem of poverty and injustice, and future generations makes this an ethical issue.

The WFC position is that carbon needs to be returned to the soil by sustainable agricultural practices. We know that nonrenewable fossil fuel energy sources need to be replaced by renewable energy sources such as wind and solar, and we know that it is technically feasible. A specific political policy to bring about the shift to renewable energy that is already proven to work is the use of Feed-In Tariffs (FITs) that offer various subsidies to sustainable energy producers. This of course is not free market, but neither are the vast government subsidies that promoted, and still promote, the development of fossil fuels. The total subsidy to the fossil fuel industry is unknown, but the International Institute for Sustainable Development (IISD)'s Global Subsidies Initiative estimates the figure at about $600 billion per year.[16] The almost unthinkable conclusion of the WFC *Renewable World* report is that "...there also has to be an actual upper limit of global per capita fossil-fuel use." This draws on another important new concept—"energy sufficiency."

The energy transition to renewables is also being encouraged by government policies that apply the principle of energy subsidiarity. This means a country drawing as much of its energy from renewable sources at the lowest possible level in a hierarchically structured energy network. This is the small nation solution. Each small nation would strive to become totally energy self-sufficient, starting at the household and local level. Reliance would be on whatever renewable source was most readily available at that level. Surplus energy could be fed into the higher levels, and the higher regional and national levels which might have more diverse renewable sources available could serve as backup suppliers for its lower level "subsidiaries." Making energy subsidiarity work requires public policies to facilitate the necessary investments, and these are more likely to occur in small nations where there are no massive energy company lobbying campaigns in favor of continued use of fossil fuels.

LOCAL GOVERNMENTS
IMPLEMENTING SUSTAINABILITY

A remarkable and very promising model for how the small nation solution can be, and *now is being*, implemented is being promoted by Local Governments for Sustainability (ICLEI), an international intergovernmental organization dedicated to sustainable development. According to the ICLEI Charter,[17] members are "local spheres of government (local and regional governments and authorities)", or associations of local governments, and in practice are primarily municipal governments. Most of the thousands of cities in the world could be considered small nations, because only about two dozen of the largest cities have more than 10 million people. A high proportion of the cities in many small nations are ICLEI members. Bhutan's two largest cities, the capital Thimphu with 62,500 people and Phuntsholing with 60,400 people, are both members. As might be expected, Scandinavian local governments are well represented. Members include six Danish cities, including Copenhagen, with 1.2 million people; fifteen Finnish cities and an association of Finnish local and regional authorities; Iceland's capital Reykjavik, with 119,000 people; Norway's capital Oslo, with 613,000 people, and ten other Norwegian cities, and an association of regional authorities; and Sweden's capital Stockholm with 871,000 people, and eleven other cities and a development association. New Zealand has twelve member cities. Even the small nation of Mauritius with a population of only 1.2 million has five member cities, including Port Louis, its capital.

There are also thousands of subnational governmental units in the world that are small enough to be considered small nations. All are potential members of ICLEI, even if their national governments are not willing or able to join. By aligning themselves with the objectives of ICLEI, small governments worldwide are now implementing sustainability policies that larger governments seem incapable of taking on, primarily because they are simply too large to reach a political consensus on sustainability. Reaching consensus on sustainability is what the small nation solution is all about.

There is a separate ICLEI headquarters in the United States. In 2012 there were some 515 member governments in forty-seven states and the District of Columbia, as well as an Indian nation, the Oglala Sioux. Only the states of Mississippi, Rhode Island, and Wyoming were unrepresented. More than half of the membership was in just five states, in descending order: California (113 members), New York (62), Florida (34), Massachusetts (29), and Washington (29). It is not surprising to see California at the top, because with more than 37 million people it is the largest state in the country, but Texas, the second largest state with nearly 26 million people, has only twelve ICLEI local governments. Unfortunately, this suggests that in the United States at least, sustainability has become a politically charged concept. It is the "Blue States" that lean toward the Democratic Party in presidential elections that also lean toward sustainability and ICLEI membership.

The politically skewed distribution of local government interest in sustainability in the United States may be related to opposition by Tea Party activists to the ICLEI, which they accuse of being part of a United Nations "conspiracy" to take away American freedoms.[18] The assumed conspiracy is attributed to a link between ICLEI and Agenda 21, the international voluntary "action plan" to guide governments and intergovernmental organizations in pursuit of sustainable development. Agenda 21 is an extensive foundational document discussing all aspects of sustainable development, and it was the central product of the United Nations Conference on Environment and Development (UNCED) which convened in Rio de Janeiro in 1992. In fact virtually any organization concerned with the environment or environmental policy, combating deforestation, conserving biodiversity, protecting the oceans, management of hazardous wastes, or urban planning is in some way related to the objectives of Agenda 21. It is hardly rational to believe that any actions related to an open international process to help governments respond to clear threats to the long-term well-being of humanity to be a dangerous "conspiracy" to be avoided at all costs.

However, the perceived threat of Agenda 21 seemed scary enough that the Republican Party included a position statement on it in their 2012 national platform prepared for the Republican National Convention in Tampa Bay. The subsection on "Sovereign American Leadership in International Organizations" in the American Exceptionalism section declared: "We strongly reject the U.N. Agenda 21 as erosive of American sovereignty, and we oppose any form of U.N. Global Tax."[19] In reality the American branch of the ICLEI is connected to Agenda 21 only in the sense that both are concerned with sustainability, but so are innumerable other American organizations. ICLEI has its own list of funders and partner organizations, none of which are UN agencies. It received funding from more than a dozen prominent American foundations and an equally extensive list of major U.S. corporations, as well as the U.S. Departments of State, and Energy, and the Environmental Protection Agency.

When several American city governments were pressured into dropping their membership in the ICLEI, the American Planning Association included a special question on Agenda 21 in a commissioned Harris Poll of 1,308 U.S. residents selected as a representative sample of the country. They learned that 85 percent had no opinion about Agenda 21, 6 percent opposed it, and 9 percent supported it.[20] Most of those polled believed that conditions in their communities were deteriorating, and wanted local planning efforts and local funding to make jobs, safety, schools, neighborhoods, and clean water top priorities. Most respondents also wanted to be involved in community planning. Of course, community planning to address the well-being of local communities is also what ICLEI and the small nation solution are all about.

ICLEI was founded in New York City in 1990 as the "International Council for Local Environmental Initiatives." Their emphasis is to promote "local action for global sustainability" so that cities can become "sustainable, resilient, resource-efficient, biodiverse, [and] low-carbon... [and] to build a smart infrastructure; and to develop an inclusive, green urban economy." ICLEI's ambitious ultimate end is "to achieve healthy and happy communities."[21] The ICLEI vision is about connecting leaders and accelerating action and being a "Gateway to Solutions." In 2012 the ICLEI international secretariat was located in Bonn, Germany, and it has offices in twelve other countries, a staff of 200, and more than 1,200-member local, mostly municipal, governments in 84 countries throughout the world. It claimed to be the largest international association of local governments in the world representing more than half a billion people.[22] The ICLEI motto is "Local Solutions to Global Challenges."[23]

EUROPE'S SMALL NATIONS: A MODEL
FOR A SMALL NATION WORLD

> RESOLVED to continue the process of creating an ever closer union among the peoples of Europe, in which decisions are taken as closely as possible to the citizen in accordance with the principle of subsidiarity, . . .—(European Union. 2010. *Consolidated Version of the Treaty on European Union*. Official Journal of the European Union.)[24]

In 1994, shortly after the ICLEI was created, the European Union (EU) set up a special assembly, the Committee of the Regions (CoR), for subnational governments to represent their views within the EU system. The CoR is a very useful real-world model for how small nations worldwide might be represented in a small nation world. In this case, "the world" is the twenty-seven member states of the EU, which in the aggregate encompass more than half a billion people with an economy of some $17 trillion dollars in 2011. This is a larger population and a larger economy than the United States and makes the EU the largest economy in the world and the third largest population in the world. This means that the way the EU is accommodating the existence and the interests of its internal small nations has enormous significance for the potential of the small nation solution to be effectively applied at a global level.

The Committee of the Regions CoR is a representative organization of 344 members, plus their alternates, and individuals who serve as representatives of regional and local governments.[25] Depending on the organization of individual countries, CoR members are selected either as existing representatives of federally recognized subnational regions within a federal system, or they are elected representatives of local authorities such as municipalities. In either case, CoR members are typically selected by associations of local and regional authorities.[26] However selected, members serve four-year terms, and it is assumed that they will answer to a democratically elected local or regional political body. The CoR holds six plenary sessions and dozens of consultations with local groups every year. Representation of local areas and communities in the CoR helps override the effects of concentrated political power in large states because when small areas can select their own representatives more people have the possibility of running for office. This opens up an entirely new political forum by means of which people can speak directly to top level decision makers.

More than half of the EU member states are themselves small nations with populations of under ten million. Eleven are small nations with populations over a million, but under ten million (by declining size: Sweden, Austria, Bulgaria, Denmark, Slovakia, Finland, Ireland, Lithuania, Latvia, Slovenia, and Estonia). Three EU small nation countries (Cyprus, Luxembourg, and Malta) are mini small nations with fewer than a million people. There are also a few European small nations (Åland, Andora, Faroe Islands, Iceland, Lichtenstein, and Norway) that are not part of the EU. This latter group, together with Denmark, Greenland, and Sweden, have formed their own cooperating economic group called Norden. In comparison to the EU, all but seven states (by descending size: California, Texas, New York, Florida, Illinois, Pennsylvania, Ohio) of the fifty U.S. states had fewer than 10 million people in 2011 and could be considered small nations. Seven states with fewer than a million people (Montana, Delaware, South Dakota, Alaska, North Dakota, Vermont, Wyoming) are small enough to be considered mini small nations.

The EU politically and economically unites twenty-seven countries under the 1993 Maastricht Treaty as amended and grew out of the European Economic Community (EEC) formed in 1958 after the chaos of World War II. The EU has three legislative bodies: the twenty-seven-member European Commission which initiates and implements legislation to be applied to all member states, the European Parliament of 754 elected representatives, which proposes changes to draft legislation, and the twenty-seven-member Council of the European Union (Council of Ministers), which adopts legislation.

The EU should not be confused with the Council of Europe, which is a larger intergovernmental organization with forty-seven member states encompassing some 800 million people. The Council of Europe is not a government. Virtually all of Europe, except Belarus, Kazakhstan, and Vatican City, are members. The Council drafts treaties, not laws, and its treaties promote international standards, human rights and cultural cooperation, and most importantly for the small nation solution, it champions and monitors self-government and democracy at local and regional levels. Like the EU, the Council of Europe has a Parliamentary Assembly and a Congress of Local and Regional Authorities. The Council of Europe drafted the European Charter of Local Self Government in 1985. This is an international treaty which requires that signatory national governments incorporate constitutional provisions for local self-government based on the subsidiarity principle, supported by transfer of decision-making powers, and financial resources from central to local governments. Article 9, Section 5 included provisions for local taxing authorities and "financial equalization" to correct unequal distribution of resources. This charter clears the way for subnational units of large nations to become self-governing small nations. As of 2012 all but two of the forty-seven members of the Council of Europe had ratified the treaty. Only San Marino and Monaco had not, but these micro-nations are already self-governing.

The Preamble of the EU Treaty cites the determination of the signing member states to promote both economic and social progress, taking the principle of sustainable development into account, assuming environmental protection, and the key principles of subsidiarity and proportionality. These two principles taken together get at the essence of the problem of elite-directed growth and concentrated power, and thereby provide the intellectual and legal basis for the small nation solution to be applied to global problems. Democracy and the will of the citizenry are applied under a third principle, conferral, which refers to powers "conferred" on governments by their citizens. For the EU, these are the powers specified by the Maastricht Treaty. Subsidiarity determines *who* decides, and proportionately determines *what and how much* they can do. The words of the treaty specify that when the subsidiarity principle is applied "decisions are taken as closely as possible to the citizen." Under proportionately, "the content and form of Union action shall not exceed what is necessary to achieve the objectives of the Treaties" (Article 5, Section 4).

In the EU context, the subsidiarity principle in effect gives the lowest levels of European government the highest possible priority in decision making and thereby empowers small nations. This sets limits on who first gets to decide. Article 5 of the Maastricht Treaty states in Section 3: "Under the principle of subsidiarity, in areas which do not fall within its exclusive competence, the Union shall act only if and in so far as the objectives of the proposed action cannot be sufficiently achieved by the Member States, either at central level, or at regional and local level, but can rather, by reason the scale or effects of the proposed action, be better achieved at Union level." This means that the first deciders are elected officials at the lowest level of government, or the small nation. If these authorities prove unable to solve the problem, make a decision, or reach a workable consensus on an appropriate policy, the matter would work its way up the political hierarchy, perhaps eventually coming to the attention of the European Commission, the European Parliament, and the EU Council of Ministers. Conceivably, if still unresolvable it might then be moved to an appropriate global forum. Obviously, the scale of an issue like the necessity of limiting carbon emissions to mitigate global warming would require global level decision making.

As important as the subsidiarity principle and the functions of the Committee of the Regions are in getting political decision making at optimum levels, these principles and institutional structures will not in themselves directly produce an equitable distribution of wealth and power. Nor do they by themselves temper the actions of giant corporations or the effects of global "free markets." Political parties and their associated manifestos, think tanks, conventions, and campaigns still play a vital role in shaping policy at all levels within the European Union. All of this will be guided by a consensus on values.

The unifying cultural values of the EU are enshrined in the Charter of Fundamental Rights of the European Union which was first drafted in 2000 and then legally codified under the Lisbon Treaty of 2009.[27]

The EU rights charter is comparable to the U.S. Bill of Rights but differs in significant ways. Most importantly for solving human problems, the EU Fundamental Rights make Europe a place where small nations and the small nation solution can thrive. The Preamble cites Europe's common spiritual and moral heritage in ". . . the indivisible, universal values of human dignity, freedom, equality and solidarity . . . based on the principles of democracy and the rule of law." The charter explicitly tips its hand toward Europe's small nations by recognizing common values, "while respecting the diversity of the cultures and traditions of the peoples of Europe . . ." and reaffirming the principle of subsidiarity. As we will show, subsidiarity is the principle that gives real power and vitality to small nations in relation to higher governing bodies or regulatory authorities. Article 22 declares that the EU "shall respect cultural, religious, and linguistic diversity." The Preamble also explicitly endorses sustainable development.

The EU Charter of Fundamental Rights resembles the American Bill of Rights, but the EU Charter covers more rights. There is no death penalty in the EU. This appears as section 2 of Article 2 as "Right to Life." Torture, slavery, and forced labor are also banned as offenses to human dignity by the EU Charter. Everyone has the right to marry and found a family (Article 9). This is worded to permit families formed by same-sex unions. Discrimination based on sexual orientation is banned, and gender equity is required (Articles 21 and 23). The right to form and join labor unions is included under the general right of peaceful assembly (Article 12). "Solidarity" (chapter 4) takes on a special meaning in the EU. Under Article 34, everyone is "entitled" to social security benefits and services to protect them "in cases such as maternity, illness, industrial accidents, dependency or old age, and in the case of loss of employment. . . ." Political discourse in the United States often disparages Social Security and health care as "entitlements" as if it were self-evident that people who receive social benefits are undeserving "takers" opposed to the "makers." In the EU this sort of political conflict is not an issue. Access to health care, including preventive care, and health protection is a specific right (Article 35). "A high level of environmental protection and the improvement of the quality of the environment" must be built into EU policies (Article 37).

EUROPEAN SMALL NATION POLITICS:
LEFT, CENTER, AND RIGHT

Recognising that the dominant patterns of human production and consumption, based on the dogma of economic growth at any cost and the excessive and wasteful use of natural resources without considering Earth's carrying capacity, are causing extreme deterioration in the environment and a massive extinction of species
Acknowledging that injustice, racism, poverty, ignorance, corruption, crime and violence, armed conflict and the search for maximum short term profit are causing widespread human suffering. . . . — preamble to the Charter of the Global Greens, as adopted in Canberra in 2001 and updated in Dakar in 2012.[28]

Political support for the small nation solution within the EU system is strongest on the political left and is to some degree resisted by the right. However, left and right in the EU are generally more diverse and to the "left" of left and right than in the United States. The European Parliament recognizes seven different political groups, some of which are individual parties, others are shifting alliances of parties. These groups have official standing and cross cut the twenty-seven national parliamentary groups. To qualify as a political group a party must have at least twenty-five members, and must represent at least one-fourth (six to seven) of member states. These rules make it difficult for really radical parties to gain a place at the table, and parties must form coalitions. The left-right ideological split is explicit. Political groups are physically arranged on a left-to-right seating arrangement when parliament is in session.

The largest political group in the EU is the European People's Party (EPP), which descended from the founders of the EU. It self-identifies as center and center-right. It promotes the Single Market, the Euro monetary system, and "sustainable" growth. It identifies populism, nationalism, and "political radicalism" as threats. The EPP's emphasis on "reforms" to perpetuate free market growth implies less support for local autonomy movements and the small nation solution. The EPP officially endorses ethno-diversity and subsidiarity and recognizes that global warming, natural resource degradation, biodiversity loss, and poverty are serious challenges that must be addressed.[29] However, there are contradictions here because EPP leaders are the intellectual descendants of those who used their political power to extend the scale of the European market, and they want to continue with the original framework of economic globalization, and neoliberal economic ideology with necessary adjustments.

The EPP endorse a "Social Market Economy based on environmental sustainability in which competitiveness and entrepreneurial freedom are balanced with social justice." They argue that "Socialism and radical environmentalism do not give the same priority to freedom, personal responsibility and subsidiarity" and are not compatible with "progress, democracy and the Social Market Economy" or a "strong and efficient European Union." The Social Market seeks to balance free market and social welfare principles in a way that will produce continuing economic growth. This is the Christian Democratic pathway followed in Germany after World War II, but many critics warn that it is too conservative and does not address the real problems of growth limits and concentrated power. It is certainly a step forward in its recognition of the severity of the unfolding social, economic, and environmental crisis facing Europe and the world. Although the EPP proposals for implementing the Social Market Economy speak of social justice, human rights, and sustainability, it clearly remains market-centric and growth-oriented. [30]

The European socialist perspectives on the political left appear to be the most supportive of the small nation solution. For example, the Greens/European Free Alliance (Greens/EFA) political group, the fourth largest group in the EU Parliament in 2012, explicitly argues that social, cultural, and ecological values need to take precedence over economic policy and markets. They are strong advocates for political self-determination, deepening democracy, and full application of the subsidiarity principle. They include representatives of "stateless nations," cultural groups who are seeking autonomy.[31] The Greens are a globally organized political party, and their basic principles are for example endorsed by Sustainable Chile and are incorporated into their political agenda. Green principles are ecological wisdom, social justice, participatory democracy, nonviolence, sustainability, and respect for diversity (see above quotations from the Charter of the Global Greens). These principles can also be a foundation for the small nation solution generally and deserve close attention because they are already being implemented by small nations.

CONSTRUCTING SMALL NATIONS:
DECENTRALIZATION AND NEW GLOBAL NETWORKS

United Cities and Local Governments (UCLG) represents and de-
fends the interests of local governments on the world stage, regardless of the size of the communities they serve. Headquartered in
Barcelona, the organisation's stated mission is: To be the united
voice and world advocate of democratic local self-government, promoting its values, objectives and interests, through cooperation between local governments, and within the wider international community. —UCLG's website[32]

While many of the problems facing cities and towns may be global,
the solutions will, in large measure, be local and unique to the specific circumstances on the ground. Good solutions will result from a
smooth collaboration amongst various levels of government that is
crafted pragmatically to get results. We look forward to a strong
partnership with UCLG. —Katherine Sierra, VP, Sustainable Development, The World Bank[33]

The potential number of small nations is enormous, depending on what
decision-making authority territories take on and how they relate to
higher-level organizations. Eurostate, the European Commission's statistical directorate's NUTS 1 classification (Nomenclature of territorial
units for statistics), distinguishes 124 major socioeconomic regions in
the twenty-seven European Union countries. Many of these regions
correspond to administrative provinces and typically range in size from
three to seven million people. All could be considered small nations.
Going smaller, at NUTS 2 there are 297 basic regions, small administrative areas ranging in size from 800,000 to 3 million people, which the
EU treats as units for the distribution of financial resources according
to its Cohesion Policy designed to reduce development disparities
across the EU, as well as for its regular financial distribution (Structural
Funds).[34] The smallest areas, at NUTS 3 are 1,321 geographic areas of
150,000 to 800,000 people identified for specific local development
issues. Many of these small areas might also decide to become small
nations.

The Assembly of European Regions (AER), formed in 1985, is a
network of regional government authorities resembling the EU Committee of the Regions, however the AER is independent of the EU

system and like the Council of Europe has a broader reach. The Assembly includes more than 250 regions in thirty-five countries, including several countries that are not part of the EU in Eastern Europe, the Adriatic, Switzerland, and Norway. Sixteen international organizations are also members, and the AER has partnership agreements with other European networks with common interests such as ERRIN, the European Regions Research and Innovation Network with 101 regional members in twenty-two countries; with The Association of Cities and Regions for Recycling and Sustainable Resource Management (ACR+), a networked organization of more than ninety local and regional authorities, and municipal associations; and with the Association of North East Asia Regional Governments (NEAR) which includes China, Japan, South Korea, North Korea, Mongolia, and Russia.

Just as small nations and subnational governments are in the process of negotiating more beneficial relations with existing larger governments, they are forming partnerships with carefully selected large commercial businesses where they have shared interests. The Assembly of European Regions created one such alliance with the EDF Group, Électricité de France, the largest producer of electricity in the world. EDF is a Forbes 2000 Corporation, approximately 85 percent owned by the French government. EDF is also heavily committed to reducing carbon emissions. It produces most of its electricity from nuclear and is investing heavily in renewable energy and energy conservation.[35]

The AER has also formed a partnership with another organization concerned with mobilizing local and regional governments on environmental issues—R20 Regions of Climate Action, a nonprofit organization formed in 2010 at the initiative of then California governor Arnold Schwarzenegger to bring subnational and local governments together from all over the world to take action to deal with the climate change crisis. R20 started with twenty-four founding subnational and local government members in Africa, Asia-Pacific, Europe, North America, and South America, and then quickly added twenty-seven more regional government members. Three small nations, Togo, Burundi, and Seychelles, are among its new members. R20 then linked up with forty-three partner organizations worldwide, including academic institutions, business corporations, many prominent NGOs, the Asian Development Bank, the UN Development Program (UNDP), and the UN Environment Program (UNEP). By also networking with the AER, the Association of North East Asia Regional Governments, and Metropolis, and the World Association of the Major Metropolises, a network of 129 city or metro region governments, R20 was able to bring together a total of 560 small regional governments by 2012.

This a move toward the long-heralded Information Society (IS), or the Global Networked-Knowledge Society (GNK), as envisioned in the European Commission's Terra-2000 futurist model for Europe and the world. What is especially exciting about these very new, twenty-first-century developments is that they are being constructed on the base of politically and economically self-reliant small nations, networked together to share information, and they are situated within higher-level decision-making governments based on the principles of democracy, diversity, subsidiarity, proportionality, solidarity, and sustainability. Small nations are the small governments, regions, and local communities in which citizens, households, and individuals can prosper and have maximum decision-making control over the conditions of their daily lives and their futures.

The AER adopted a formal declaration on regionalism in 1996.[36] Their preamble noted that states with regional governments empowered to control their own finances are optimally situated to solve their economic and social problems. The AER declaration defined the region as the top subnational territorial body with self-government. In the EU context, this would mean that they would be NUTS 1 level, with populations in the 3 to 7 million range. They would be in effect small nations. They would have full legal status, recognized by their parent state government, but they would have their own political identity with an official insignia and a democratically elected representative assembly. They would have specific powers, or "competencies," according to principles of decentralization and subsidiarity.

Following up on their declaration on regionalism, the AER commissioned a special study on how to measure the degree of autonomy of politically decentralized territories and how autonomy might affect their economic performance. There were two issues. The first asked how decentralized was the state itself. The second asked how much autonomy the subnational region had. The more regulatory power (competencies) the regions have, the more decentralized the state and the more autonomous the region. The project was carried out by analysts at BAK Basel Economics, an independent consultant firm in Basel,

Switzerland.[37] BAK researchers first produced a Decentralization Index by collecting information on 185 indicator qualities and measurable quantities relevant to political decision making and financial matters at different tiers in the political hierarchy. Adding up the score for all of these indicators gives a good picture of how much autonomy regions have in each country.

The small nation of Switzerland showed the highest level of decentralization with a score of 70 and Bulgaria the lowest with 25. Switzerland has 7.6 million people (2010), a three-tiered constitutional federal system, with twenty-six cantons, 2,763 municipalities, and four official languages: German, French, Italian, and Romansh. Each canton is like an independent small nation with its own constitution. Swiss cantons have high decision-making authority and a very high degree of financial autonomy with the power to set their own tax base and rate. They keep their tax revenues and receive a share of the national tax. In contrast, Bulgaria is a parliamentary republic of 7.4 million people in twenty-eight provinces and 264 municipalities. Bulgaria receives such a low score for decentralization because regional officials are simply agents of the central government. Local officials have no control over taxes and receive only a small amount from the central government.

The BAK researchers carefully examined the economic performance of the countries in their survey and concluded that more decentralized countries and regions with more autonomy in fact did better than more centrally controlled countries and regions. Among the factors that might have influenced this outcome is the role of government policy, or public finance, in affecting more efficient and equitable resource allocation and distribution between regions, and maintaining a stable economic system.[38] Governments in very small polities can be expected to know much better than more remote authorities what specific public goods their citizens want, and this can make for greater efficiency. This of course assumes the existence of considerable cultural diversity. Not everyone in the world wants exactly the same goods, or will satisfy their needs in exactly the same way, even though they have the same basic needs.

Knowledge of the local culture makes government planning and decision making easier and less costly. Citizens are also more likely to trust their government and more willingly pay local taxes. The administrative costs in general are likely to be lower in decentralized systems when there is a consensus on how government should work, and citizens will have more ready access to government.[39] Locals are also in a position to see what government is doing and demand greater efficiency. Local governments can buy their own goods and services locally; they may also be more able and willing to experiment with innovative approaches to their tasks. Some government will always be more efficiently produced centrally, because of returns to scale in some operations, but even then a smaller central government may be more efficient overall than larger. Where governments are small and local, citizens may also opt to move from one to another if they become dissatisfied. Such competition for citizen loyalty may encourage more efficient government services. In the final analysis many diverse things can best be provided by small or regional governments, whereas some things will require a central government, or even, in the case of small nations, an association of nations for them to be provided. Costly science and technology services, central banks, superior courts, or military defense may require either a large nation-state or a consortium of international providers.

United Cities and Local Governments (UCLG) is the newest and now largest network of subnational governments and has quickly become the most prominent international proponent of decentralization, local and regional self-government (see opening quotations above). This new organization was created by a merger of the International Union of Local Authorities (IULA), the World Federation of United Cities (FMCU-UTO), and Metropolis. Small-scale subnational governments are in effect small nations that are not fully sovereign independent nations, but they are nevertheless well positioned to implement the small nation solution. The UCLG was founded in 2004 and is headquartered in Barcelona in the autonomous community of Catalonia, Spain. By 2012 the UCLG claimed that the local governments that it networked together represented more than half of the world's people living in 140 states in all regions of the world and more than 1,000 cities and regions. This must be a more complete and more democratic representation of humanity than the UN General Assembly which represents 191 states.

What is remarkable about all of these networked societies representing local and regional governments is that economic development by itself is conspicuously not the most important issue. It is as if when

government gets close to citizens as demanded by the subsidiarity principle and actually respond to the real interests of the democratic majority, then the real human issues of justice, social sustainability, the needs
of future generations, and the environment jump out as the issues that
really matter. It is not an oversight that under "Issues" on its website in
2012 the UCLG listed the following: Policy and Advocacy; Decentralization and Local Democracy; Cooperation; and Urban Sustainability,
not increasing GDP and global competitiveness. Climate change was
the first item under Policy and Advocacy.

MAKING THE WORLD SAFE FOR SMALL NATIONS

Key dimensions of the small nation solution can be found within the
futurist scenarios explored in three prominent futurist proposals produced by intergovernmental organizations to help national policy makers choose the most promising pathway to a sustainable world, which
would of course also be a world in which small nations could thrive.
These proposals are GEO-3 produced by the UN Environment Program (UNEP) in 1993[40] ; the European Commission's TERRA-2000
Project[41] ; and the UN Intergovernmental Panel on Climate Change
(IPCC) Special Report on Emissions Scenarios (SRES).[42] Each proposal contains four major scenarios, and in each case one stands out as
clearly compatible with the small nation solution, and it would produce
the most promising pathway to sustainability. The GEO-3 report considered four alternative futures which were called Markets First, Security First, Sustainability First, and Policy First, each respectively corre-
sponding closely to scenarios A, B, C, D in TERRA-2000. Even though
they used somewhat different computer programs and modeling techniques, the results pointed to GEO-3's Sustainability First or TERRA-
2000's eco-social market scenario C as the only really viable futures.
Under Sustainability First there are "more equitable values" and "fuller
collaboration between governments, citizens and other stakeholder
groups in decision-making ..." TERRA-2000's Scenario C would limit
growth to protect the environment and would distribute benefits in a
way that maximized justice and equity. This would require a knowledgeable citizenry and a highly democratic and participatory government in a society where political and economic power was decentral-

ized. This could best be achieved in small nations. The four IPCC scenarios were called A1, A2, B1, and B2. As emphasize policy choices favoring economic growth, and Bs emphasize social equity and environmental protection; 1s and 2s reflect predominance of either global or regional decision making, respectively. A1 is a world that maximizes market globalization. Sustainable small nations would most likely be B2, because their economies would be more regional and they would emphasize environment over economic growth. All of three of these sustainable small nation scenarios, like their agoria, ecodemia, and arcadia counterparts in the Great Transition futurist scenarios, would succeed because they set limits to growth, are less materialist, and emphasize social justice.

Small Nations also conform remarkably well to the conditions for "perpetual peace" among nations proposed by German Enlightenment philosopher Immanuel Kant (1724–1804) in 1795.[43] Kant was critical of the close connection between economic growth and arms races financed by government debt. He advocated the complete abolition of standing armies, arguing that their very existence constituted a constant threat to other states. The World Bank's 2008 figures on military expenditures by 191 nations[44] support Kant's contention that absolute size of a national economy is strongly correlated with the size and power of standing armies. These 191 countries spent more than $1.6 trillion on their militaries in 2010, but these expenditures were highly concentrated with over half in just three nations: the United States, China, and Russia. Military expenditures tended to increase predictably in pace with economic growth, except for the thirty-six small nations with economies of less than $10 billion that virtually dropped off the military scale. Many small nations, such as Andorra, Antigua and Barbuda, Channel Islands, Costa Rica, Iceland, Isle of Man, Kiribati, Palau, Samoa, St. Kitts and Nevis, St. Lucia, St. Vincent and the Grenadines, and Vanuatu either had only token militaries or maintained only very small police forces.

Small nations with small economies could not of course finance many important weapons systems and that can be a good thing. It is no surprise that only a handful of counties have nuclear weapons, and all those that do also have very large economies, or they impose severe sacrifices on their citizens. Forty-four small nations had individual GDPs that were smaller than the $6 billion construction cost of a single

American nuclear aircraft carrier in 2005. There were ten such ships in the U.S. Navy. A single M-1 Abrams tank cost more than $4 million, which was more than the entire military budget of Trinidad in 2008. The primary corporations that produce costly military hardware have annual revenues of tens of billions of dollars, and their shares are held by investment corporations that manage hundreds of billions or trillions in financial assets. These giant corporations, the stock markets, and other financial service institutions that support them are all critical parts of the military-industrial complex that Kant considered a major obstacle to perpetual peace. He was right, and the small nation solution would solve that problem as well.

NOTES

PREFACE

1. Smith, Anthony D. 2001. *Nationalism: Theory, Ideology, History.* Cambridge, UK: Polity Press, Table 1.1, p. 13.
2. Aristotle. *The Politics*, Book I, 1252b27. Translated by T. A. Sinclair, Revised by Trevor J. Sanders. 1981. London: Penguin.
3. Aristotle. *The Politics*, Book I, 1253a1.

ACKNOWLEDGMENTS

1. Bodley, John H. 2012. "Sol Tax's Global Futurist Model and Small-Nation Solutions". In *Action Anthropology and Sol Tax in 2012: The Final Word?* Edited by Darby C. Stapp, pp. 165–182. Richland, WA: Journal of Northwest Anthropology.

I. THE BIG PROBLEM

1. Bodley, John H. 2012. "Small Nation Happiness: A Scale and Power Perspective." Vital Topics Forum on Happiness. *American Anthropologist* 114(1) (March): pp. 10-11.
2. Madison, James. 1787. "The Union a Check on Faction." *Federalist Paper No. 10.* http://en.wikipedia.org/wiki/Federalist_No._10

3. Hölldobler, Bert, and Edward O. Wilson. 1990. *The Ants*. Cambridge, MA: Belknap Press of Harvard University Press.

4. Alexander, Richard D. 1987. *The Biology of Moral Systems*. Hawthorne, NY: A. de Gruyter.

5. Humphrey N. K. 1976. " The social function of intellect. " In P P. G. Bateson and R. A. Hinde, editors. *Growing Points in Ethology* . Cambridge, UK: Cambridge University Press. pp. 303 – 317.

6. Dunbar, Robin I. 1993. "Neocortex Size as a Constraint on Group Size in Primates." *Journal of Human Evolution* 20:469–493.

7. Mandeville, Bernard. 1924. *The Fable of the Bees: or, Private vices, publick benefits*. (commentary critical, historical, and explanatory by F. B. Kaye) 2 volumes. Oxford: The Clarendon Press (first edition 1705).

8. Bodley, John H. 2012. *Anthropology and Contemporary Human Problems*. 6th edition. Lanham, MD: AltaMira Press. Chapter 3, pp. 103–111.

9. Fischer-Kowalski, Marina, and Helmut Haberl. 2002. "Sustainable Development: Socio-Economic Metabolism and Colonization of Nature." *International Social Science Journal* 50(158): 573–587.

10. Vitousek, Peter M., Paul R. Ehrlich, Anne H. Ehrlich, and Pamela A. Matson. 1986. "Human Appropriation of the Products of Photosynthesis." *BioScience* 36(6): 368–373; Wright, David Hamilton. 1990. "Human Impacts on Energy Flow Through Natural Ecosystems, and Implications for Species Endangerment." *Ambio* 19(4): 189–194; Imhoff, Marc L., Lahouari Bounoua, Taylor Ricketts, Colby Loucks, Robert Harriss, and William T. Lawrence. 2004. "Global Patterns in Human Consumption of Net Primary Production." *Nature* 429: 870–873.

11. Smil, Vaclav. 2002. *The Earth's Biosphere: Evolution, Dynamics, and Change*. Cambridge, MA: The MIT Press.

12. Thurow, Lester C. 1996. *The Future of Capitalism: How Today's Economic Forces Shape Tomorrow's World*. New York: W. Morrow.

13. Gates, Bill, with Nathan Myhrvold and Peter Rinearson. 1996. *The Road Ahead*, 2nd ed. New York: Penguin Books.

14. Levi-Strauss, Claude. 1966. *The Savage Mind*. Chicago: University of Chicago Press.

15. These brief examples are summarized from more extended accounts in Bodley, John H. 2003. *The Power of Scale: A Global History Approach*. Armonk, NY: M. E. Sharpe.

16. Seya, Hiromichi (editor). 2010. *Conditions for Survival: Toward a "Solar Energy-Based Society " Full of Vibrant Life*. Tokyo: The Asahi Glass Foundation. www.af-info.or.jp/en/doc/ survival .pdf , p. 1

17. Pinker, Steven. 2011. *The Better Angels of Our Nature: Why Violence Has Declined*. New York: Viking.

18. Rummel, R. J. 1997. *Death by Government*. New Brunswick, NJ: Transaction.

19. United Nations Development Program. 2011. 2011 Human Development Index Press Release. http://hdr.undp.org/en/media/PR2-HDI-2011HDR-English.pdf

20. United Nations Development Program. 2011. Human Development Report 2011 Sustainability and Equity: A Better Future for All. New York: Palgrave Macmillan. http://hdr.undp.org/en/reports/global/hdr2011/download/

21. Farmer, Paul. 2003. *Pathologies of Power: Health, Human Rights, and the New War on the Poor*. Berkeley: University of California Press.

22. Bodley, John H. 2012. *Anthropology and Contemporary Human Problems*. Sixth edition. Lanham, MD: AltaMira Press. Chapter 6, pp. 215–242.

23. Bodley, John H. 2012. "Small Nation Happiness: A Scale and Power Perspective." Vital Topics Forum on Happiness. *American Anthropologist* 114(1) (March); World Values Survey, www.worldvaluessurvey.org/organization/index.html

24. Capgemini. 2012. *World Wealth Report 2012*. www.capgemini.com

25. Costanza, Robert, Lisa Graumlich, Will Steffen, Carole Crumley, John Dearing, Kathy Hibbard, Rik Leemans, Charles Redman, and David Schimel. 2007. "Sustainability or Collapse: What Can We Learn from Integrating the History of Humans and the Rest of Nature?" *Ambio* 36(7): 522–527.

26. Crutzen, Paul J., and Eugene F. Stoermer. 2000. "The 'Anthropocene.'" *IGBP Newsletter* No. 41: 17–18. The International Geosphere-Biosphere Programme (IGBP): A Study of Global Change of the International Council for Science (ICSU).

27. Millennium Ecosystem Assessment. 2005. *Ecosystems and Human Well-being: Synthesis*. Washington, D.C.: Island Press www.maweb.org/documents/document.356.aspx.pdf ; Millennium Ecosystem Assessment. 2005. *Living Beyond Our Means: Natural Assets and Human Well-Being*. Statement from the Board. Technical Volume. Washington, DC: Island Press. www.maweb.org/documents/document.429.aspx.pdf

28. WWF. 2011. *Living Planet Report 2010 Biodiversity, Biocapacity and Development*. Gland, Switzerland: WWF International. www.worldwildlife.org/sites/living-planet-report/WWFBinaryitem18260.pdf, p. 7, figure 2.

29. Rockström, Johan, et al. 2009. "Planetary Boundaries: Exploring the Safe Operating Space for Humanity." *Ecology and Society* 14(2), article 32.

30. Watson, Sir Bob, et al. 2012. *Environment and Development Challenges: The Imperative to Act*. The Blue Planet Prize Laureates, The Asahi Glass Foundation (February 20). www.af-info.or.jp/en/bpplaureates/doc/2012jp_fp_en.pdf

31. Stern, Nicholas. 2007. *The Economics of Climate Change: The Stern Review*. Cambridge, UK: Cambridge University Press; UK Treasury. 2006. *Stern Review: Economics of Climate Change, Executive Summary*. www.hm-treasury.gov.uk/d/Executive_Summary.pdf

32. Watson, Sir Bob, et al. 2012. *Environment and Development Challenges*, p. 3.

33. Union of Concerned Scientists. 1992. "World Scientists' Warning to Humanity." www.ucsusa.org/ucs/about/1992-world-scientists-warning-to-humanity.html

34. Meadows, Donella H., Dennis L. Meadows, Jørgen Randers, and William W. Behrens III. 1972. *The Limits to Growth*. New York: Universe.

35. Diamond, Jared. 1997. *Guns, Germs, and Steel: The Fates of Human Societies*. New York: W. W. Norton & Co.

36. Bodley, John H. 2003. *The Power of Scale: A Global History Approach*. Armonk, NY: M.E. Sharpe.

37. Davis, Mike. 2001. *Late Victorian Holocausts: El Niño Famines and the Making of the Third World*. London: Verso.

2. FINDING THE RIGHT SIZE

1. Montesquieu, Baron de (Charles-Louis de Secondat). 1899 (1748). *The Spirit of the Laws*. Vol. 1, Book 8, Chapter 16. (Translated by Thomas Nugent). New York: Colonial Press, p. 120.

2. Bodley, John H. 1976. *Anthropology and Contemporary Human Problems*. Menlo Park, CA: Cummings Publishing Co., p. viii.

3. Bodley, John H. 1983. *Anthropology and Contemporary Human Problems* (2nd edition). Palo Alto, CA: Mayfield Publishers.

4. Tax, Sol. 1977. "Anthropology for the World of the Future: Thirteen Professions and Three Proposals." *Human Organization* 36(3):225-234.

5. Goldsmith, Edward, et al. 1972. *Blueprint for Survival*. Boston: Houghton Mifflin.

6. Bodley, John H. 1994. *Cultural Anthropology: Tribes, States, and the Global System*. Mountain View, CA: Mayfield Publishing Co.

7. Bodley, John H. 1999. "Socio-Economic Growth, Culture Scale, and Household Well-Being: A Test of the Power-Elite Hypothesis." *Current Anthropology* 40(5):595–620.

8. Pareto, Vilfredo. 1971. *Manual of Political Economy*. Translated by Ann S. Schwier and Alfred N. Page. New York: A. M. Kelley.

9. Axtell, Robert L. 2001a. "Zipf distribution of U.S. firm sizes." *Science* 293(5536):1818-1820; Axtell, Robert L. 2001b. *The emergence of firms in a*

population of agents: local increasing returns, unstable Nash equilibria, and power law size distributions. CSED Working Paper No. 3. Brookings Institution.

10. Bodley, John H. 2003. *The Power of Scale: A Global History Approach.* Armonk, NY: M.E. Sharpe.

11. Kohr, Leopold. 1978. *The Breakdown of Nations.* New York: Dutton, p.79 [originally published 1957].

12. Kohr, Hans [Leopold]. 1941. "Disunion Now: A Plea for a Society based upon Small Autonomous Units." *The Commonweal*, Sept. 26. http://www.panarchy.org/kohr/1941.eng.html

13. Schumacher, E. F., 1973. *Small Is Beautiful: A Study of Economics as If People Mattered.* London: Blond and Briggs.

14. Rasmussen, Morten et.al. 2011. "An Aboriginal Australian Genome Reveals Dispersals into Asia." *Science* 334(6052): 94-98.

15. Sahlins, Marshall. 1968. "Notes on the Original Affluent Society." In *Man the Hunter*, edited by Richard B. Lee and Irven DeVore, 85–89. Chicago: Aldine.

16. Bodley, John H. 2012. *Anthropology and Contemporary Human Problems.* Sixth edition. Lanham, MD: AltaMira Press, pp. 85-90.

17. Loh, Jonathan, and Mathis Wackernagel. 2004. *Living Planet Report 2004.* Gland, Switzerland: World Wide Fund for Nature.

18. Hiatt, L. R. 2002. *Edward Westermark and the Origin of Moral Ideas.* Presented at the Ninth International Conference on Hunting and Gathering Societies, Heriot-Watt University, Edinburgh, Scotland.

19. Bodley, John H. 1973. "Romanticism in Anthropology." Northwest Anthropological Conference, La Grande, Oregon.

20. Montesquieu. 1899. *The Spirit of the Laws*, Vol. 1, Book 8, Chapter 20, p. 122.

21. Dahl, Robert A. and Edward R. Tufte. 1973. *Size and Democracy.* Stanford, CA: Stanford University Press.

22. Kohr, Leopold. 1978. *The Breakdown of Nations.* New York: Dutton. Originally published in 1957.

23. Sandel, Michael J. 2009. *Justice: What's the Right Thing to Do?* New York: Farrar, Straus and Giroux.

24. Marks, Nic, and Saamah Abdallah, Andrew Simms, and Sam Thompson. 2006. *The Happy Planet Index: An Index of Human Well-Being and Environmental Impact.* London: New Economics Foundation. www.neweconomics.org/gen/z_sys_PublicationDetail.aspx?PID=225

25. World Bank. World databank. World Bank Development Indicators 9WDI) & Global Development Finance (GDF). http://databank.worldbank.org/data/home.aspx

26. Bodley, John H. 2011. *Cultural Anthropology: Tribes, States, and the Global System*. Fifth edition. Lanham, MD: AltaMira Press, pp. 520-521, Table 14.4.

27. Wilkinson, Richard G. 1996. *Unhealthy Societies: The Afflictions of Inequality*. London and New York: Routledge; Pickett, Kate and Richard Wilkinson. 2010. *The Spirit Level: Why Greater Equality Makes Societies Stronger*. New York: Bloomsbury Press; Bezruchka, Stephen. 2001. "Societal Inequality and the Health Olympics." *Canadian Medical Association Journal* 164(12): 1701-03; De Vogli, Roberto, Ritesh Mistry, Roberto Gnesotto, Giovanni Andrea Cornia. 2005. "Has the relation between income inequality and life expectancy disappeared? Evidence from Italy and top industrialized countries." *Journal of Epidemiology and Community Health* 59: 158-162.

28. Chadwick, Sir Edwin. 1842. *Report to her Majesty's principal secretary of state for the Home Department, from the Poor Law Commissioners, on an inquiry into the sanitary condition of the laboring population of Great Britain*. London: W. Clowes and Sons.

29. Wilkinson, Richard and Kate Pickett. 2009. *The Spirit Level: Why Equality Is Better for Everyone*." London: Allen Lane, Penguin.

30. United Nations Development Program. 2011. *Human Development Report 2011: Sustainability and Equity: A Better Future for All*. New York: Palgrave Macmillan; U.S. Central Intelligence Agency. Distribution of Family Income, Gini Index. www.cia.gov/library/publications/the-world-factbook/fields/2172.html (accessed May, 2012).

31. Credit Suisse. 2010. *Global Wealth Databook*. Credit Suisse Research Institute. www.credit-suisse.com/news/doc/credit_suisse_global_wealth_databook.pdf

32. Collier, Paul. 2007. *The Bottom Billion: Why the Poorest Countries Are Failing and What Can Be Done About It*. New York: Oxford University Press.

33. Sachs, Jeffrey D. 2005. *The End of Poverty: Economic Possibilities of Our Time*. New York: Penguin Press, p. 19.

34. Acemoglu, Daron and James A. Robinson. 2012. *Why Nations Fail: The Origins of Power, Prosperity, and Poverty*. New York: Crown.

35. The Royal Society. 2012. *People and the Planet*. The Royal Society Science Policy Centre Report 01/12, p. 14. http://royalsociety.org/uploadedFiles/Royal_Society_Content/policy/projects/people-planet/2012-04-25-PeoplePlanet.pdf

36. The Royal Society. 2012. *People and the Planet*, p. 14.

37. Millennium Ecosystem Assessment. 2005. *Ecosystems and Human Wellbeing: General Synthesis*. Washington, D.C.: Island Press.

38. Sen, Amartya. 2001. *Development as Freedom*. New York: Oxford University Press.

39. Jackson, Tim. 2006. "Beyond the 'Wellbeing Paradox': - wellbeing, consumption growth and sustainability." Centre for Environmental Strategy. University of Surrey, Guildford (Surrey). www.surrey.ac.uk/ces/files/pdf/0606_WP_Wellbeing_and_SD.pdf ; Jackson, Tim. 2009. *Prosperity Without Growth: Economics for a Finite Planet*. London: Earthscan.

40. Friedman, Benjamin M. 2005. *The Moral Consequences of Economic Growth*. New York: Alfred A. Knopf.
NEF, New Economic Foundation. 2012. *NEF Review of the Year 2010-2011*. www.neweconomics.org/sites/neweconomics.org/files/Review_of_the_Year_2010-2011.pdf

41. Jackson, "Beyond the 'Wellbeing Paradox'...", p. 15.

3. SMALL NATION MARKET CAPITALISM

1. Arbeiderpartiet. 2012. *The Norwegian labour Party – a brief presentation*. http://arbeiderpartiet.no/Kontakt/Information-in-English

2. Tellus Institute. 2005. *Great Transition Initiative: Visions and Pathways for a Hopeful Future*. GTI Brochure. www.gtinitiative.org/default.asp?action=42

3. United Nations Development Programme (UNDP). 2011. *Human Development Report 2011, Sustainability and Equity: A Better Future for All*. New York: Palgrave Macmillan. Statistical Tables, p.126. http://hdr.undp.org/en/media/HDR_2011_EN_Tables.pdf

4. Hails, Chris, Sarah Humphrey, Jonathan Loh, Steven Goldfinger. 2008. *Living Planet Report 2008*. Gland, Switzerland: World Wide Fund for Nature.

5. U.S. Energy Information Administration. 2009. *Annual Energy Review*. Total Carbon Dioxide Emissions from the Consumption of Energy (Million Metric Tons). www.eia.doe.gov/emeu/international/contents.html

6. Norway, Ministry of Finance. 2008. *Norway's Strategy for Sustainable Development*, published as part of the National Budget. R-0617E. www.regjeringen.no/upload/FIN/rapporter/R-0617E.pdf

7. Great Britain, United Kingdom, Treasury. 2007. *The Economics of Climate Change*, (Nicholas Stern, Editor). Cambridge and New York: Cambridge University Press. Also available: H.M. Treasury website: www.hm-treasury.gov.uk/stern_review_report.htm

8. Great Britain, 2007, *Economics of Climate Change*, Full Executive Summary, i.

9. Ahrne, Göran and Erik Olin Wright. 1983. "Class in the United States and Sweden: A Comparison." *Acta Sociologica* 26(3/4), 211-235.

10. Chydenius, Anders. 1931. *The National Gain*. London: Ernest Benn Ltd. (original 1766).

11. Higley, John, G. Lowell Field, and Knut Grøholt. 1976. *Elite Structure and Ideology: A Theory with Applications to Norway*. New York: Columbia University Press.

12. Norway, Ministry of Finance. 2005. *The Government Pension Fund: The Ethical Guidelines*. www.regjeringen.no/en/dep/fin/Selected-topics/the-government-pension-fund/responsible-investments/Guidelines-for-observa-tion-and-exclusion-from-the-Government-Pension-Fund-Globals-investment-universe.html?id=594254 (accessed April 2010).

13. Norway, Ministry of Finance. 2008. *Council on Ethics, Government Pension Fund. Annual Report 2008*. www.regjeringen.no/en/sub/styrer-rad-ut-valg/ethics_council/annual-reports.html?id=458699

14. Medrano, Jaime Diez. 2005. *WVS 2005 Codebook*, Variables 10, 11, 22, 46, 214. Data from online World Values Survey 2005-2008 www.worldvaluessurvey.org/

15. Medrano, *WVS 2005 Codebook*, Variables 132, 136, 137, 138, 140, 141. www.worldvaluessurvey.org

16. Andersen, Torben M., Bengt Holmstrom, Seppo Honkapohja, Sixten Korkman, Hans Tson Soderstrom, Juliana Vartiainen. 2007. *The Nordic Model: Embracing Globalization and Sharing Risks*. Research Institute of the Finish Economy (ETLA), Helsinki: Taloustieto Oy. www.etla.fi/Files/1892 the_nordic_model_complete.pdf.

17. Anderson, et al. 2007. *The Nordic Model*, 16-18.

18. CONICYT, Comisión Nacional de Investigación Científica y Tecnológica; FONDAP, Fondo de Financiamiento de Centros de Excelencia en Investigación. www.conicyt.cl/573/channel.html

19. Maddison, Angus. 2003. *The World Economy: Historical Statistics*. OECD: Development Centre Studies, Paris.

20. Zeitlin, Maurice, Lynda Ann Ewen, and Richard Earl Ratcliff. 1974. "'New Princes' for Old? The Large Corporation and the Capitalist Class in Chile." *American Journal of Sociology* 80(1):87-123.

21. Klein, Naomi. 2007. *The Shock Doctrine: The Rise of Disaster Capital-ism*. New York: Picador, Henry Holt & Co. See especially Introduction and Chapter 3.

22. Friedman, Milton. 2005. "The Promise of Vouchers." *Wall Street Jour-nal*. Dec. 5.

23. United States Institute of Peace. 2000. *Report of the Chilean National Commission on Truth and Reconciliation*. www.usip.org/files/resources/collec-tions/truth_commissions/Chile90-Report/Chile90-Report.pdf by permission of the University of Notre Dame Press, also known as the Rettig Report originally

issued in 1991; see also the National Commission on Political Imprisonment and Torture (Comisión Nacional Sobre Prisón Politica y Tortura), the Valech Commission, issued 2004, and 2005.

24. Instituto de Ecología Política. 1995. "Critica de Libros: El Tigre Sin Selva." *Ecología Política* No. 9, p. 181.

25. Mitchell, Daniel J. and Julia Morriss. 2012. "The Remarkable Story of Chile's Economic Renaissance." *Daily Caller*, July 18, 2012. Reprinted by the Cato Institute. www.cato.org/publications/commentary/remarkable-story-chiles-economic-renaissance

26. Quiroga, Rayén. 1994. *El tigre sin selva. Consecuencias Ambientales de la transformación económica de Chile: 1974-1993*. Santiago, Chile: Instituto de Ecología Política.

27. IWGIA, International Work Group for Indigenous Affairs, Copenhagen. Founded in 1968. www.iwgia.org/

28. Mariquero, Vicente. 1979. *The Mapuche Tragedy*. IWGIA Document No. 38. Copenhagen. www.iwgia.org/iwgia_files_publications_files/0104_38Chile.pdf

29. Montalba Navarro, René, Noelia Carrasco Henríquez, José Araya Cornejo. 2005. *The Economic and Social Context of Monoculture Tree Plantations in Chile: The Case of the Commune of Lunaco, Araucania region*. World Rainforest Movement www.wrm.org.uy/countries/Chile/booklumaco.pdf

30. http://skyscraperpage.com/cities/maps/?cityID=906

31. http://skyscraperpage.com/cities/?cityID=906

32. Taylor, P.J., and D.R.F. Walker. 2002. "Measurement of the World City Network." *Urban Studies* 39(13):2367-2376; Data Set 11: Taylor, P.J. and G. Catalano. World City Network: The Basic Data. www.lboro.ac.uk/gawc/datasets/da11.html

33. Taylor, Peter J. et.al. 2009. "The way we were: command-and-control centres in the global space-economy on the eve of the 2008 geo-economic transition." *Environment and Planning* A 41:7-12.

34. Cuadros, Alex, and Eduardo Thomson. 2012. "Billionaire Catching Wal-Mart Brazil as Cencosud Surges." www.bloomberg.com/news/2012-06-19/billionaire-catching-wal-mart-in-brazil-as-cencosud-quadruples.html

35. Vitali, Stefania, James B. Glattfelder, and Stefano Battiston. 2011. "The network of global corporate control." *arXiv* (July 28), Cornell University.

36. *500 Las Mayores Empresas de Chile*. http://rankings.americaeconomia.com/2011/500-chile/ranking-500-chile.php

37. Lagos, Ricardo. 1962. *La Concentracion del Poder Economico: Su Teoria, Realidad Chilena*. Memoria de Prueba para optar al Grado de Licenciado en Ciencias Jurídicas y Sociales de la Universidad de Chile. www.cybertesis.uchile.cl/tesis/uchile/1962/lagos_r/html/index-frames.html

38. Lagos, 1962. *Concentration del Poder Economico*, section 61.

39. Undurraga, Tomás. 2010. "Recomposición de Elites Económicas y Renovación Ideológica del Empresariado de Chile 1980-2010. El Apogeo del Management." Latin American Studies Association 2010 Congress, Toronto. http://xa.yimg.com/kq/groups/26452858/1086320237/name/Undurraga+LASA+2010+Elites+economicas+Chile+061010.pdf

40. Max-Neef, Manfred, Antonio Elizalde, and Martin Hopenhayn et al. 1989. "Human Scale Development: An Option for the Future." *Development Dialogue* 1989:1, pp. 5-80. Uppsala: Dag Hammarskjöld Foundation.

41. Max-Neef, Manfred. 1992. *From the Outside Looking in: Experiences in "Barefoot Economics."* London: Zed Books. Originally published, 1982, Uppsala Sweden: Dag Hammarskjöld Foundation.

42. Max-Neef, Manfred. 1992. *From the Outside Looking in...* p. 53-54. Smith, Philip B. and Manfred Max-Neef. 2011. *Economics Unmasked: From power and greed to compassion and the common good.* Totnes, Devon, UK: Green Books; Max-Neef, Manfred. 2007. "Economía a Escala Humana." *Revista Mundo Nuevo* 9(56):10-15.

43. Rees, William E. (October 1992). "Ecological footprints and appropriated carrying capacity: what urban economics leaves out." *Environment and Urbanisation* 4 (2): 121 – 130.

4. SMALL NATION ECONOMIC DEMOCRACIES

1. International Co-operative Alliance (ICA). 2012. "Co-operative identity, values & principles." http://2012.coop/en/what-co-op/co-operative-identity-values-principles

2. Mondragón Corporation. 2012. *Corporate Profile 2011 Perfil corporativo.* p. 1. www.mondragon-corporation.com/mcc_dotnetnuke/Portals/0/documentos/cas/Perfil-Anual/Perfil-Corporativo.html

3. International Co-operative Alliance (ICA). 2012. "Co-operative identity, values & principles." http://2012.coop/en/what-co-op/co-operative-identity-values-principles

4. Donnachie, Ian. 2000. *Robert Owen: Owen of New Lanark and New Harmony.* East Lothian, Scotland: Tuckwell Press. Donnachie, Ian and George Hewitt. 1993. *Historic New Lanark.* Edinburgh, Scotland: Edinburgh University Press; New Lanark Conservation Trust. 1993. *New Lanark Village Store and the Development of the Co-operative Movement.* New Lanark Mills: New Lanark Conservation Trust.

5. International Co-operative Alliance. 2012. *Co-operative facts and figures.* http://2012.coop/en/ica/co-operative-facts-figures

6. United Nations, Department of Economic and Social Affairs. 2012. *International Year of Cooperatives 2012*. Division for Social Policy and Development. http://social.un.org/coopsyear/

7. The Co-operative Group. 2012. *The Co-operative Group Building for the future Interim report 2012*. http://www.co-operative.coop/PageFiles/376400294/cooperative_interim_report_2012.pdf. The Co-operative Group. 2011. *The Co-operative Group Building for the Future, Annual Report & Accounts 2011*. www.co-operative.coop/Corporate/PDFs/Annual-Report/Annual_Report_2011.pdf The Co-operative Group. 2011. Inspiring Through Co-Operation, Sustainability Report 2011. The Co-operative Group. www.co-operative.coop/Corporate/sustainability-report-2011/downloads/sustainability-report-2011.pdf

8. From the brief of the Nunavut Constitutional Forum (NCF) to the Royal Commission on the Economic Union and Development Prospects for Canada, cited in Patterson, Dennis. 1984. "Canada: Inuit and Nunavut." *IWGIA Newsletter*, no. 37:39-52, 52.

9. Nunavut Planning Commission. *Agreement Between the Inuit of the Nunavut Settlement Area and Her Majesty the Queen in Right of Canada*, Articles 1, and 35. http://npc.nunavut.ca/eng/nunavut/nlca.pdf

10. IWGIA. 1983. *Newsletter*. 33:114.

11. Patterson "Inuit and Nunavut," 39-52.

12. Nunavut Tunngavik Inc. 2006. *Iniksaqattiarniq, Inuusiqattiarniq: Housing in Nunavut – The Time for Action is Now*. Annual Report on the State of Inuit Culture and Society 2003/04 and 2004/05. www.tunngavik.com/english/pub.html

13. Nunavut Tunngavik Inc. 2007. Inuit Firm Registry – Approved Businesses as of Sep 07, 2007. www.inuitfirm.com/public/pdfreport.php

14. Sivummut Economic Development Strategy Group. 2003. *Nunavut Economic Development Strategy: Building a Foundation for the Future*. http://edt.gov.nu.ca/docs/nes/NUNAVUTE.pdf, I.

15. Sivummut Economic Development Strategy Group, *Nunavut Economic Development Strategy*, VI.

16. The Conference Board of Canada. 2001.*Nunavut Economic Outlook*: An Examination of the Nunavut Economy. http://www.gov.nu.ca/frv21.pdf

17. Nunasi Corporation. Operations. Consolidated Balance Sheet, December 31, 2005. http://www.nunasi.com/operations.htm

18. Berger, Thomas R. 2006. *The Nunavut Project. Conciliator's Final Report*. Nunavut Land Claims Agreement Implementation Contract Negotiations for the Second Planning Period 2003-2013. www.ainc-inac.gc.ca/pr/agr/nu/lca/nlc_e.pdf

19. Steury, Tim. 2011. "Back in the Earth: Putting ancestors to rest, or destroying the past?" *Washington State Magazine* (Spring). http://wsm.wsu.edu/s/index.php?id=844#.UJ0jg4Z4D4Y ; National Park Service, Department of the Interior. 2010. "Notice of Inventory Completion: U.S. Department of Defense, Army Corps of Engineers, Walla Walla District, Walla Walla, WA, and Museum of Anthropology, Washington State University, Pullman, WA." *Federal Register* 75(92). (Thursday, May 13, 2010). www.gpo.gov/fdsys/pkg/FR-2010-05-13/html/2010-11456.htm; Hicks, Brent A. 2004. *Marmes Rockshelter: a final report on 11,000 years of cultural use*. Pullman: Washington State University Press.

20. Walker, Deward E. 1967. *Mutual cross-utilization of economic resources in the plateau: an example from aboriginal Nez Perce Fishing Practices*. Reports of Investigations No. 41. Pullman, WA: Washington State University, Laboratory of Anthropology; Hunn, Eugene S. 1990. *Nch'i-wána, "the Big River': Mid-Columbia Indians and their Land*. Seattle: University of Washington Press.

21. United States Census. 2012. *The 2012 Statistical Abstract*. Population: Estimates and Projections by Age, Sex, Race/Ethnicity. Table 6. Resident Population by Sex, Race, and Hispanic-Origin Status: 2000 to 2009; Malcolm Wiener Center for Social Policy. Harvard Project on American Indian Economic Development. 2008. *The state of the Native Nations: conditions under U.S. policies of self-determination*. New York: Oxford University Press, Preface.

22. Taylor, Jonathan B. 2012. *The Economic and Fiscal Impacts of Indian Tribes in Washington*. Olympia: Washington Indian Gaming Association. www.washingtontribes.org/pdfs/WIGA%20Taylor%20September%202012%20Web%20Version.pdf

23. U.S. Department of Energy. Western Area Power Administration, Renewable Resources Program. 2010. *Tribal Authority Process Case Studies: The Conversion of On-reservation Electric Utilities to Tribal Ownership and Operation*. Tribal Energy Program. http://apps1.eere.energy.gov/tribalenergy/pdfs/tribal_authority.pdf ; U.S. Department of Energy, Office of Energy Efficiency and Renewable Energy (EERE). Yakama Nation Hydropower Project. http://apps1.eere.energy.gov/tribalenergy/pdfs/0811review_15lewis.pdf

24. Forbes Magazine. 2012. "The World's Billionaires." www.forbes.com/billionaires/

25. Ruff, Joe. 2005. "Buffett expands energy holdings." *Spokesman Review*, May 25, A12, A18.

26. U.S. Department of Energy. Case Study: Yakama Nation Housing Authority Wapato, WA. http://apps1.eere.energy.gov/buildings/publications/pdfs/building_america/ba_cs_retrofit_yakama.pdf

27. United States Department of Energy, Federal Energy Regulatory Commission. 2008. *Order Issuing New License*. 123 FERC 61,049. www.ferc.gov/whats-new/comm-meet/2008/041708/H-1.pdf

28. Grant County PUD. 2007. *Settlement between Yakama Nation and Grant County PUD*. www.gcpud.org/pudDocuments/naturalResourcesDocs/yakamaNationSettlementAgreement061107.pdf

29. Grant County PUC. 2005. *Priest Rapids Project Salmon and Steelhead Settlement Agreement*. www.gcpud.org/prcc/pdfs/Salmon%20&%20Steelhead%20Settlement%20Agreement%20-%20Executed081006.pdf

30. National Indian Gaming Commission. 2012. Tribal Gaming Revenues (in thousands) by Region Fiscal Year 2011 and 2010. www.nigc.gov/Portals/0/NIGC%20Uploads/Tribal%20Data/GamingRevenuesByRegion2010and2011.pdf

31. Las Vegas Sands Corporation. 2012. *Proxy Statement*, Principal Stockholders, p. 5. http://files.shareholder.com/downloads/ABEA-242MDE/2163521511x0x564198/FB6B4BB0-F001-41AD-A961-6FEBACC0D695/LVS_2012_Proxy_Statement.pdf ; Sands Las Vegas Corporation 2012. *Annual Report 2012*. http://files.shareholder.com/downloads/ABEA-242MDE/2163521511x0x564189/05AE746E-AF52-4E5E-8221-9E20F02760F5/LVS_2011_Annual_Report.pdf

32. Las Vegas Sands Corporation. 2012. *Environmental Responsibility Policy April 12, 2012*. http://sands.com/sands-eco-360/our-strategy/360-sustain-policy/

33. Las Vegas Sands Corporation. 2012. *More than just an idea… 2011 Environmental Report*. http://sands.com/wp-content/themes/lvs/files/EnvironmentalReport.pdf

34. Yakama Nation. Title LXXI (71) – Yakama Nation Tribal Employment Rights Ordinance. www.yakamanation-nsn.gov/Ordinance%202009%20Title%2071%20%28LXXI%29%20-%20TERO%20-%20First%20DCR%20Ed.%20%28v.%2002.09.02%29.pdf

35. Assad, Matt. 2012. "Security guards form first union in Las Vegas Sands' empire." *LA Times*, June 2, 2012. http://articles.latimes.com/2012/jun/02/business/la-fi-sands-union-20120602

36. Corporations (Aboriginal and Torres Strait Islander Act) 2006. www.comlaw.gov.au/ComLaw/Management.nsf/lookupindexpagesbyid/IP200626899?OpenDocument

37. Australia, Office of the Registrar of Indigenous Corporations. 2009. *Yearbook 2008-09*, p. 16, Table 4. www.orac.gov.au/html/publications/Yearbooks/Yearbook2008-09_72dpi_104pp.pdf\; Bawinanga Aboriginal Corporation website www.bawinanga.com.au/index.htm accessed January 2010.

38. Altman, Jon. 2008. "Different governance for difference: the Bawinanga Aboriginal Corporation." In Hunt, Janet, Diane Smith, Stephanie Garling, and Will Sanders (editors). *Contested Governance: Culture, power and institutions in Indigenous Australia*, pp. 177-203. Centre for Aboriginal Economic Policy Research. Research Monograph. No. 29.Canberra: Australia National University Press.

39. Morrison, Roy. 1991. *We Build the Road as We Travel*. Philadelphia: New Society Publishers; Whyte, William Foote, and Kathleen King Whyte. 1988. *Making Mondragón: The Growth and Dynamics of the Worker Cooperative Complex*. Ithaca, NY: ILR Press.

40. Mondragón Corporation. 2008 *Annual Report*. www.mondragon-corporation.com/language/en-US/ENG/General-Information/Downloads.aspx

41. MCC (Mondragón Corporación Cooperativa). 2006. *2005 Annual Report*. www.mcc.es/

42. Mondragón. 2011. *Corporate Profile 2011*. www.mondragon-corporation.com/language/en-US/ENG/Economic-Data/Corporate-Profile.aspx

43. Eurostat. 2007. *Europe in figures: Eurostat yearbook 2006–2007*. ec.europa.eu/eurostat

5 . ARCADIA

1. Bolivia, La Asamblea Legislative Plurnacional. 2010. *Decreta: Ley de Derechos de la Madre Tierra*. http://www.scribd.com/doc/44900268/Ley-de-Derechos-de-la-Madre-Tierra-Estado-Plurinacional-de-Bolivia#archive

2. Esty, Daniel C., M.A. Levy, C.H. Kim, A. de Sherbinin, T. Srebotnjak, and V. Mara. 2008. *2008 Environmental Performance Index*. New Haven, CT: Yale Center for Environmental Law and Policy. http://sedac.ciesin.columbia.edu/es/epi/downloads.html#summary

3. Metz, B., O.R. Davidson, P.R. Bosch, R. Dave, L.A. Meyer (editors). 2007. *Climate Change 2007: Mitigation of Climate Change. Contribution of Working Group III to the Fourth Assessment Report of the Intergovernmental Panel on Climate Change, 2007*. Cambridge, UK, and New York: Cambridge University Press. www.ipcc.ch/publications_and_data/publications_ipcc_fourth_assessment_report_wg3_report_mitigation_of_climate_change.htm

4. Kaya, Y. 1990. "Impact of Carbon Dioxide Emission Control on GNP Growth: Interpretation of Proposed Scenarios." Paper presented to the IPCC Energy and Industry Subgroup, Response Strategies Working Group, Paris (cited in Metz, et al. *Climate Change 2007*, p. 180-183).

5. Hansen, James et. al. 2008. "Target Atmospheric CO2: Where Should Humanity Aim?" *The Open Atmospheric Science Journal* 2:217-231. www.bentham.org/open/articles.htm

6. Meinshausen, Malte, et al. 2009. "Greenhouse-gas emission targets for limiting global warming to 2°C." *Nature* 458 (30 April): 1158-1162.

7. Matthews, H. Damon. 2008. "Stabilizing climate requires near-zero emissions." *Geophysical Research Letters* 35, L04705, doi:10.1029/2007GL032388, 208.

8. Baer, Paul, Tom Athanasiou, Sivan Kartha, and Eric Kemp-Benedict. 2008. *The Greenhouse Development Rights Framework: The Right to Development in a Climate Constrained World.* Heinrich Böll Foundation, Christian Aid, Ecoequity, and the Stockholm Environment Institute. http://gdrights.org/2009/02/16/second-edition-of-the-greenhouse-develoment-rights.

9. United States Energy Information Administration. 2009. "Total Carbon Emissions from the Consumption of Energy." www.eia.doe.gov/emeu/international/contents.html

10. Much of this material is taken directly with modifications from chapters 2 and 13 of Bodley, John H. 2011. *Cultural Anthropology: Tribe, State, and the Global System.* 5th Edition. Lanham, MD: AltaMira Press, and chapter 2, Bodley, John H. 2012. *Anthropology and Contemporary Human Problems.* 6th Edition. Lanham, MD: AltaMira Press. The general outlines of Amazonian prehistory are based on Donald W. Lathrap, 1970. *The Upper Amazon.* London: Thames & Hudson.

11. To qualify as a "hotspot" an area must contain at least 1,500 endemic vascular plant species (0.5 percent of the world's 300,000 known plants found nowhere else in the world), and it must have lost at least 70 percent of its original area. The originally designated twenty-four Hotspots now cover less than 1.4 percent of the terrestrial earth, but they contain 60 percent of the world's plants and animal species.

12. Critical Ecosystem Partnership Fund. 2005. *Tropical Andes Hotspot: Vilcabamba-Amoró Conservation Corridor: Peru and Bolivia Briefing Book.* www.cepf.net/Documents/final.tropicalandes.vilcabambaamboro.briefingbook.pdf (Accessed May 12, 2008).

13. Killeen, Timothy J. 2007. *A Perfect Storm in the Amazon Wilderness: Development and Conservation in the Context of the Initiative for the Integration of the Regional Infrastructure of South America (IIRSA),* 8, 12. AABS, Advances in Applied Biodiversity Science, No. 7. Arlington, VA: Conservation International. www.conservation.org/publications/Pages/perfect_storm.aspx (accessed April 27, 2009).

14. Goulding, Michael. 1980. *The Fishes and the Forest: Explorations in Amazonian Natural History*. Berkeley: University of California Press.

15. Mittermeier, Russell, Cristina Goettsch Mittermeier, Patricio Robles Gil, Gustavo Fonseca, Thomas Brooks, John Pilgrim, and William R. Konstant. 2003. *Wilderness: Earth's Last Wild Places*. Chicago: University of Chicago Press; Mittermeier, Russell, Norman Myers, Cristina Goettsch Mittermeier. 2000. *Hotspots: Earth's Biologically Richest and Most Endangered Terrestrial Ecoregions*. Arlington, VA: Conservation International; Mittermeier, Russell, Patricio Robles Gil, Michael Hoffman, John Pilgrim, Thomas Brooks, Cristina Goettsch Mittermeier, John Lamoreux, Gustavo A. B. da Fonseca, Peter A. Seligmann, Harrison Ford. 2005. *Hotspots Revisited: Earth's Biologically Richest and Most Endangered Terrestrial Ecoregions*. Arlington, VA: Conservation International. Myers, Normal, Russell A. Mittermeier, Christina G. Mittermeier, Gustavo A. B. da Fonseca, and Jennifer Kent. 2000. "Biodiversity Hotspots for Conservation Priorities." *Nature* 403, 24 February, 853–58.

16. Ellis, Erle C., and Navin Ramankutty. 2008. "Putting People in the Map: Anthropogenic Biomes of the World." *Frontiers in Ecology and the Environment* 6(8):439–47. www.ecotope.org/people/ellis/papers/ellis_2008.pdf (accessed May 18, 2009).

17. Schulenberg, Thomas S., Douglas F. Stotz, Daniel F. Lane, John P. O'Neill, and Theodore A. Parker III. 2007. *Birds of Peru*. Princeton, NJ: Princeton University Press.

18. Fittkau, E., and H. Klinge. 1973. "On Biomass and Trophic Structure of the Central Amazonian Rain Forest Ecosystem." *Biotropica* 5(1):2–14.

19. Bailey, Robert C., G. Head, M. Jenike, B. Own, R. Rechtman, and E. Zechenter. 1989 "Hunting and Gathering in Tropical Rain Forest: Is It Possible?" *American Anthropologist* 91(1):59–82.

20. My translation. Pizango Chota, Alberto. 2012. Que Queremos? AIDESEP. www.aidesep.org.pe/saludo/

21. AIDESEP, Asociación Interétnica de Desarrollo de la Selva Peruana. www.aidesep.org.pe/

22. Bodley, John H. 1972b. *Tribal Survival in the Amazon*.

23. Bodley, John H. 1975. *Victims of Progress*. 1st edition, 169; reprinted in Bodley, John H. 2008. *Victims of Progress*, 5th edition, 293-294.

24. Permanent Forum on Indigenous Issues (UNPFII). 2010. *United Nations Declaration on the Rights of Indigenous Peoples*. www.un.org/esa/socdev/unpfii/en/drip.html

25. Instituto de Bien Común. www.ibcperu.org/ (accessed January 2010); Smith, Richard Chase, Margarita Benavides, Mario Pariona, and Ermeto Tuesta. 2003. "Mapping the Past and the Future: Geomatics and Indigenous Territories in the Peruvian Amazon. *Human Organization* 62(4):357-368.

26. CEDIA, Centro para el Desarrollo del Indígena Amazónico. www.cedia. org.pe/index.php (accessed January 2010).

27. Benavides, Margarita. 2005. "Conservación, derechos indígenàs y poder en la gestión de los bienes communes: El caso de la reserve communal El Sira en la Amazonía Peruana." Originally presented at the International Association for the Study of the Commons. Global Meeting, Oaxaca City, Mexico, 2004. www.ibcperu.org/doc/isis/5316.pdf (accessed January 2010); ParksWatch. 2003. *Profile of Protected Area: Peru El Sira Communal Reserve.* www.parkswatch.org/parkprofiles/pdf/escr_eng.pdf (accessed January 2010); Servicio Nacional de Areas Naturales Protegidas por el Estado Peruano (SER-NANP), Instituto Nacional de Recursos Naturals (INRENA), and Interdencia de Areas Naturales Protegidas (IANP). 2009. *Plan Maestro de la Reserva Comunal El Sira 2009-2013.* www.sernanp.gob.pe/sernanp/archivos/biblioteca/publicaciones/RC_ElSira/PlanMaestro-2009-2013-RCElSira.pdf

28. For background on Asháninka (Campa) ethnography and ethnohistory, see: Varese, Stefano. 1973. *La Sal de los Cerros: Una aproximación al mundo Campa.* Lima: Instituto Nacional de Investigación y Desarrollo de Educación; Varese, Stefano. 2002. *Salt of the Mountain: Campa Asháninka History and Resistance in the Peruvian Jungle.* Norman: University of Oklahoma Press; Johnson, Allen. 2003. *Families of the Forest: The Matsigenka Indians of the Peruvian Amazon.* Berkeley: University of California Press.

29. RAISG, Red Amazónica de Información Socioambiental Georeferenciada. 2009. Amazonia 2009 *Áreas Protegidas Territorios Indígenas.* www.raisg.socioambiental.org (accessed April 14, 2009).

30. Quinlan, Marsha B. 2004. *From the Bush: The Front Line of Health Care in a Caribbean Village.* Case Studies in Cultural Anthropology. Belmont, CA: Thomson Wadsworth.

31. Honychurch, Lennox. 1975. *The Dominica Story: A History of the Island.* Oxford: Macmillan.

32. Marks, Nic, and Saamah Abdallah, Andrew Simms, and Sam Thompson. 2006. *The Happy Planet Index: An Index of Human Well-Being and Environmental Impact.* London: New Economics Foundation. www.neweconomics.org/gen/z_sys_PublicationDetail.aspx?PID=225

33. Halcrow Group Limited. 2003. *Dominica Country Poverty Assessment. Final Report.* Caribbean Development Bank, Government of the Commonwealth of Dominica.

34. Halcrow Group, 2003, *Dominica Country Poverty Assessment,* vi.

35. Kauai, County of. 2004. *Kaua'i Economic Development Plan: Kaua'i's Comprehensive Economic Development Strategy (CEDS) Report 2005-2015.* Office of Economic Development, Kauai'i Economic Development Board.

36. Kauai, 2004, *Economic Development Plan,* 38-40.

37. Bolivia, La Asamblea Legislative Plurinacional. 2010. *Decreta: Ley de Derechos de la Madre Tierra.* http://www.scribd.com/doc/44900268/Ley-de-Derechos-de-la-Madre-Tierra-Estado-Plurinacional-de-Bolivia#archive

38. Lewis, M. Paul (editor). 2009. *Ethnologue: Languages of the World.* 16th edition. Dallas, TX: SIL International.

39. Astete, Álvaro Díez. 2006. "Sobre Antropología de Urgencia en Bolivia: Pueblos Étnicos de Tierras Bajas en Situación de Alta Vulnerabilidad y en Aislamiento Voluntario." www.wrm.org.uy/paises/Bolivia/ANTROPOLO-GIA_URGENCIA_BOLIVIA.pdf

40. Kroll, Luisa and Allison Fass. 2007. "The World's Billionaires." *Forbes Magazine* (March). www.forbes.com/2007/03/07/billionaires-worlds-richest_07billionaires_cz_lk_af_0308billie_land.html

41. Nash, June. 1992. "Interpreting Social Movements: Bolivian Resistance to Economic Conditions Imposed by the International Monetary Fund." *American Anthropologist* 19(2):275-293.

42. Forbes Magazine. 2011. *America's Largest Private Companies.* www.forbes.com/lists/2010/21/private-companies-10_land.html

43. Forbes Magazine. 2007. The World's Billionaires. www.forbes.com/lists/2007/10/07billionaires_Riley-Bechtel_QGCP.html

44. Movement for Socialism—Political Instrument for the Sovereignty of the Peoples (Movimiento al Socialismo-Instrumento Politico por la Soberania de los Pueblos, MAS-IPSP).

45. My translation. Bolivia, Asamblea Constituyente de Bolivia. 2008. *Nueva Constitución Política del Estado.* Congreso Nacional. (Octubre). www.presidencia.gob.bo/download/constitucion.pdf

46. World Conference on Climate Change and the Rights of Mother Earth. http://pwccc.wordpress.com/ (accessed Sept. 2011).

47. Global Island Partnership. 2008. GLISPA Brochure. www.cbd.int/island/glispa.shtml

48. United Nations. 1992. *Agenda 21.* Department of Economic and Social Affairs, Division for Sustainable Development, Chapter 17, Part G. Sustainable development of small islands, sections 123-136. www.un.org/esa/dsd/agenda21/res_agenda21_17.shtml

49. *Agenda 21,* G 17.123.

50. Convention on Biological Diversity. 2009. Global Island Partnership. www.cbd.int/island/glispa.shtml

51. UN General Assembly. 1994. *Report of the Global Conference on the Sustainable Development of Small Island Developing States.* A/CONF.167/9. Annex II Programme of Action for the Sustainable Development of Small Island Developing States, Preamble, Article 14. www.sidsnet.org/docshare/other/BPOA.pdf

52. UN General Assembly. 1994. *Report of the Global Conference, Annex II Programme of Action for the Sustainable Development of Small Island Developing States*, Preamble, Article 13.

53. Cook Islands Government. 2004. *Cook Islands Constitution. Preamble.* www.parliament.gov.ck/Constitution.pdf

54. Cook Islands Government. 2004. *Cook Islands National Environment Strategic Action Framework 2005-2009.* National Environment Service, p. 15. www.thegef.org/gef/sites/thegef.org/files/documents/NESAF-Final-Draft-30-June.pdf

55. Cook Islands Government. 2002. *Cook Islands Biodiversity Strategy and Action Plan.* National Steering Committee on behalf of the Government of the Cook Islands. www.sprep.org/attachments/12.pdf

56. McCormack, Gerald M. 2006. "Rimatara Lorikeet Reintroduction Programme." Cook Islands Natural Heritage Trust. http://cookislands.bishopmuseum.org/showarticle.asp?id=24

57. Cook Islands, Statistics Office.2003. *Cook Islands 2001 Census of Population and Dwellings Main Report*. Table 14. www.stats.gov.ck

6. SMALL NATION SOLUTIONS FOR THE PACIFIC NORTHWEST, 2025

1. Batker, David, Rowan Schmidt, Jennifer Harrison-Cox, and Briana Lovell. 2010. *The Whole Economy of the Snohomish Basin: The Essential Economics of Ecosystem Services*. P. 10. www.eartheconomics.org/FileLibrary/file/Reports/Snohomish/Earth_Economics_Snohomish_Basin_Report.pdf

2. Callenbach, Ernest. 1975. *Ecotopia: the notebooks and reports of William Weston*. Berkeley, CA: Banyan Tree Books.

3. Webley, Kayla. 2011. "To Be or Not To Be: The Republic of Cascadia." *Newsweek* (January 10). www.time.com/time/specials/packages/article/0,28804,2041365_2041364_2041373,00.html

4. Bob Connell. 2010. "Pacific politics and the far-off dream of an independent Cascadia." Letter, *The Guardian*, March 3. www.guardian.co.uk/world/2010/mar/04/pacific-politics-america-northwest

5. Republic of Cascadia The Bioregional Cooperative Commonwealth of Cascadia. Website. http://republic-of-cascadia.tripod.com/

6. Sustainable Seattle. 2012. Who We Are. www.sustainableseattle.org/whoweare/whoweare

7. Arha, Kaush, Hal Salwasser, and Gail Achtermaqn. 2003. *The Oregon Plan for Salmon and Watersheds: A Perspective.* Institute for Natural Resources, INR Policy Paper 2003-03. Corvallis: Oregon State University.

8. The Willamette Valley Livability Forum. 1999. *Choices for the Future: The Willamette Valley.* www.upa.pdx.edu/IMS/currentprojects/TAHv3/Content/PDFs/WVLF_Choices_Future_Revisited.pdf

9. Pernick, Ron, Clint Wilder, Dexter Gauntlett. 2008. *Carbon-Free Prosperity 2025: How the Northwest Can Create Green Jobs, Deliver Energy Security, And Thrive in the Global Clean-Tech Marketplace.* Clean Edge, Inc. and Climate Solutions. http://climatesolutions.org/resources/reports/carbon-free-prosperity/CarbonFreeProsperity.pdf

10. Clean Edge. 2011. *Oregon's Clean Energy Economy: A Clean Edge State Clean Energy Leadership Index Report.* Clean Edge, Inc. www.pdxeconomicdevelopment.com/docs/cleantech/Oregon-Clean-Energy-Economy.pdf

11. Regional Plan Association. 2006. *America 2050*: A Prospectus." (September). New York. www.america2050.org/pdf/America2050prospectus.pdf

12. Fishman, Robert. 2000. "The Metropolitan Tradition in American Planning." In Robert Fishman, editor, *The American Planning Tradition: Culture and Policy*, pp. 65-88.Baltimore: The John Hopkins University Press.

13. Pacific NorthWest Economic Region. 2012. "About Us." www.pnwer.org/AboutUs/Background.aspx

14. Pacific NorthWest Economic Region. 2012. *Pacific NorthWest Economic Region 2011 Annual Report.* P. 6. www.pnwer.org/Portals/0/2011%20Annual%20Report%20-%20Web%20Version.pdf

15. House Journal of the Third Legislature of the State of Washington, 1893. *Inaugural Address of Governor McGraw.* pp. 44-45. Olympia, Washington.

16. House Journal of the Fifth Legislature of the State of Washington. 1897, pp. 34-46. Olympia, Washington.

17. Johnson, David H. and Thomas A. O'Neil (editors). 2001. *Wildlife-Habitat Relationships in Oregon and Washington.* Corvallis: Oregon State University Press.

18. Hunn, Eugene S. 1990. *Nch'i-Wána " The Big River " : Mid-Columbia Indians and their Land.* Seattle and London: University of Washington Press.

19. *St'át'imc (PC) Settlement Agreement Among St'át'imc (PC) St'át'imc Authority British Columbia Hydro and Power Authority and Her Majesty the Queen in Right of the Province of British Columbia.* May 10, 2011. www.cohencommission.ca/DownloadExhibit.php?ExhibitID=2025 ; Paley, Dawn. 2011. "BC Hydro-St'át'imc Authority Agreement Creates a Wave of Opposition." Vancouver Media Co-op, April 17. http://vancouver.mediacoop.ca/story/bc-hydro-st%C3%A1timc-authority-agreement-creates-wave-opposition/6973 ; BC Hydro. 2012. *BC Hydro Annual Report 2012.* P. 18-19. www.bchydro.com/etc/medialib/internet/documents/annu-

al_report/2012_BCH_AnnualReport.Par.0001.File.2012-BCH-Annual-Report.pdf

20. Jensen, Derrick, George Draffan, and John Osborn. 1995. *Railroads and Clearcuts: Legacy of Congress' s 1864 Northern Pacific Railroad Land Grant*. Spokane: Inland Empire Public Lands Council.

21. Augerot, Xanthippe with Dana Nadel Foley. 2005. *Atlas of Pacific Salmon: The First Map-Based Status Assessment of Salmon the the North Pacific*. Berkeley: University of California Press, p. 54.

22. CRITFC, Columbia River Inter-Tribal Fish Commission. 2011. Columbia River Treaty Tribes. www.critfc.org/text/tribes.html

23. CRITFC, Columbia River Inter-Tribal Fish Commission. 2011. Columbia River Treaty Tribes Salmon Culture. www.critfc.org/text/trilogy.html; CRITFC. 2011. *Message from the Executive Director, Paul Lumley*. www.critfc.org/text/ex_dir.html;

24. Columbia River Inter-Tribal Fish Commission. 2011. *What is CRITFC?* www.critfc.org/text/work.html

25. CRITFC. 1996. *Wy-Kan-Ush-Mi Wa-Kish-Wit Spirit of the Salmon: The Columbia River Anadromous Fish Restoration Plan of the Nez Perce, Umatilla, Warm Springs, and Yakama Tribes*. Columbia River Inter-Tribal Fish Commission. www.critfc.org/text/trptext.html

26. Lakoff, George. 2010. "We are the polar bears: what's wrong with the way that the environment is understood." In, Sylvia Rowley and Rebekah Phillips (editors), *From Hot Air to Happy Endings: How to Inspire Public Support for a Low Carbon Society*, pp. 12-15. London: Green Alliance. http:// www.green-alliance.org.uk/uploadedFiles/Publications/ Hot%20Air_online%282%29.pdf

27. WAC 222-22-100(1).

28. Washington State Department of Natural Resources. 2005. *Forest Practices Habitat Conservation Plan*. Dec. 2005. www.dnr.wa.gov

29. Jensen, Derrick, George Draffan, and John Osborn. 1995. *Railroads and Clearcuts: Legacy of Congress's 1864 Northern Pacific Railroad Land Grant*. Spokane: Inland Empire Public Lands Council.

30. Myers, Gustavus 1936. *History of the Great American Fortunes*. New York: Random House.

31. Hirt, Paul W. 1994. *A Conspiracy of Optimism: Management of the National Forests since World War Two*. Lincoln and London: University of Nebraska Press.

32. U.S. Department of Agriculture, Forest Service. 2003. *Report of the Forest Service FY 2002: Healthy Forests and Grasslands—Financial and Performance Accountability*. Table 1, P. 225. www.fs.fed.us/publications/documents/report-of-fs-2002-low-res.pdf

33. Hirt, Paul W. 1994. *A Conspiracy of Optimism: Management of the National Forests since World War Two.* Lincoln and London: University of Nebraska Press.

34. Bolsinger, Charles L., Neil McKay, Donald R. Gednev, and Carol Alerich. 1997. *Washington's Public and Private Forests.* Resource Bulletin. PNW-RB-218. USDA Forest Service, Pacific Northwest Research Station, p. 45.

35. Bolsinger, Charles L. 1973. *Changes in Commercial Forest Area in Oregon and Washington 1945-70.* Resource Bulletin. PNW-RB-46. USDA Forest Service, Pacific Northwest Research Station.

36. Based on corporate annual reports and SEC filings.

37. Greenpeace. 2011. *Koch Industries: Still Fueling Climate Denial: 2011 Update.* www.greenpeace.org/usa/Global/usa/planet3/publications/gwe/Koch-Ind-Still-Fueling-Climate-Denial.pdf

38. Whitesides, George M., and George W. Crabtree. 2007. "Don't Forget Long-Term Fundamental Research in Energy." *Science* 315: 796–98, Fig. 1.

39. Venetoulis, Jason, and Cliff Cobb. 2004. *The Genuine Progress Indicator 1950 – 2002 (2004 Update).* Oakland, CA: Redefining Progress.

40. U.S. Department of Agriculture (USDA), Economic Research Service. 2002. *The U.S. Food Marketing System, 2002.* Agricultural Economic Report No. 811.

41. Bodley, John H. 2001. "Growth, Scale, and Power in Washington State." *Human Organization* 60(4): 367-379.

42. Bucks, Brian K., Arthur B. Kennickell, and Kevin B. Moore. 2006. "Recent Changes in U.S. Family Finances: Evidence from the 2001 and 2004 Survey of Consumer Finances." *Federal Reserve Bulletin* 2006 (March 22).

43. Bernstein, Peter W. and Annalyn Swan, editors. 2007. *All the Money in the World: How the Forbes 400 Make —and Spend —Their Fortunes.* New York: Knopf; Frank, Robert. 2007. *Richistan: A Journey Through the American Wealth Boom and the Lives of the New Rich.* New York: Crown, Random House; Lundberg, Ferdinand. 1968. *The Rich and the Super-Rich: A Study in the Power of Money Today.* New York: Bantam.

44. Civic Economics and Urban Conservancy. 2009. *Thinking Outside the Box: A Report on Independent Merchants and the New Orleans Economy.* http://civiceconomics.com/app/download/5841600904/Magazine+Street+2009.pdf

45. Civic Economics and Urban Conservancy. 2009. *Thinking Outside the Box: A Report on Independent Merchants and the New Orleans Economy.* http://civiceconomics.com/app/download/5841600904/Magazine+Street+2009.pdf

46. Maxwell, James R. et.al. 1995. *A Hierarchical Framework of Aquatic Ecological Units in North America* (Nearctic Zone). Gen. Tech. Rep. NC-176.

St. Paul, MN: U.S. Department of Agriculture, Forest Service, North Central Forest Experiment Station.

47. Pentec Environmental. 1999. *Snohomish River Basin Conditions and Issues Report*. Prepared for The Snohomish River Basin Work Group, p. i. www.co.snohomish.wa.us/documents/Departments/Public_Works/SWM/H-SnoRivBasinConditions-IssuesRpt-Dec1999.pdf

48. Center for Biological Diversity and Friends of the San Juans. 2005. *The Puget Sound Basin: A Biodiversity Assessment*. Portland, OR: Center for Biological Diversity, Friday Harbor, WA: Friends of the San Juans. www.sanjuans.org/pdf_document/PugetSoundBasinBiodiversityAssessment.pdf

49. Batker, David, Rowan Schmidt, Jennifer Harrison-Cox, and Briana Lovell. 2010. *The Whole Economy of the Snohomish Basin: The Essential Economics of Ecosystem Services*. www.eartheconomics.org/FileLibrary/file/Reports/Snohomish/Earth_Economics_Snohomish_Basin_Report.pdf

50. Brian K. Bucks, Arthur B. Kennickell, Traci L. Mach, and Kevin B.Moore. 2009. "Changes in U.S. Family Finances from 2004 to 2007: Evidence from the Survey of Consumer Finances." *Federal Reserve Bulletin* Vol. 95 (February), pp. A1-A55. www.federalreserve.gov/econresdata/scf/files/2007_scf09.pdf

51. These estimates used the Federal Reserve 2007 Survey of Consumer Finances average income figures of $396,400 for top 10 percent of households for superelite households; $116,000 for the 80 to 89.9 percentile for elites; $57,900 for the 40-59.9 percentile for maintenance-level households; and $12,300 for the under 20 percentile, for poor households.

52. Washington State Department of Revenue. 2011. *Property Tax Statistics 2011*. P. 41, Table 22.

53. Schultheis. 2012. *Poverty in America, Living Wage Calculator for Snohomish County, Washington*. http://livingwage.mit.edu/counties/53061

7. UNITED SMALL NATIONS OF AMERICA

1. Barnes, Peter. 2006. *Capitalism 3.0: A Guide to Reclaiming the Commons*. San Francisco: BK, Berrett-Koehler Publishers, p. 80, commenting on Marjorie Kelly. 2009. *The Divine Right of Capital: Dethroning the Corporate Aristocracy*. San Francisco: Berrett-Koehler.

2. Barnes, 2006. *Capitalism 3.0*, pp. xiii–xiv.

3. U.S. Energy Information Administration. 2009. *International Energy Statistics*. Total Primary Energy Consumption (Quadrillion Btu), Table: Total

Carbon Dioxide Emissions from the Consumption of Energy (Million Metric Tons). www.eia.doe.gov/emeu/international/contents.html

4. Vermont Business Magazine. 2011. *Vermont 100+*. http://vtdigger.org/2011/01/07/vermont-business-magazine-releases-vermont-100/

5. Puget Sound Business Journal. 2008. *Book of Lists*. (December 29).

6. U.S. Bureau of the Census. 1963. *Statistical Abstract 1963*. Table No. 648. Sole Proprietorships, Partnerships, and Corporations—Number, Business Receipts, and net Profit by Industry and Size of Receipts, 1960, p. 490.

7. U.S. Internal Revenue Service. 2012. Table 1. Number of Returns, Total Receipts, Business Receipts, Net Income (less deficit), Net Income, and Deficit by Form of Business Tax Years 1980-2008. www.irs.gov/uac/SOI-Tax-Stats---Integrated-Business-Data

8. U.S. Bureau of the Census. 1953. *U.S. Statistical Abstract. 1953*. 74th edition. Income Tax Returns, Table 381. Individual Income Tax Returns, by Adjusted Income Classes: 1949 and 1950. www2.census.gov/prod2/statcomp/documents/1953-04.pdf ; U.S. Internal Revenue Service. 2012. *SOI Tax Stats –* Individual Statistical Tables by Size of Adjusted Gross Income. Table 1.4 All Returns: Sources of Income, Adjustments, and Tax Items. hwww.irs.gov/uac/SOI-Tax-Stats---Individual-Statistical-Tables-by-Size-of-Adjusted-Gross-Income by Size of Adjusted Gross Income, Tax Year 2009.

9. U.S. Internal Revenue Service. 2011. *SOI Tax Stats*, Historical Table 24. U.S. Corporation Income Tax: Tax Brackets and Rates, 1909-2010. www.irs.gov/taxstats/article/0,,id=175911,00.html

10. Smith, Greg. 2012. "Why I Am Leaving Goldman Sachs." Op-Ed, *New York Times*. www.nytimes.com/2012/03/14/opinion/why-i-am-leaving-goldman-sachs.html

11. *Forbes Magazine*. 2011. "The World's Biggest Public Companies." Global 2000 Leading Companies (as of April 2011), www.forbes.com/global2000/list/ ; "Global 2000 Methodology: How we crunch the numbers." www.forbes.com/2011/04/20/global-2000-11-methodology.html

12. Vitali, Stefania, James B. Glattfelder, and Stefano Battiston. 2011. "The network of global corporate control." *arXiv* (July 28), Cornell University.

13. Schwartz, Nelson D. 2012. "A Public Exit From Goldman Sachs Hits at a Wounded Wall Street." *New York Times*, March 14. www.nytimes.com/2012/03/15/business/a-public-exit-from-goldman-sachs-hits-a-wounded-wall-street.html?_r=1&hp=&pagewanted=all

14. Rosenblum, Harvey. 2012. "Choosing the Road to Prosperity: Why We Must End Too Big to Fail—Now." Federal Reserve Bank of Dallas 2011 *Annual Report*, p. 21. www.dallasfed.org/assets/documents/fed/annual/2011/ar11.pdf.

15. Fisher, Richard W. 2011. "Taming the Too-Big-to Fails: Will Dodd-Frank Be the Ticket or Is Lap-Band Surgery Required?" Remarks before Columbia University's Politics and Business Club, Nov. 15, 2011.

16. Financial Crisis Inquiry Commission. 2011. *The Financial Crisis Inquiry Report: Final Report of the National Commission on the Causes of the Financial and Economic Crisis in the United States*. www.gpoaccess.gov/fcic/fcic.pdf; Levin, Carl (chair) and Tom Coburn. 2011. *Wall Street and the Financial Crisis: Anatomy of a Financial Crisis*. Majority and Minority Report, Staff Report, Permanent Subcommittee on Investigations, United States Senate (April 13, 2011); Johnson, Simon. 2009. "The Quiet Coup." *The Atlantic*. May. Www.theatlantic.com/doc/200905/imf-advice; Johnson, Simon and James Kwak. 2010. *13 Bankers: the Wall Street takeover and the Next Financial Meltdown*. New York: Pantheon Books.

17. Igan, Deniz, Prachi Mishra, and Thierry Tressel. 2011. "A Fistful of Dollars: Lobbying and the Financial Crisis." *National Bureau of Economic Research*, NBER Working Paper 17076. www.nbr.org/papers/w17076

18. Rosenblum, Harvey. 2012. "Choosing the Road to Prosperity: Why We Must End Too Big to Fail—Now." p. 3. www.dallasfed.org/assets/documents/fed/annual/2011/ar11.pdf.

19. Silver-Greenberg, Jessica and Peter Eavis. 2012. "JPMorgan Discloses $2 Billion in Trading Losses." *New York Times*, May 10, http://dealbook.nytimes.com/2012/05/10/jpmorgan-discloses-significant-losses-in-trading-group/

20. Federal Financial Institutions Examination Council. 2011. *Annual Report 2010*. Table Assets, Liabilities, and Net Worth of U.S. Commercial Banks, Thrift Institutions, and Credit Unions as of December 31, 2010, p. 29. www.ffiec.gov/PDF/annrpt10.pdf

21. Haldane, Andrew G. 2011. "Control Rights (and Wrongs)." Wincott Annual Memorial Lecture, Westminster London. www.bis.org/review/r111026a.pdf

22. Tax, Sol. 1977. "Anthropology for the World of the Future: Thirteen Professions and Three Proposals." *Human Organization* 36(3):225–234.

23. Hart, Keith. 2011. "The Financial Crisis and the End of All-Purpose Money." *Economic Sociology* 12(2): 4–10.

24. Stiglitz, Joseph E., Amartya Sen, and Jean-Paul Fitoussi. 2009. *Report by the Commission on the Measurement of Economic Performance and Social Progress*, p. 8. www.stiglitz-sen-fitoussi.fr/documents/rapport_anglais.pdf

25. Kuznets, Simon (editor), with Lillian Epstein and Elizabeth Jenks. 1941. *National Income and Its Composition, 1919-1938*, Vol. 1. New York: National Bureau of Economic Research, Publications of the NBER No. 40, p. 6–8. www.nber.org/chapters/c4225.pdf

26. Daly, Herman. 1991. *Steady-State Economics*, 2nd edition. Washington, D.C.: Island Press.

27. Redefining Progress. 2012. About Redefining Progress. http://rprogress.org/about_us/about_us.htm

28. Venetoulis, Jason, and Cliff Cobb. 2004. *The Genuine Progress Indicator 1950 – 2002 (2004 Update)*. Oakland, CA: Redefining Progress. www2.medioambiente.gov.ar/ciplycs/documentos/archivos/Archivo_243.pdf

29. Stiglitz, Joseph E., Amartya Sen, and Jean-Paul Fitoussi. 2009. *Report by the Commission on the Measurement of Economic Performance and Social Progress*. www.stiglitz-sen-fitoussi.fr/en/index.htm

30. Kapur, Ajay, Niall Macleod, and Narendra Singh 2005. *Plutonomy: Buying Luxury, Explaining Global Imbalances*. Citigroup Global Markets. www.scribd.com/doc/6674234/Citigroup-Oct-16-2005-Plutonomy-Report-Part-1, pp. 1

31. Citigroup. 2012. *200 Years Citi: 2011 Annual Report*. www.citigroup.com/citi/fin/data/ar11c_en.pdf?ieNocache=413 , p. 28.

32. Kapur, Macleod, and Singh. 2005, *Plutonomy*, p. 2.

33. Barclays Capital. 2012. "Skyscraper Index Bubble Building." http://static.nzz.ch/files/6/2/0/Skyscraper+Index+-+Bubble+building+100112+%282%29_1.14300620.pdf

34. Hamilton, Clive. 2011. "Overheated debate." *New Scientist* 211(2824):28-29; Hamilton, Clive. 2010. *Requiem for a Species: Why we resist the truth about climate change*. London: Earthscan.

35. Data from www.opensecrets.org

36. Greenpeace. 2010. *Koch Industries Secretly Funding the Climate Denial Machine*. www.greenpeace.org/usa/Global/usa/report/2010/3/koch-industries-secretly-fund.pdf; Greenpeace. 2011. *Koch Industries: Still Fueling Climate Denial 2011 Update*. www.greenpeace.org/usa/Global/usa/planet3/publications/gwe/Koch-Ind-Still-Fueling-Climate-Denial.pdf

37. Americans for Prosperity. 2012. About Americans for Prosperity. Our Missions. www.americansforprosperity.org/about, accessed March 14, 2012.

38. Americans for Prosperity. Issues: Energy and Environment www.americansforprosperity.org/energy-environment, accessed March 14, 2012.

39. PERI, Political Economy Research Institute. 2010. *Toxic 100 Air Polluters*. University of Massachusetts Amherst, www.peri.umass.edu/toxic_index

40. Johnson, Brad. 2011. "Koch Industries: The 100-Million Ton Carbon Gorilla." http://thinkprogress.org/green/2011/01/30/174900/koch-carbon-footprint/

41. Barnes, Peter. 2006. *Capitalism 3.0: A Guide to Reclaiming the Commons*. San Francisco: BK, Berrett-Koehler Publishers, p. xiii.

42. Hardt, Michel and Antonio Negri. 2009. *Commonwealth*. Cambridge, MA: Belknap Press, Harvard University Press, p. viii.

43. Alperovitz, Gar and Lew Daly. 2008. *Unjust Deserts: How the Rich are Taking Our Common Inheritance*. New York: The New Press, p. 1; see also: Alperovitz, Gar. 2005. *America Beyond Capitalism: Reclaiming Our Wealth, Our Liberty, and our Democracy*. Hoboken, NJ: John Wiley & Sons.

44. Hess, Charlotte. 2008. *Mapping the New Commons*. http://common-strust.global-negotiations.org/resources/ Hess,%20C.%20Mapping_the_New_Commons.pdf

45. Galbraith, John Kenneth. 1958. *The Affluent Society*. Boston: Houghton Mifflin.

46. Barnes, 2006, *Capitalism 3.0*, p. 22.

47. Barnes, 2006, *Capitalism 3.0*, Figure 2.1, p. 22.

48. Barnes, 2006, *Capitalism 3.0*, p. 25.

49. Olson, Mancur. 1965. *The Logic of Collective Action*. Cambridge, MA: Harvard University Press.

50. Naylor, Thomas H. and William H. Willimon. 1997. *Downsizing the U.S.A.* Grand Rapids, MI: William B. Eerdmans Publishing.

51. Garreau, Joel. 1981. *The Nine Nations of North America*. Boston: Houghton Mifflin.

52. Chinni, Dante. 2008."About the Patchwork Nation Project." *Christian Science Monitor*. http://patchworknation.csmonitor.com/about/ (accessed March 2010); Gimpel, James G., Jason E. Schuknecht. 2003. *Patchwork Nation: Sectionalism and Political Change in American Politics*. Ann Arbor: University of Michigan Press; Chinni, Dante and James Gimpel. 2010. *Our Patchwork Nation: The Surprising Truth About the "Real" America*. New York: Gotham Books, Penguin.

53. Rand McNally. 2002. *Commercial Atlas and Marketing Guide*. 133rd edition. Chicago: Rand McNally.

54. Johnson, Kenneth P. and John R. Kort. 2004. "2004 Redefinition of the BEA Economic Areas." *Survey of Current Business* (November): 68–75.

55. Drake-Terry, Joanne. 1989. *The Same as Yesterday: The Lillooet Chronicle the Theft of their Lands and Resources*. Lillooet, BC: Lillooet Tribal Council.

56. Brian K. Bucks, Arthur B. Kennickell, Traci L. Mach, and Kevin B.Moore. 2009. "Changes in U.S. Family Finances from 2004 to 2007: Evidence from the Survey of Consumer Finances." *Federal Reserve Bulletin* Vol. 95 (February), pp. A1-A55. www.federalreserve.gov/econresdata/scf/files/2007_scf09.pdf

57. Shorrocks, Anthony, James B. Davies, and Rodrigo Lluberas. 2010. *Global Wealth Databook*. Credit Suisse Research Institute. Zurich, Switzerland: Credit Suise Group AG.

58. U.S. Federal Reserve. [quarterly]. *Flow of Funds Accounts of the United States*. Z.1 Statistical Release.

59. World Bank. 2011. *The Changing Wealth of Nations: Measuring Sustainable Development in the New Millennium*. Washington DC: The International Bank for Reconstruction and Development / World Bank. http://issuu.com/world.bank.publications/docs/9780821384886 ; Wealth of Nations dataset :World Bank total_and_per_capita_wealth_of nations 1995-2005.xls http://data.worldbank.org/data-catalog/wealth-of-nations

60. Sutton, Paul C. and Robert Costanza. 2002. "Global estimates of market and non-market values derivedfrom nighttime satellite imagery, land cover, and ecosystem service valuation." *Ecological Economics* 41:509-527.

61. Venetoulis, Jason, and Cliff Cobb. 2004. *The Genuine Progress Indicator 1950 – 2002 (2004 Update)*. Oakland, CA: Redefining Progress.

62. Whitesides, George M., and George W. Crabtree. 2007. "Don't Forget Long-Term Fundamental Research in Energy." *Science* 315: 796–98.

63. U.S. Department of Education, National Center for Education Statistics. (2005). *Revenues and Expenditures for Public Elementary and Secondary Education: School Year 2002–2003* (NCES 2005-353).

64. U.S. Department of Commerce, Bureau of the Census. 2007. *Statistical Abstract of the United States*. Various annual editions. Washington, D.C.: U.S. Government Printing Office.

65. Heller, Martin C., and Gregory A. Keoleian. 2000. "Life Cycle-based Sustainability Indicators for Assessment of the U.S. Food System." Report no. CSS00-04 Center for Sustainable Systems. University of Michigan. Ann Arbor, MI.

66. Garvin, Lewis, Natalie Henry, Melissa Vernon. 2000. *Community Materials Flow Analysis: A Case Study of Ann Arbor, Michigan*. Center for Sustainable Systems, University of Michigan. Report no. CSS00-02.

8. UNITED SMALL NATIONS
OF THE WORLD

1. Global Greens. 2012. *Charter of the Global Greens as adopted in Canberra 2001 and updated in Dakar 2012*. Principles. www.globalgreens.org/sites/globalgreens.org/files/Charter%202012_1.pdf

2. World Bank. 2006. *Where is the Wealth of Nations?: Measuring Capital for the 21st Century*. World Bank: Washington, D.C.; World Bank. 2011. *The*

Changing Wealth of Nations: Measuring Sustainable Development in the New Millennium. http://issuu.com/world.bank.publications/docs/9780821384886 . The World Bank's primary data on the wealth of nations is available at http://data.worldbank.org/sites/default/files/to-tal_and_per_capita_wealth_of_nations.xls

3. Costanza, Robert, Maureen Hart, Stephen Posner, and John Talberth. 2009. *Beyond GDP: The Need for New Measures of Progress.* The Pardee Papers No. 4 (January). Boston University, The Frederick S. Pardee Center for the Study of the Longer-Range Future; EPA. 2009. *Valuing the Protection of Ecological Systems and Services: A Report of the EPA Science Advisory Board.* United States Environmental Protection Agency. EPA-SAB-09-012. .www.epa.gov/sab

4. Costanza, Robert, et al. 1997. "The Value of the World's Ecosystem Services and Natural Capital." *Nature* 387 (15 May): 253–60.

5. Shorrocks, Anthony, James B. Davies, and Rodrigo Lluberas. 2010. *Global Wealth Databook.* Credit Suisse Research Institute. Zurich, Switzerland: Credit Suisse Group AG.

6. Forbes. 2011. "The World's Biggest Public Companies." (April 20). www.forbes.com/global2000/

7. Brown, Lester R. 2009. *Plan B 4.0: Mobilizing to Save Civilization.* Earth Policy Institute. New York: W.W. Norton. www.earth-policy.org/images/uploads/book_files/pb4book.pdf

8. I am borrowing from two websites for these graphic calculations: http://usdebt.kleptocracy.us/ ; www.pagetutor.com/trillion/index.html

9. Shaxson, Nicholas, John Christensen, and Nick Matnhiason. 2012. *Inequality: You Don't Know the Half of It* (Or why inequality is worse than we thought)." Tax justice network. www.taxjustice.net/cms/upload/pdf/Inequality_120722_You_dont_know_the_half_of_it.pdf

10. Forbes. 2012. "The World's Billionaires." www.forbes.com/billionaires/

11. Taylor, P. J. 2009. "The way we were: command-and-control centres in the global space-economy on the eve of the 2008 geo-economic transition." *Environment and Planning* A 41:7-12.

12. Climate Analysis Indicators Tool (CAIT) Version 9.0. Washington, D.C.: World Resources Institute, 2012.

13. World Future Council. 2012. Website: Vision, Mission and Values. www.worldfuturecouncil.org/vision.html

14. Girardet, Herbert and Miguel Mendonça. 2009. *A Renewable World: energy, Ecology, Equality: A Report for the World Future Council.* Totnes, Devon, UK: Green Books.

15. IUCN, International Union for the Conservation of Nature. 2012. *2011 IUCN Annual Report: Solutions, Naturally*. Gland, Switzerland: IUCN, Frontpiece. http://data.iucn.org/dbtw-wpd/edocs/2012-051.pdf

16. International Institute for Sustainable Development. 2012. "Fossil Fuels – At What Cost?" www.iisd.org/gsi/fossil-fuel-subsidies/fossil-fuels-what-cost

17. ICLEI, 2011. Charter, Revised and approved by consensus by Executive Committee on 6 June 2011. www.iclei.org/fileadmin/user_upload/documents/Global/governance/Charter/Charter_approved_FINALforCOUNCIL20110912.pdf

18. Kaufman, Leslie and Kate Zernike. 2012. "Activists Fight Green Projects, Seeing U.N. Plot." *New York Times* February 3, 2012. www.nytimes.com/2012/02/04/us/activists-fight-green-projects-seeing-un-plot.html?pagewanted=all&_r=0

19. Republican National Committee. 2012. *Republican Platform 2012: We Believe in America*. P. 45. www.gop.com/wp-content/uploads/2012/08/2012GOPPlatform.pdf

20. American Planning Association. 2012. *Planning in America: Perceptions and Priorities: A Research Summary June2012*. http://planning.org/policy/economicrecovery/pdf/planninginamerica.pdf

21. ICLEI 2012. About ICLEI. www.iclei.org/index.php?id=about

22. Low Cap. 2012 Low Carbon Regions in the North Sea. ILCI. www.lowcap.eu/PartnerProjects/ICLEI.aspx

23. ICLEI.

24. European Union. 2010. *Consolidated Version of the Treaty on European Union*. Official Journal of the European Union. 30.2.2010,C83/13. Preamble. http://eur-lex.europa.eu/LexUriServ/LexUriServ.do?uri=OJ:C:2010:083:0013:0046:en:PDF

25. European Union. 2010. "Rules of Procedure Committee of the Regions." *Official Journal of the European Union* L 6/14, 9.1.2010. http://cor.europa.eu/en/documentation/Documents/Rules-of-Procedure-of-the-Committee-of-the-Regions/EN.pdf; European Union. 2012. *Structure of the Committee of the Regions (CoR)*. http://cor.europa.eu/en/documentation/brochures/Documents/CoR%20At%20a%20Glance%202012/EN.pdf

26. European Union. 2009. *The selection process for Committee of the Regions members Procedures in the Member States*. http://cor.europa.eu/en/Archived/Documents/840ed860-60ca-4af6-8be9-70b795f42207.pdf

27. European Union. 2000. *Charter of Fundamental Rights of the European Union*. www.europarl.europa.eu/charter/pdf/text_en.pdf

28. Global Greens. 2012. *Charter of the Global Greens a s adopted in Canberra 2001 and updated in Dakar 2012*. www.globalgreens.org/sites/globalgreens.org/files/Charter%202012_1.pdf

29. European People's Party, EPP. 2012. *EPP Manifesto* (Adopted at the EPP Congress in Bucharest, 17th and 18th October 2012). http://images.europaemail.net/client_id_5328/attachments/1._EPP_Manifesto,_EN.pdf

30. European People's Party, EPP. 2012. *Party Platform EPP Statutory Congress* 17-18, October 2012, Bucharest, Romania. http://images.europaemail.net/client_id_5328/attachments/1._EPP_Platform,_EN.pdf

31. The Greens / European Free Alliance. 2012. "Who we are." www.greens-efa.eu/about-us/48-who-we-are.html

32. UCLG The Global Network of Cities, Local and Regional Governments. 2012. "About UCLG." www.uclg.org/en/organisation/about

33. UCLG The Global Network of Cities, Local and Regional Governments. 2008. *Decentralization and local democracy in the world: First Global Report by United Cities and Local Governments*. Co-publication of the World Bank and United Cities and Local Governments. www.cities-localgovernments.org/gold/Upload/gold_report/01_introduction_en.pdf

34. EU, Eurostat. 2007. *Regions in the European Union: Nomenclature of territorial units for statistics*, NUTS 2006 /EU-27. http://epp.eurostat.ec.europa.eu/cache/ITY_OFFPUB/KS-RA-11-011/EN/KS-RA-11-011-EN.PDF

35. EDF Group. 2012. *EDF Group Sustainable Development Indicators 2011*. www.edf.com/html/RA2011/en/pdf/EDF2011_cahierDD_va.pdf

36. Assembly of European Regions. 1996. *Declaration on Regionalism in Europe*. The Assembly of European Regions meeting in Basel on 4th December 1996. www.aer.eu/fileadmin/user_upload/PressComm/Publications/DeclarationRegionalism/DR_GB.pdf

37. BAK Basel Economics. 2009. *From Subsidiarity to Success: The Impact of Decentralisation on Economic Growth. Part I. Creating a Decentralization Index*. A Study commissioned by the Assembly of European Regions (AER). www.aer.eu/fileadmin/user_upload/PressComm/Publications/AER_Study_on_decentralisation/Studies/BAK-Part1-FINAL ; BAK Basel Economics. 2009. *From Subsidiarity to Success: The Impact of Decentralisation on Economic Growth. Part II. Decentralization and Economic Performance*. A Study commissioned by the Assembly of European Regions (AER). www.aer.eu/fileadmin/user_upload/PressComm/Publications/AER_Study_on_decentralisation/Studies/BAK-Part2-FINAL_cover.pdf ; BAK Basel Economics. 2009. *From Subsidiarity to Success: The Impact of Decentralisation on Economic Growth. Summary and Conclusions*. A Study commissioned by the Assembly of European Regions (AER). www.aer.eu/fileadmin/

user_upload/PressComm/Publications/AER_Study_on_decentralisation/Studies/GB-FINAL_cover.pdf

38. Richard A. Musgrave. 1959. *The Theory of Public Finance: A Study in Public Economy*. New York: McGraw-Hill; Linder, Wolf. 2004. *Political Challenges of Decentralization*. Written for the World Bank Institute, Washington, D.C. 2002. http://info.worldbank.org/etools/docs/library/136160/tslg/pdf/challenges.pdf

39. Shah, Anwar. 1998. *Fiscal Federalism and Macroeconomic Governance: For Better or For Worse?* World Bank, Policy Research Working Paper No. 2005. www-wds.worldbank.org/external/default/WDSContentServer/IW3P/IB/2000/02/24/000094946_99031911104728/Rendered/PDF/multi_page.pdf

40. UNEP (United Nations Environment Programme). 2002. *Global Environment Outlook 3: Past, Present and Future Perspectives*. London: Earthscan.

41. Cave, Jonathan. 2003. *Towards a Sustainable Information Society*. TERRA 2000 IST-2000-26332.

42. Nakicenovic, Nebojsa, and Robert Swart, ed. 2000. *Special Report on Emissions Scenarios: A Special Report of Working Group III of the Intergovernmental Panel on Climate Change*. Cambridge and New York: Cambridge University Press.

43. Kant, Immanuel. 1917 [1795]. *Perpetual Peace: A Philosophical Essay*. Edited and translated by M. Campbell Smith. London: Allen & Unwin.

44. World Bank, WDI Online. World Development Indicators. Military expenditure (% of GDP). http://ddp-ext.worldbank.org/ext/DDPQQ/member.do?method=getMembers&userid=1&queryId=6 (accessed Nov 2009).

SELECTED BIBLIOGRAPHY

Acemoglu, Daron and James A. Robinson. 2012. *Why Nations Fail: The Origins of Power, Prosperity, and Poverty*. New York: Crown.

Alperovitz, Gar. 2005. *America Beyond Capitalism: Reclaiming Our Wealth, Our Liberty, and our Democracy*. Hoboken, NJ: John Wiley & Sons.

Alperovitz, Gar and Lew Daly. 2008. *Unjust Deserts: How the Rich Are Taking Our Common Inheritance*. New York: The New Press.

Barnes, Peter. 2006. *Capitalism 3.0: A Guide to Reclaiming the Commons*. San Francisco: BK, Berrett-Koehler Publishers, P. 80, commenting on Marjorie Kelly. 2009.*The Divine Right of Capital: Dethroning the Corporate Aristocracy*. San Francisco: Berrett-Koehler.

Batker, David, Rowan Schmidt, Jennifer Harrison-Cox, and Briana Lovell. 2010. *The Whole Economy of the Snohomish Basin: The Essential Economics of Ecosystem Services*. www.eartheconomics.org/FileLibrary/file/Reports/Snohomish/ Earth_Economics_Snohomish_Basin_Report.pdf

Bodley, John H. 2003. *The Power of Scale: A Global History Approach*. Armonk, New York and London: M. E. Sharpe.

Bodley, John H. 2011. *Cultural Anthropology: Tribes, States, and the Global System*. Fifth edition. Lanham, Maryland: AltaMira Press.

Bodley, John H. 2012. "Small Nation Happiness: A Scale and Power Perspective." Vital Topics Forum On Happiness. *American Anthropologist* 114(1) (March): pp. 10-11.

Bodley, John H. 2012. *Anthropology and Contemporary Human Problems*. 6th edition. Lanham, Maryland: AltaMira Press.

Brown, Lester R. 2009. Plan B 4.0: *Mobilizing to Save Civilization*. Earth Policy Institute. New York: W.W. Norton. www.earth-policy.org/images/uploads/book_files/pb4book.pdf

Capgemini. 2012. *World Wealth Report 2012*. www.capgemini.com

Costanza, Robert, et al. 1997. "The Value of the World's Ecosystem Services and Natural Capital." *Nature* 387 (15 May): 253–60.

Costanza, Robert, Lisa Graumlich, Will Steffen, Carole Crumley, John Dearing, Kathy Hibbard, Rik Leemans, Charles Redman, and David Schimel. 2007. "Sustainability or Collapse: What Can We Learn from Integrating the History of Humans and the Rest of Nature?" *Ambio* 36(7): 522-527.

Credit Suisse. 2010. *Global Wealth Databook*. Credit Suisse Research Institute. www.credit-suisse.com/news/doc/credit_suisse_global_wealth_databook.pdf

Daly, Herman. 1991. *Steady-State Economics*, 2nd edition. Washington, D.C.: Island Press.

Hardt, Michel and Antonio Negri. 2009. *Commonwealth*. Cambridge, Mass.: Belknap Press, Harvard University Press.

Jackson, Tim. 2006. "Beyond the 'Wellbeing Paradox': - wellbeing, consumption growth and sustainability." Centre for Environmental Strategy. University of Surrey, Guildford (Surrey). www.surrey.ac.uk/ces/files/pdf/0606_WP_Wellbeing_and_SD.pdf

Jackson, Tim. 2009. *Prosperity Without Growth: Economics for a Finite Planet.* London: Earthscan.

Klein, Naomi. 2007. *The Shock Doctrine: The Rise of Disaster Capitalism.* New York: Picador, Henry Holt & Co.

Kohr, Leopold. 1978. *The Breakdown of Nations.* New York: Dutton, p.79 [originally published 1957].

Marks, Nic, and Saamah Abdallah, Andrew Simms, and Sam Thompson. 2006. *The Happy Planet Index: An Index of Human Well-Being and Environmental Impact.* London: New Economics Foundation. www.neweconomics.org/gen/z_sys_PublicationDetail.aspx?PID= 225

Max-Neef, Manfred, Antonio Elizalde, and Martin Hopenhayn et al. 1989. "Human Scale Development: An Option for the Future." *Development Dialogue* 1989:1, pp. 5-80. Uppsala: Dag Hammarskjöld Foundation.

Max-Neef, Manfred. 1992. *From the Outside Looking in: Experiences in "Barefoot Economics."* London: Zed Books. Originally published, 1982, Uppsala Sweden: Dag Hammarskjöld Foundation.

Max-Neef, Manfred. 2011. *Economics Unmasked: From power and greed to compassion and the common good.* Totnes, Devon, UK: Green Books

Pickett, Kate and Richard Wilkinson. 2010. *The Spirit Level: Why Greater Equality Makes Societies Stronger.* New York: Bloomsbury Press.

Raskin, Paul, Tariq Banuri, Gilberto Gallopín, Pablo Gutman, Al Hammond, Robert Kates, and Rob Swart. 2002. *Great Transition: The Promise and Lure of the Times Ahead.* Global Scenario Group. Boston: Stockholm Environment Institute, Tellus Institute.

Raskin, Paul D. 2006. *The Great Transition Today: A Report from the Future.* GTI Paper Series 2, Frontiers of a Great Transition. Boston: Tellus Institute.

Rosenblum, Harvey. 2012. "Choosing the Road to Prosperity: Why We Must End Too Big to Fail—Now." Federal Reserve Bank of Dallas 2011 *Annual Report.* www.dallasfed.org/ assets/documents/fed/annual/2011/ar11.pdf

The Royal Society. 2012. *People and the Planet.* The Royal Society Science Policy Centre Report 01/12. http://royalsociety.org/uploadedFiles/Royal_Society_Content/policy/projects/ people-planet/2012-04-25-PeoplePlanet.pdf

Sandel, Michael J. 2009. *Justice: What's the Right Thing to Do?* New York: Farrar, Straus and Giroux.

Shaxson, Nicholas, John Christensen, and Nick Matnhiason. 2012. *Inequality: You Don't Know the Half of It* (Or why inequality is worse than we thought)." Tax justice network. www.taxjustice.net/cms/upload/pdf/Inequality_120722_You_dont_know_the_half_of_it.pdf

Shorrocks, Anthony, James B. Davies, and Rodrigo Lluberas. 2010. *Global Wealth Databook.* Credit Suisse Research Institute. Zurich, Switzerland: Credit Suisse Group AG.

Stiglitz, Joseph E., Amartya Sen, and Jean-Paul Fitoussi. 2009. *Report by the Commission on the Measurement of Economic Performance and Social Progress,* p. 8. www.stiglitz-senfitoussi.fr/documents/rapport_anglais.pdf

Tax, Sol. 1977. "Anthropology for the World of the Future: Thirteen Professions and Three Proposals." *Human Organization* 36(3):225-234.

Tellus Institute. 2005. *Great Transition Initiative: Visions and Pathways for a Hopeful Future.* GTI Brochure. www.gtinitiative.org/default.asp?action=42

Watson, Sir Bob, et.al. 2012. *Environment and Development Challenges: the Imperative to Act.* The Blue Planet Prize Laureates, The Asahi Glass Foundation (February 20). : www.afinfo.or.jp/en/bpplaureates/doc/2012jp_fp_en.pdf

Venetoulis, Jason, and Cliff Cobb. 2004. *The Genuine Progress Indicator 1950–2002 (2004 Update).* Oakland, CA: Redefining Progress. www2.medioambiente.gov.ar/ciplycs/documentos/archivos/Archivo_243.pdf

Vitali, Stefania, James B. Glattfelder, and Stefano Battiston. 2011. "The network of global corporate control." *arXiv* (July 28), Cornell University.

INDEX

ABOUT THE AUTHOR

John H. Bodley, known for his trenchant critiques of capitalism and the elite corporate power structure, is Regents Professor in the Department of Anthropology at Washington State University. In addition to his book *The Power of Scale* (2003), he is the author of *Cultural Anthropology*, 5th edition (2011), *Anthropology and Contemporary Human Problems*, 6th edition (2012), and *Victims of Progress*, 5th edition (2008), all published by AltaMira Press.